We dedicate this book to
our daughter, Molisa Meier

Counselling and Therapy Techniques

Theory and Practice

Augustine Meier *and* Micheline Boivin

Los Angeles | London | New Delhi
Singapore | Washington DC

First published 2011

SAGE Publications Ltd
1 Oliver's Yard
55 City Road
London EC1Y 1SP

SAGE Publications Inc.
2455 Teller Road
Thousand Oaks, California 91320

SAGE Publications India Pvt Ltd
B 1/I 1 Mohan Cooperative Industrial Area
Mathura Road
New Delhi 110 044

SAGE Publications Asia-Pacific Pte Ltd
33 Pekin Street #02-01
Far East Square
Singapore 048763

Library of Congress Control Number: 2009941545

British Library Cataloguing in Publication data

A catalogue record for this book is available from the British Library

ISBN 978-1-84787-957-8
ISBN 978-1-84787-958-5 (pbk)

Typeset by C&M Digitals (P) Ltd, Chennai, India
Printed and bound in Great Britain by TJ International Ltd, Padstow, Cornwall
Printed on paper from sustainable resources

Mixed Sources
Product group from well-managed
forests and other controlled sources
www.fsc.org Cert no. SGS-COC-2483
© 1996 Forest Stewardship Council
FSC

Contents

Author Biographies

Augustine Meier, Ph.D., Clinical Psychologist, Professor Emeritus, Saint Paul University, is the Founder and President of the Ottawa Institute for Object Relations Therapy. He trains and supervises candidates pursuing Certification as Object Relations Therapists and Supervisors. He taught graduate courses on Psychotherapy and Psychopathology and trained and supervised graduate students in counselling and research and doctoral students in psychology. Dr. Meier edited five books including *The Helping Relationship: Healing and Change in Community Context* (in press) and with his wife, Micheline Boivin, published over forty articles in refereed journals and as chapters in books on psychotherapy process and outcome. He has a private practice where he specializes in posttraumatic stress disorder, abuse, trauma and personality disorders.

Micheline Boivin, M.A., is a Certified Clinical Psychologist and a Certified Object Relations Therapist working with troubled and traumatized children and their parents at the Services psychologiques du Programme Enfance Jeunesse Famille du Centre de santé et des services psychosociaux de l'Outaouais, Gatineau, Québec (Psychological Services of the Family, Youth and Children's Program at the Psychosocial and Health Center of Gatineau, Québec). She has presented workshops on child sexual abuse and play therapy and with her husband, Augustine Meier, she has presented more than a dozen workshops on psychotherapy techniques such as Experiential Focusing, Task-Directed Imagery and Gestalt Two-Chair technique.

Acknowledgments

For decades the authors have been interested in integrating psychotherapy theory and practice and wrote the first article on the topic over twenty five years ago. In the development of their ideas over the years, the authors are particularly grateful for the comments, questions and feedback from their graduate students who were enrolled in therapy and counselling courses, took graduate-level training and practicum in counselling, and received supervision for their clinical work. The authors also wish to acknowledge the contributions of the persons who requested professional therapy and counselling to resolve their self, relational and emotional problems. They helped us to assess when, how and which techniques are helpful to achieve their therapy goals.

Special thanks to our cherished daughter, Molisa Meier, for having carefully reviewed each of the chapters and for posing challenging questions and providing us with helpful suggestions. Thanks for assisting us in preparing the glossary. We enjoyed our many lively, thought provoking and stimulating discussions that helped to sustain our efforts to stay with our project, to move it forward and bring it to its ultimate conclusion. We are extremely happy that we were able to share with you our joy in writing this book.

We wish to thank Shelley Briscoe-Dimock, our dear friend and colleague, for having meticulously read and commented on each chapter and helped formulate the title of the final chapter *Self-in-Relationship Psychotherapy*. You were very generous in giving of your time and were prompt in providing us with your comments and suggestions. Your excitement for and belief in our book was a constant source of inspiration.

This book would not have been possible without the professional help of the editorial staff of Sage Publications. The authors wish to express their appreciation to Alison Poyner, Senior Commissioning Editor, Susannah Trefgarne, Commissioning Editor, Alice Oven, Associate Editor, Counselling, and Emma Paterson, Editorial Assistant. Your patience, kindness, enthusiasm and guidance made the writing of our book a sheer delight and joy and a very positive experience. Thank you for your encouragement and support. The authors wish to acknowledge the meticulous work of Imogen Roome who took the book through the copyediting and proofing stage.

Lastly, we wish to express our appreciation to our families, colleagues and friends who took particular interest in our endeavours.

1   Theoretical Bridges and the Psychotherapy Process

Chapter Summary

This chapter presents the place of techniques within the complex process of psychotherapy. Each of the techniques was originally designed for a specific task such as developing new behaviours, uncovering encoded experiences, resolving internal conflicts, and promoting movement through the phases of the psychotherapy process. Techniques are simply techniques or, as Freud says, they are the scaffolds and not the building. Techniques become meaningful when they bridge the conceptualization of a client's problem with the therapeutic goal to be achieved.

For each of the techniques presented in this book, the theory from which it emerged, the procedures for its implementation, and a demonstration of its use are presented (All of the demonstrations were conducted by the first author, A.M.). Theory is believed to be a therapist's greatest tool as it provides the therapist with the conceptual skills to be innovative, creative, and flexible in applying a technique in achieving the therapeutic goal. The theoretical orientation for each of the techniques is presented according to the terms specific to it and in the "voice" of the theorist.

Introduction

This book presents a set of techniques used by therapists of varying orientations. Techniques form one part of the very complex psychotherapy process that includes theory, conceptualization, treatment plans, and their implementation. Therapy practice includes, as well, cultural and gender issues, professional and ethical guidelines, and the therapist–client relationship. Techniques become meaningful primarily when they are used within the context of theory and the goal of therapy and together they determine the techniques that are selected and how they are to be applied to bring about the desired changes.

Theory is fundamental to the practice of psychotherapy. Theory provides the bridge – the understanding – of that which takes place, for example, between a precipitating factor (e.g., loss of a loved one) and an emotional response (e.g., depression) and between a therapeutic intervention (e.g., task-directed imagery) and the therapeutic outcome (e.g., become assertive). Theory influences all of the components that become part of a therapeutic approach including its underlying philosophy, focus of therapy content (e.g., emotions), encoding of experiences, formation of psychic organization (e.g., schemas), target of change (e.g., behaviours), phases of the change process, and therapist–client relationship. Theories differ on the position that they take towards these topics and thereby determine the goal of therapy and the means taken to achieve it.

To make the text of this book more reader friendly, the male form of third-person noun and pronoun are used in the odd numbered chapters and the female form of third-person noun and pronoun are used in the even-numbered chapters.

These topics together with the discriminate and ethical use of the techniques are presented with reference to different therapeutic approaches.

Epistemological Foundations

Epistemological assumptions lie at the heart of virtually all psychotherapy theories and indirectly influence technical approaches to treatment. Epistemology poses the question, "What is knowledge?" or "How do we know what we know?" When epistemology is applied to psychotherapy the questions that arise are: Is a therapist able to understand the client's subjective world? Does the therapist have the knowledge to guide the treatment process? If yes, how is the therapist able to arrive at this knowledge? If no, what keeps the therapist from gaining such an understanding?

The two dominant epistemologies that influence psychotherapy orientations are modernism and postmodernism, and prior to that there was premodernism. The three represent different world views or "metanarratives" (Butler, 2002, p. 13). This section will describe and critique these three world views with reference to the practice of psychotherapy.

Premodernism

In the premodern era there was a strong sense of unity and coherence. Human persons were viewed as unified beings that discovered their meaning, purpose, and identity primarily in relationship and in the recognition of their proper place in a clearly ordered world of social arrangements (Downey, 1994). Relationality and interdependence were its hallmarks. Personal tragedies and sufferings were comprehended in view of a larger picture according to which everything had its place and everyone a purpose. A theocentric view (God-centreed) of one's purpose in life, human relationships, suffering and healing prevailed in this era (Kearney, 2001). Persons who healed others were perceived to function, not according to their proper authority (competency), but in virtue of a Higher Power (e.g., God).

Modernism

Modernism accepts premodernity's belief in order, unity, coherence, and history as inevitably progressive according to some plan, but situated this in the human and in human reason. The theocentric paradigm and a Higher Power were replaced by the anthropocentric paradigm that considered that the person to be the centre of reality and the human person as artist, scientist, inventor, explorer, and engineer (Kearney, 2001). The hallmarks of modernism are individuality, self-subsistent autonomy, superiority of reason, transcendence and the superiority of spirit over matter and body. Modernism believes that there is a "givenness" in the world that humans can come to know although partially and in a limited way (Downey, 1994). It believes that the mind is capable of knowing some external reality (Held, 1995) particularly through experimentation or the empirical method by which the principles and laws of the natural order are uncovered. By the same token, it is believed that therapists are able to arrive at principles and methods through research that can improve a client's reality contact and foster the actualization of a person's true self. In brief, modernism is a trend of thought that rejects previous traditions and affirms that human beings with the help of scientific knowledge, empirical methods, and technology are able to improve and reshape their environment.

Postmodernism

Postmodernism rejects the idea that there is a "givenness" in the world to be known (Butler, 2002) and that there are principles, dynamics, and forces underlying the "givenness" (e.g., depression) that can be uncovered. Postmodernism holds that knowing is a subjective phenomenon and that the mind is not capable of knowing anything outside of itself, that is, it is not capable of knowing objective truth (Held, 1995). The hallmarks of postmodernism are relationality, interdependence, community, and traditions. In place of a theocentric and an anthropocentric world view, postmodernism subscribes to an "ex-centric" view, meaning that a person does not "function as a controlling origin of self-expression" (Kearney, 2001, p. 11). Postmodernists believe that the theories and models that we have of any human phenomena are simply constructions of the mind and do not correspond to reality, thus, there is no possibility of arriving at the truth of anything. They believe that reality is co-constructed and changes from moment to moment. Postmodernism replaces the idea of a single reality, including the self, with multiple realities conditioned by individual, social, and temporal factors. In brief, postmodernism rejects the assumed certainty of the scientific endeavours to understand and explain reality and asserts that reality is not simply reflected in human understanding of it but is constructed as the mind tries to understand its own personal reality.

Critique

When applied to human conditions, it is not a question of modernism or postmodernism, rather, the question is: How do the two views contribute to our understanding of a human condition and its treatment? It can be seen that psychotherapy, for instance, incorporates aspects from both modernism and postmodernism. Take for instance, modernism's concept of "givenness" and postmodernism's concept of "social construction." An example is a child's movement away from the significant parent in order to achieve separation and individuation, a phenomenon observed in children across cultures. This "force" to move away is innate, it is the "givenness," it is not socially constructed. However the unique manner in which this "givenness" is realized in a child's life represents a social construction on part of the child and environmental conditions in which it finds itself. Not everything can be reduced to social construction. If everything is socially constructed, if there is no givenness, then the statement itself is socially constructed and not "an accurate reflection of how things really are" (Detmer, 2003, p. 38).

Psychotherapeutic Content – Client Experiences

Current psychological theories tend to be built around a model of feelings, thoughts, and behaviour interacting with the environment as instrumental to change. When applied to psychotherapy, the major models focus on and address one or more of the client's inner experiences when discussing the change process. Cognitive therapists, for example, focus on thoughts and pay attention to emotion only in the sense that it leads them to the automatic thoughts and irrational beliefs (e.g., schemas) (Beck, 1976). Experientially oriented therapists focus on the client's emotions and link unexpressed emotions (affect) to the development of emotional problems and the releasing of emotions to healthy responses (Rogers, 1961; Gendlin, 1996).

Current therapy models, however, fail to take into account other important dimensions of the human experience, such as needs, wants, longings, and desires. One exception is Caplan's (2008) Needs ABC model that places emphasis on the relational needs underlying maladaptive behaviours rather than on the behaviours themselves. Few empirical studies have investigated the role of needs in the change process.

Theorists during the past four decades have pointed out the importance of considering needs and wants in theory building and in clinical practice. Freud (1938) gave needs and impulses a central place in his psychoanalytic theory. Murray (1938) postulated a central role for needs in normal development and presented a taxonomy of needs. Maslow (1954) gave a place for needs and wants in normal development and offered a hierarchy of needs beginning with physiological needs (e.g. food) and extending to the need for self-actualization. For Gestalt therapists, needs are primary, for without them there would be no human motivation and people would have no future (Perls, 1969). Yalom (1989) observed that people regardless of their emotional state are driven (pulled) by their need (want) to matter, to be important, to be remembered, and to be loved. Blanck and Blanck (1979) differentiated between affect and drive and held that each must go its separate way so that a more unified theory can be constructed. Stumpf suggests that the mind does not just consist of intellectual representations (cognitions) and raw feelings, but also desires and wishes of all kinds (Reisenzein & Schnpflug, 1992).

It seems apparent then that the model of cognition, emotion, and behaviour is inadequate to fully explain the development of both adaptive and maladaptive human behaviour. By expanding this model to include needs/wants one could conceive of a triad comprised of cognitions, emotions, and needs/wants which influence the acquisition and modification of behaviour (Meier & Boivin, 1983). In this context, cognitions, emotions, and needs/wants form three parallel but independent systems which interact in the acquisition and modification of behaviour (Stumpf in Reisenzein & Schnpflug, 1992). The independent systems comprising emotion and cognition (Zajonc, 1980; Benesh & Weiner, 1982; Lazarus, 1984) would thereby be expanded to include needs/wants.

Within this triad, needs/wants are conceived to be prime directional motivators of behaviours, emotions are perceived to be responses to either the satisfaction or the frustration of needs/wants, and thoughts pertain to the stylistic ways of construing reality, to solving problems, to managing reality, and to evaluating experiences (Meier & Boivin, 1983). The emotional response to need deprivation (e.g., the need for a sense of belonging, the need to feel worthwhile) is also referred to as emotional intelligence that can help to identify the deprived needs and serve as a guide to new thinking and behaviour (Mayer, Salovey, & Caruso, 2008). The triad of emotions, cognitions, and needs/wants do not operate in isolation, but within the context of the person's social and physical milieu (Meier & Boivin, 1993) (see Figure 1.1). The triad

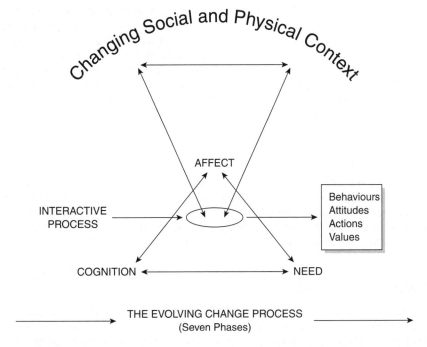

Figure 1.1   The interactive process of affect, cognition and needs/wants in the development of actions, behaviours, attitudes, and values within a social and physical context

continuously interacts with the social and physical context in the development of behaviours, actions, attitudes, values, and so on. This interactive process evolves according to a pattern marked by phases or stages that are summarized below.

Encoding Experiences

For psychotherapists who believe that a person's style of relating and behaviour is influenced by subjective experience and that to bring about change it is necessary to access and retrieve the subjective experience, the manner in which a person stored the experiences is important as this determines the techniques to be used. Such therapists believe that a person begins to psychologically store experiences, in some fashion, beginning in intrauterine existence and extending into childhood, adolescence, and adulthood, for potential retrieval. One can think of the manner of storage and the storage "location" in classical terms such as the Unconscious, Preconscious, and Conscious (Freud, 1938). These represent three different mechanisms of storage and three levels of awareness at which they are stored. One can also conceive of storing experiences with reference to the level of intelligence development. The manner in which the human mind encodes experiences, therefore, is dependent upon the level of intelligence development. At the initial level of intelligence, the human mind encodes experiences at the sensorial or physical level. With the development of perceptual skills, the human mind encodes experiences at the perceptual and conceptual levels. Lastly, with the ability to abstract and form and manipulate concepts, the human mind encodes experiences at the symbolic level. Thus the level of encoding is dependent upon the human mind's ability to form abstractions from the lived experiences.

The human mind encodes and represents experiences in three different ways with each having a different function (Tompkins & Lawley, 1996). The three ways of encoding experiences (sensorial, conceptual, symbolic) use different processes, have their own syntax and logic, and require a specific model of communication to access the information.

Sensory Encoding

Sensory encoding implies that the person stores experiences at the level of the senses, the physical. This is at times referred to as bodily memory. Thus a person in remembering a traumatic experience may indeed experience the same physical pain, smell, sounds, etc., as he experienced at the time of the trauma. The experience of the event is encoded bodily. The encoded sensorial information may trigger the memory of a past event.

Conceptual Encoding

Conceptual encoding refers to using perceptual and conceptual skills to encode experiences. Conceptual level encoding may be at the primitive level which is at the level of perception or at the higher level which is abstract and at the level of concepts. For example, Gendlin's (1996) experiential focusing technique addresses a client's problem at the preverbal level, that is, at the level of perception. Milton Erickson's hypnotherapy is also designed to access this layer of encoded experience (Tompkins & Lawley, 1996).

Symbolic Encoding

Symbolic encoding refers to storing experiences at the level of symbols, images, metaphors, scripts, narratives, etc. The symbols and images embody a wealth of affective, cognitive, motivational, value-related, etc., information. Not only do symbols and images contain experiences of the past but they also give direction for future growth and development.

These different levels of encoding require different techniques to bring to light their content. For example, experiential focusing (Gendlin, 1996) is able to access sensory encoded memories by getting in touch with bodily felt feelings. Empathic responding (Rogers, 1961) and experiential focusing are able to access perceptually encoded memories. Metaphor therapy (Kopp, 1995) is a linguistic method designed to access experiences encoded symbolically.

Psychic Organizations and Processes

Beginning in intrauterine life (Verny, 1981; Verny & Weintraub, 2002) and extending into infancy, childhood, adolescence, and adulthood, a person encodes psychological and physiological experiences to form "organized cognitive–affective–motivational systems" (OCAMS).

These OCAMS have elsewhere been referred to as ego states (Watkins & Watkins, 1997; Fairbairn, 1944), schemas (Young, 2005) internal representations (Klein, 1961) and psychic structures (Freud, 1923). The OCAMS, henceforth referred to as ego states, comprise sensory, memory, affective, cognitive, behavioural, and motivational aspects that influence the processing of information and give direction to the person's behaviours, actions, attitudes, values and so on. The ego states represent primitive and enduring, but changeable organizations that can serve the person well in daily living or can interfere with it. The ego states may interfere with daily living when they are formed, for example, from childhood experiences of tragedies, abuse, and parental neglect. The associated feelings of anger, fear, rage, and hate might dominate such ego states that are instrumental in bringing about attitudes, beliefs, behaviours, and actions harmful to the person and to others.

Psychodynamic and cognitive-behavioural oriented therapists assume that ego states or schemas underlie covert and overt behaviours. To illustrate, one can use as an analogy that of a tree with its branches/trunk/roots and foliage. One could say that as the branches/trunk/roots are to the foliage and give life to it, so too the ego states are to behaviour and trigger it. By extension, then, it is assumed that hidden ego states are the source of emotional challenges such as depression and anxiety.

According to this perspective, treatment entails uncovering these ego states and reworking them, or the relationship between them, so as to be able to bring about new behaviours. To accomplish this task, ego-state therapy (Watkins & Watkins, 1993), for example, have devised techniques to uncover the hidden and maladaptive ego states and to heal and transform them into more adaptive ego states. For example, a 35-year-old male was troubled, as an adult, by feelings of abandonment. Therapeutic work uncovered his first experience of abandonment as a child – called an abandonment ego state (Young, 2005) – at the age of two. Ego-state therapy offers a technique to heal the "abandonment schema" and then use the "healed schema" to work through current experiences of abandonment.

Target of Change: Behaviour or Reworking and Rebuilding Psychic Organizations

With regards to the goal of therapy, therapist are divided into two camps with one camp arguing that change takes place at the level of behaviour and the second camp arguing that change takes place at the level of reworking and rebuilding psychic organizations (e.g., ego states, schemas, structures). That is, the one camp holds that one changes that which is observed (e.g., felt, heard, seen) and is objective. The second camp holds that one changes that which is hidden and subjective (e.g., schemas, ego states). This divergent thinking between the objective versus the subjective can be traced back to Freud (1938) who at first thought that when symptoms were ameliorated, treatment was complete, only to realize later, that the mere removal of symptoms did not constitute lasting change. Change took place at the level of reworking structure. The moderate view is that there is no behaviour change without at least some structural change and there is no structural change without some accompanying behaviour change.

The issue is not that black and white. There are clear instances when changing the behaviour is the primary target of the therapeutic work and there are clear situations when reworking the structure is the primary target of therapeutic work. For example, in the cases of acting out anger or aggression, as in road rage, or trying to come to terms with phobias, the initial therapeutic work addresses the behaviour with the goal of diminishing it. Once the behaviours have been diminished, one can then address underlying dynamics and structural issues such as low self-esteem and impoverished inner resources. In the case of recovery from childhood abuse, for example, with the associated memories, flashbacks, and interpersonal and intimacy problems, effective therapy needs to address and rework the underlying structures that initiate and maintain these symptoms.

In bringing about behavioural or structural changes, the therapist will use techniques that are designed for such tasks. For example, to help a person become more assertive, one might use imagery, a technique that helps not only to bring about change, but also to empower the person. To help a survivor of childhood trauma and abuse to behave and relate in a new way, the therapist might use ego-state therapy to bring to light the hidden dynamics or forces that are creating anxieties and conflicts regarding interpersonal relationships, sexuality, and intimacy.

Phases of the Change Process and Techniques

Insight-oriented psychotherapists hold that psychotherapeutic change takes place across time and space which is described in terms of phases or stages. For example, psychoanalysis postulates four treatment phases: opening phase, development of transference, working through, and resolution of transference (Arlow, 1989). Rogers (1961) proposed seven successive stages in changing from fixity to flowingness, and from the rigid end of the continuum to a point nearer the "in-motion" end of the continuum. Tosi (1974) outlined five phases: awareness, exploration, commitment, skill development, and redirection–change. These professionals hold that change is not an all-or-nothing phenomenon but a gradual forward movement through specific stages or phases.

Although psychotherapy phases or stages have been identified and described in the literature, these have only recently been operationalized and empirically investigated. Among these models are the *The Seven-Phase Model of the Change Process* (SPMCP) (Meier & Boivin, 1983, 1998, 2000; Meier, Boivin & Meier, 2006, 2008), *The Assimilation Model* (Stiles et al., 1990), and the *Transtheoretical Model* (Prochaska, 2003).

For the purpose of this chapter, the SPMCP will serve as a model of the change process. The SPMCP emerged from a therapy approach, the goal of which was to facilitate the awareness, emergence, and expression of the authentic/real self (Masterson, 1993) and to enact these in new behaviours and actions. The therapeutic approach combines exploration (of client problem), gaining insight and action.

The seven phases of the SPMCP are briefly present in Table 1.1. In an ideal therapy session, the client begins the session by presenting the problem followed by exploring the underlying feelings, thoughts, desires, values, and so on. The exploration typically leads to greater awareness or to an insight. This new awareness brings about a commitment to change and to trying out different ways of relating and being. From the trying out, the client retains those ways of being and relating that are consistent with the experience of himself. With repetition, the new experiences become consolidated. If at this point the client has achieved his goal, therapy is terminated.

Hypothetically, the client requires technical help to move through the seven cyclical phases. For example, to work through the Exploration Phase, Empathic Responding and Experiential Focusing can be particularly helpful. To move towards the Insight phase, Empathic Responding,

Table 1.1 The seven-phase model of the change process

Phase 1: Problem Definition: The client presents and discloses personal and/or interpersonal difficulties, concerns, feelings, etc. The therapist helps the client to identify and articulate the parameters of the problem in terms of its nature, intensity, duration, and extent. Psychotherapy goals are established.

Phase 2: Exploration: The client, with the help of the therapist, uncovers the dynamics of the problem in terms of its etiology and maintenance with reference to affective, cognitive, motivational, and behavioural constituents. The style of relating to others is examined. This phase represents a shift from complaining and emoting to that of wanting to better understand the presenting problems and concerns and to bring about change.

Phase 3: Awareness/Insight: The client has a better understanding of how unexpressed feelings, inappropriate cognitions, unfulfiled needs and wants, and lost meanings are related to the present problem. This new perspective (e.g. insight, awareness) provides a handle for taking responsibility for self and provides a direction for change. The uncovering process leads to a new perspective on the etiology, maintenance, meaning, and significance of the problem.

Phase 4: Commitment/Decision: The client implicitly or explicitly expresses a determination to change behaviours, manner of relating, and perspectives, and assumes responsibility for the direction of life.

Phase 5: Experimentation/Action: The client responds, relates, feels, behaves, and thinks in new and different ways and in accordance with the new perspective. He tries out (experiments with) the new awareness in everyday life situations. The experimentation takes place between therapy session and/or is rehearsed within therapy sessions.

Phase 6: Integration/Consolidation: The client makes his own and solidifies those new actions, feelings, perceptions, etc., which are consistent with his sense of self.

Phase 7: Termination: The client, having achieved the counselling goals, prepares to live without the support of the therapy sessions. The client's feelings regarding termination are addressed and worked through.

Source: Meier & Boivin, 2000; © 2000 by the Society for Psychotherapy Research. Reprinted with permission.

Experiential Focusing and the Gestalt techniques can be effective. Task-Directed Imagery, Metaphor Therapy, Ego-State Therapy, Solution-Focused Therapy, Cognitive-Behavioural Therapy, and Narrative Therapy can help a client at the Experimentation/Action phases to acquire new skills and competencies to relate in new ways. The movement from one phase to the next phase, therefore, requires specific interventions; however, certain techniques are better suited than others in facilitating this process.

Techniques and the Therapeutic Relationship

Techniques have always been considered an essential aspect of psychotherapy. They act like bridges that carry a person from "troubled" waters to land securely on the "ground," that is, from unwanted situations (e.g., abuse) or experiences (e.g., depression) to those that are wanted. Techniques do not work magically; they receive their potency from an accurate conceptualization of the task to be achieved, and their timely application in the clinical work, and from a therapeutic relationship in which the therapist knows when to nurture and when to challenge and nudge the client towards continued growth.

Psychotherapy techniques are not like medications that operate on the person to deal with feelings of depression, anxiety, anger, and so on. Rather, the client operates on the techniques and takes from them what is needed at the moment (Meier, 2010). An analogy is that of a hungry person to whom a plate of food is brought. The person will take from the plate that which satisfies his hunger. Obviously, the better we understand the person's needs, the better we will be able to provide the appropriate food. Similarly, in therapy, the more we understand the needs of the client and what he is able to receive, the better we will be able to offer what he needs in terms of the therapeutic relationship and technical help. Given all of this, the client, not the therapist, determines what he will take from therapy.

Research has demonstrated time and time again that it is not the theoretical orientation nor the technique that is fundamental in psychotherapy research outcome; rather, the determining factor is the therapeutic relationship. Assay and Lambert (1999) identified the common factors in successful helping relationships. According to their study 15% of the variance is attributable to the technique, 30% to relationship factors, 15% to hope and expectancy, and 40% to extra therapeutic factors.

Although techniques account for a small percentage of effect in bringing about change, this should not cause one to devalue their purpose and importance. Techniques are tools for the therapist and aids for the client to help the latter move forward. It is important for the therapist to become skillful in using techniques, to time their use according to the needs of the client, and to make techniques a natural and integrated extension of his thinking and therapeutic approach in working with clients.

Therapist–Client Collaboration

The psychotherapeutic process has, from the very beginning, been considered to be a collaborative endeavour between therapist and client. Freud (1938) requested that the patient be open, honest, and forthcoming of all that he experiences during the analytic hour and that he, as psychoanalyst, would bring to the session all of his understanding and discretion in helping the patient. Today, the shape that the therapist–client collaboration takes varies according to theoretical approaches with some, such as cognitive-behavioural therapy (Beck, 1976) requiring a formal expression of the work to be done, while others, such as experiential therapy (Gendlin, 1996), require merely an informal expression. The collaborative work also varies according to whether the therapist and client take on active or passive, directive or nondirective roles.

Effective therapy integrates both client-directed and therapist-directed interventions. In the majority of cases it is the client who presents the material that becomes part of the therapeutic process and the therapist agrees to collaborate with the client to deal with it. In such cases, the client works on the concern without much help from the therapist, who assumes a more or less passive role. There are times, however, when the client is stuck or goes around in a circle, and the therapist must intervene more actively and directly by suggesting an exercise or posing a question that will help the client to become less stuck. The rule of the thumb is that if the client is able to manage on his own, the therapist takes more of a passive role and lets the client direct the process.

The willingness to collaborate and the nature of this collaboration are continuously reworked throughout the therapy sessions. For example, a client working on issues of intimacy might become aware that these issues are related to childhood abandonment experiences, but the client might not know how to get at them. The therapist might suggest the use of a technique such as Experiential Focusing (Gendlin, 1996) and seek the client's collaboration to engage in the exercise. As therapy progresses there might be numerous occasions for the therapist to seek collaboration from the client to introduce a technique to work on a new issue that arose. It is imperative that the therapist seek the client's collaboration each time a new technique is introduced.

The counselling and therapy techniques discussed in this book are briefly presented in Table 1.2. The techniques are compared on five dimensions, namely, psychological content of

Table 1.2   Techniques compared on five dimensions

Approach	Content of therapy work	Goal to achieve	Therapy Process Phase	Nature of encoded material	Therapeutic relationship
Empathy	Feelings	Express feelings	Exploration	Perceptual	Rogers's core conditions
Focusing	Bodily felt feelings	Gain awareness	Exploration	Sensorial, perceptual	Rogers's core conditions
Gestalt Empty-Chair	Feelings	Express feelings	Exploration	Sensorial, perceptual	Interactional
Gestalt Two-Chair	Internal conflicts	Resolve conflicts	Awareness	Perceptual	Interactional
Metaphor	Symbols, images	Change perspective	Awareness	Symbolic	Interactional
Imagery	Desired relational behaviour	Empower person	Action	Perceptual, symbolic	Interactional
Ego-state therapy	Hidden ego state	Empower person	Awareness	Perceptual	Interactional
Solution focused	Behaviour that works	Change behaviour	Action	Perceptual	Collaborative
Cognitive therapy	Automatic thoughts and irrational beliefs	Change thinking	Action	Perceptual	Collaborative
Narrative	Dominant life story	Build preferred story	Action	Perceptual	Collaborative
Self-in-relationship psychotherapy	Relational and self needs	Reorient way of life anchored in primary needs	Exploration, awareness, action	Perceptual	Self and relationally immersed with boundaries

therapeutic work, goal to achieve, therapy process phase for which they are suited, type of encoded experience addressed, and the nature of the therapeutic relationship. It will be noticed that the first seven entries (empathy to ego-state therapy) under the column "Approaches" refer directly to techniques. The remainder of the entries refer more broadly to a therapeutic approach that includes more than one technique.

Discriminate Use of a Technique

Techniques are potentially powerful therapeutic interventions that are able to bring to consciousness forgotten, hidden, traumatic, and early childhood experiences that might deeply affect the client and the therapeutic process and progress. For this reason, the therapist, when inviting a client to engage in a technique, needs to exercise "sound clinical judgment based on solid understanding of psychodynamics and psychopathology" (Kopp, 1995, p. 5). A technique should be seen for what it is, an instrument to further the therapy process; in the words of Freud (1900), one "should not mistake the scaffolding for the building" (p. 536).

Timing of Intervention

The timing for the inclusion of a technique in the therapy session must be right. One introduces a technique only when there is a high probability that it will be effective and help the client with the task at hand. One could say that there is a high probability that it will be effective when it appears that the client is ready to engage in the activity for which the technique is designed to be helpful. For example, if a client is carrying on an internal dialogue, it is highly probable that the client is ready to externalize the dialogue using a technique such as the Gestalt Two-Chair technique (Perls, 1969). This is consistent with Freud's (1938) recommendation that one makes an interpretation when the patient has already arrived at the insight himself (p. 43).

Provide Rationale for Use of Technique

It is important for the therapist to provide a rationale for its use and link the technique to the achievement of the therapeutic goal. It is also important for the therapist to discuss with the client the technique that will be used in the session, give clear instructions regarding its use, allow the client the freedom to terminate the use of the technique, and, if completed, give the client time to describe the experience following the session.

Informal Use of Techniques

In the hands of an experienced therapist, techniques can be modified and informally used in the therapy sessions. For example, one might introduce Experiential Focusing (Gendlin, 1996) in an informal way by asking the client who is distraught – angry, depressed, anxious – to get in touch with what he is experiencing bodily. This modified form might be used to help the client get a grip on his distraught feeling without going to the other steps that are part of the formal use of Experiential Focusing (see Chapter 3).

Ethical Considerations and the Use of Techniques

The techniques described in this book are potentially powerful therapeutic tools and interventions. Therapists should use them only if they have adequate training. It is assumed that therapists who have a graduate-level training in the helping profession will be able to teach themselves how to use the techniques. For this, it is best to form a small group and practice the technique using each other as therapists and clients. For a beginning or inexperienced therapist, the techniques should only be used under the supervision of a supervisor who is, himself, competent to use the techniques.

In using the techniques, one must be careful not to impose one's ideas or preferences on the client or to manipulate the client into a certain way of thinking or behaving. As mentioned earlier, one uses a technique to support that which the client has already started, such as resolving an internal conflict by dialoguing or engaging in new behaviours such as assertiveness.

It is important to pay attention to cultural and gender issues when one engages a client in a technique. For example, some cultures value relationships and family whereas other cultures value competence and independence. One uses a technique in keeping with the client's cultural, family and personal values and helps a client to sort these out and to live according to their values.

Lastly, clients need to be informed that they are free to discontinue with a technique when they wish to do so. They also need to be informed as clearly as possible how they will participate in the technique and the risks of their engagement.

Something to Think About

1. What is meant by postmodernism?

2. Does adding needs/wants to a psychotherapeutic model make a difference?

3. In what way does psychotherapeutic change take place at the level of both behaviour and internal states such as schemas?

4. Which techniques are helpful to transform ego states?

5. What are some cautions that one must exercise when using techniques?

References

Arlow, J.A. (1989). Psychoanalysis. In R. Corsini (Ed.), *Current psychotherapies* (pp.1–43). Itasca, IL: F.E. Peacock Publishers.

Assay, T.P., & Lambert, M.J. (1999). The empirical case for the common factors in therapy: Quantitative findings. In M.A. Hubble, B.L. Duncan, & S.D. Miller (Eds.), *The heart and soul of change: What works in therapy* (pp. 33–56). Washington, DC: APA Press.

Beck, A.T. (1976). *Cognitive therapy and the emotional disorders.* New York: International Universities Press.

Benesh, M., & Weiner, B. (1982). Emotion and motivation: From the notebooks of Fritz Heider. *American Psychologist, 37,* 887–895.

Blanck, G., & Blanck, R. (1979). *Ego psychology II: Psychoanalytic developmental psychology.* New York: Columbia University Press.

Butler, C. (2002). *Postmodernism: A very short introduction.* Oxford: Oxford University Press.

Caplan, T. (2008). Needs ABC: Needs acquisition and behaviour change – An integrative model for couples therapy. *Journal of Psychotherapy Integration, 18*(4), 421–436.

Detmer, D. (2003). *Challenging postmodernism: Philosophy and the politics of truth.* New York: Humanity Books.

Downey, M. (1994). In the ache of absence: Spirituality at the juncture of modernity and postmodernity. *Liturgical Ministry, 3,* 92–99.

Fairbairn, W.R.D. (1944). Endopsychic structure considered in terms of object relationships. In W.R.D. Fairbairn, *An object relations theory of personality* (pp. 82–136). New York: Basic Books.

Freud, S. (1900). The interpretation of dreams. *Standard Edition* (Vol. 5). London: Hogarth Press.

Freud, S. (1923). *The ego and the id.* New York: Norton.

Freud, S. (1938). *An outline of psycho-analysis.* London: Hogarth Press.

Gendlin, E.T. (1996). *Focusing-oriented psychotherapy: A manual of the experiential method.* New York: Guilford Press.

Held, B.S. (1995). *Back to reality: A critique of postmodern theory in psychotherapy.* New York: W.W. Norton & Company.

Kearney, R. (2001). *The wake of the imagination: Toward a postmodern culture.* London: Routledge.

Klein, M. (1961). *Narrative of a child analysis.* London: Hogarth Press. (Volume 2).

Kopp, R. R. (1995). *Metaphor therapy: Using client-generated metaphors in psychotherapy.* New York: Brunner/Mazel.

Lazarus, R. (1984). On the primacy of cognition. *American Psychologist, 32*(2), 124–129.

Maslow, A.H. (1954). *Motivation and personality.* New York: Harper.

Masterson, J.E. (1993). *The emerging self: A developmental, self, and object relations approach to the treatment of the closet narcissistic disorder of the self.* New York: Brunner/Mazel.

Mayer, J.D., Salovey, P., & Caruso, D.R. (2008). Emotional intelligence: New ability or eclectic traits? *American Psychologist, 63*(6), 503–517.

Meier, A. (2010). The therapeutic relationship and techniques: How the clients take from them what is needed to bring about the desired change. In A. Meier & M. Rovers (Eds.), *The helping relationship.* Ottawa, Ontario: University of Ottawa Press, in press.

Meier, A., & Boivin, M. (1983). Towards a synthetic model of psychotherapy. *Pastoral Sciences, II,* 137–176.

Meier, A., & Boivin, M. (1993). *The interplay of affect, cognitions, and needs in a model of psychotherapeutic change.* Paper presented at the 9th Annual Conference of the Society for the Exploration of Psychotherapy Integration. New York, 23 April.

Meier, A., & Boivin, M. (1998). *The seven-phase model of the change process: Theoretical foundation, definitions, coding guidelines, training procedures, and research data* (5th Ed.). Unpublished MS. Ottawa, Ontario: Saint Paul University.

Meier, A., & Boivin, M. (2000). The achievement of greater selfhood: The application of theme-analysis to a case study. *Psychotherapy Research, 10*(1), 60.

Meier, A., Boivin, M., & Meier, M. (2006). The treatment of depression: A case study using theme-analysis. *Counselling & Psychotherapy Research, 6*(2), 115–125.

Meier, A., Boivin, M., & Meier, M. (2008). Theme-analysis: Procedures and application for psychotherapy research. *Qualitative Research in Psychology, 5*, 289–310.

Murray, H.A. (1938). *Explorations in personality.* New York: Oxford Press.

Perls, F.S. (1969). *Gestalt therapy verbatim.* Toronto: Bantam Books.

Prochaska, J.O. (2003). An eclectic and integrative approach: Transtheoretical therapy. In A.S. Gurman & S.B. Messer (Eds.), *Essential psychotherapies: Theory and practice* (pp. 403–440). New York: The Guilford Press.

Reisenzein, R., & Schnpflug, W. (1992). Stumpf's cognitive-evaluative theory of emotion. *American Psychologist, 47*(1), 34–45.

Rogers, C.R. (1961). *On becoming a person: A therapist's view of psychotherapy.* Boston: Houghton Mifflin.

Stiles, W.B., Elliott, R., Llewelyn, S.P., Firth-Cozens, J., Margison, F.R., Shapiro, D.A., & Hardy, G. (1990). Assimilation of problematic experiences by clients in psychotherapy. *Psychotherapy: Theory, Research and Practice, 27*, 411–420.

Tompkins, P., & Lawley, J. (1996). Meta, Milton and metaphor: Models of subjective experience. *Rapport Magazine, 36*, August. (Also at http://www.davidgrove. com/articles/mmm.html)

Tosi, D.J. (1974). *Youth: Toward person growth, a rational-emotive approach.* Columbus, OH: Merrill.

Verny, T.R. (1981). *The secret life of the unborn child.* New York: Dell Publishing.

Verny, T. R., & Weintraub, P. (2002). *Tomorrow's baby: The art and science of parenting from conception through infancy.* New York: Simon & Schuster.

Watkins, J.G., & Watkins, H.H. (1997). *Ego states: Theory and therapy.* New York: Norton.

Yalom, I.D. (1989). *Love's executioner and other tales of psychotherapy.* New York: Harper Perennial.

Young, J.E. (2005). Schema-focused cognitive therapy and the case of Mrs. S. *Journal of Psychotherapy Integration, 15*(1), 115–126.

Zajonc, R.B. (1980). Feeling and thinking: Preferences need no inferences. *American Psychologist, 35*, 151–175.

2 Empathic Responses

Chapter Summary

A fundamental prerequisite for effective psychotherapy is for the therapist to empathically understand not only the client's problem but also their subjective experience that is the basis for change and gives it direction. This chapter presents the notion of empathy, differentiates various levels of empathic responding, extends the notion of empathy to include desires/yearnings and commitment to change, and outlines procedures to develop the skill to respond empathically to client statements. A transcript of an actual session demonstrates the use of primary and advanced levels of empathic responding and illustrates how paying attention to client need statements and to commitment to change enhanced the therapy session. Empathic responding is most effective with resourceful clients, but with less resourceful clients it is necessary to complement empathic responding with action-oriented techniques such as imagery, metaphor therapy, narrative therapy, and cognitive-behavioural therapy.

Introduction

Empathic listening is one of the most potent and effective tools available to therapists to understand the client deeply and to conceptualize the client's strengths. Empathic listening is practiced to one degree or another by psychotherapists regardless of their theoretical orientation. Despite its importance in effective therapy, empathic listening is the most difficult skill to master, partly because our culture does not encourage this kind of response and partly because we may not have acquired the verbal and intuitive skills to access our own inner world and the inner world of the client (Nichols, 1995). It usually takes many years of experience for a therapist to develop a strong conviction that empathic listening without talking contributes the most to a client getting better (Strean, 1994).

This chapter begins by presenting the origin of the word empathy. This is followed by theoretical aspects related to empathic responding. The subsequent sections present measures of accurate empathy, the empathic cycle, guidelines for formulating and communicating empathic responses, and common problems and empathic inhibitors. The chapter ends with a transcript of a therapy session that illustrates the integration of empathic responding.

Empathy: Origin and Definitions

The word empathy has a long history going back to the times of the Greeks and Romans (Barrett-Lennard, 1981). The early Greeks coined the word, *empatheia*, meaning affection and passion with a quality of suffering. The "em" means "in" or "into" and there is the idea at least of going into a strong feeling-connection with another. The Latin equivalent was largely borrowed from the Greeks. *Pathos* is from Latin and, as the modern suffix "pathy", it can mean feeling-perception.

A German psychologist, Theodor Lipps (1897) (cited by Barrett-Lennard, 1981), used the term *Einfühlung* to refer to the process of becoming totally absorbed in an external object, such as a work of art, with meaning for the perceiver. *Fühlung* means feeling and *ein* means into. Thus *Einfühlung* is a process of feeling-into, through the creative work of another or of an object in nature, but not specifically into the experience of another person. Lipps (1903) wrote: "There are three spheres of knowledge. I know about things, about myself, and about others ... The source of the third type of knowledge is empathy" (Allport, 1937, p. 351). The concept *Einfühlung* implies apprehending the personal qualities or individuality of the other from a position as participant–observer. Edward B. Titchener introduced the concept of empathy as the English equivalent of *Einfühlung* (cited by Barrett-Lennard, 1981).

The first definitions of empathic responding within the context of psychotherapy were provided by Freud, Fliess, and Adler. Freud defined empathy as a "form of emotional knowing, the experiencing of another's feelings" (Arlow, 1979, p. 29). Fliess (1942) defined empathy as the ability to put oneself in the client's place, "to step into his shoes, and to obtain in this way inside knowledge that is almost first-hand" (p. 212). For Adler (1931) empathy is being "able to see with [the client's] eyes and listen with his ears" (p. 172) and feel with the heart of another (cited by Barrett-Lennard, 1981, p. 92). Adler did not distinguish between the process of feeling-into and feeling-with. This was left for Rogers to do (Barrett-Lennard, 1981).

Theoretical Aspects

Empathy and empathic responding as we know it today stem from Carl Rogers's person-centreed therapy. To provide the theoretical background to this technique, a brief overview of Rogers's theory is presented. This is followed by a more detailed presentation of the meaning of empathic responding, the broadening of empathic responding to include client needs, desires, values, and commitment to change, and the levels of accurate empathy.

Overview of Person-Centred Therapy

Rogers maintains that the human organism has an underlying actualizing tendency that subsumes all other needs and aims to develop all capacities in ways that maintain or enhance the organism and move it towards autonomy (Raskin & Rogers, 1989). This tendency is directional and constructive. It can be suppressed but not destroyed in a living organism. The movement towards self-actualization is guided by the "organismic valuing process" that is an "inherent ability to value positively experiences he perceives as enhancing his organism" (Meador & Rogers, 1979, p. 143). This keeps the person's movement towards self-actualization within the bounds of personal and social expectations and norms.

The human organism is the locus of all experiences available or potentially available to the person. These experiences, conscious or unconscious, are collectively referred to as the person's phenomenal field, that is, the person's subjective reality (Raskin & Rogers, 1989). As the infant grows and matures, a portion of the total subjective reality becomes differentiated into a conscious perception of self that through evaluational interactions with the environment becomes recognized as "me," "I," or "myself" (p. 166). The self-image is the patterned characteristics that a person considers to be unique to herself. This stable pattern of self-perception emerges from the individual's interaction with her environment and is shaped by the values and judgments of others. Experiences that are inconsistent with the self-image are ignored or disowned. The person may, however, discriminate and react to an experience which is not symbolized. Rogers (1966) refers to this as "subception," that is, "discrimination without awareness" (p. 406).

To grow into an emotional healthy person, the child requires positive regard from others, that is, approval, acceptance, and affection (Rogers, 1966). The provision of such approval, acceptance, and affection leads to positive self-regard and to the person feeling proud of herself and esteemed.

When significant others in the person's world provide positive regard that is conditional rather than unconditional, the person internalizes the desired values, makes them her own, and acquires conditions of worth (Rogers, 1959). The person develops a self-concept which is based on these standards of value rather than on organismic evaluation. The experiences perceived to be in accordance with these conditions are perceived and symbolized accurately in awareness while the experiences that are not are distorted or denied in awareness.

The establishment of conditions of worth leads to an incongruence between self as experienced and the actual experience of the organism. This results in alienation, estrangement from self, and the development of emotional problems including anxiety, depression, and maladaptive behaviour (Rogers, 1966). The root of these problems is that the self-actualizing tendencies and organismic needs have been suppressed by the conditions of worth. To resolve these emotional problems, Raskin and Rogers (1989) recommend empathic responding by which the therapist helps the client to dissolve the conditions of worth, achieve a self that is congruent with experience, reactivate the self-actualizing tendency, restore a unified organismic valuing process as the regulation of behaviour, and undo the estrangement in her functioning.

Empathy and Empathic Responses

Rogers and Barrett-Lennard are considered advocates for the modern day use of empathic understanding. Empathic understanding is viewed as the manner in which a therapist experiences the client at a given moment. To quote Rogers, Gendlin, Kiesler, and Truax (1967):

Accurate empathic understanding means that the therapist is completely at home in the universe of the patient. It is a moment-to-moment sensitivity that is in the 'here and now,' the immediate present. It is the sensing of the client's inner world of private personal meanings 'as if' it were the therapist's own, but without ever losing the 'as if' quality. (p. 104)

Rogers et al. (1967) add that a major part of empathic responding is the ability to communicate these inner experiences to the client in a way that fits her mood and allows the client to receive them as her own. The client clearly receives the message that the therapist is with her. Accurate empathy, therefore, means being able to enter into the "internal frame of reference of another with accuracy and with the emotional components and meanings which pertain thereto, as if one were with the other person but without losing the 'as if' condition" (Rogers, 1959, pp. 210–211). This is communicated in a way that shows that the therapist understands the client's experiences and feelings (Egan, 1982). Empathy or active listening, according to Nichols (1995), requires "a submersion of the self and the immersion of the other" (p. 62).

Subjective Experiences and Empathic Responding

Empathic responding has primarily been used to reflect back to the client her feelings and meanings. Empathic responding, as a counsellor's activity, can be extended to include feeding back to the client her needs (e.g., to feel safe, to be protected), wants and desires (e.g., an intimate relationship), values (e.g., integrity, authenticity), and commitment to change.

The authors of this book contend that it is not sufficient to pay attention only to a client's feelings. The client's desires, aspirations, yearnings, and commitment to change also need to be addressed (see Chapter 1 for more details). One might argue that a client's feelings are akin to a thermometer that indicates hot or cold (Meier & Boivin, 2001). Underlying a client's feelings of depression, for example, might be unfulfiled desires, aspirations, and yearnings. Every person can be said to have two sets of basic needs. The first set includes feeling connected to a significant other and at the same time to feel separate and individuated, that is, to feel being part of a relationship while at the same time maintaining one's sense of autonomy and individuality (Mahler, Pine, & Bergman,1975). The second set of basic needs involves being acknowledged and affirmed for what one is able to do and for who one is, that is, being affirmed for being a competent and a lovable person (Kohut, 1977). It is assumed that all human needs are associated with or derived from these two sets of basic needs.

The procedure in reflecting desires, aspirations, yearnings, and commitment to change is the same as for reflecting feelings and meanings. The difference is that one often begins by listening to the feelings expressed by the client and at the same time one listens for what has brought about the feelings. Often underlying feelings are unfulfiled aspirations and desires or a conflict between one's own values or desires and the expectations of the other. In this sense, empathic responding shifts from paying attention to feelings to paying attention to unmet or unexpressed desires, yearnings, commitment to change, and so on. The following examples represent empathic responses to a client's feelings, aspirations, and commitment to act differently.

Reflection of Feelings

Client: I get upset that they don't understand me. I'm so afraid of people rejecting me, or laughing at me. If I'm assertive and say "I always feel that I'm not good enough," they will not know how to handle it, they'll think that I am nuts.

Therapist: You fear that you will not be accepted for being assertive since they do not know you that way.

Reflection of Aspirations/Desires

Client: It is so important for me to be strong and to be myself and to know who I am and have people respect me for that and to have someone hold my hand and to have a shoulder to cry on. And yet I'm so afraid of just losing myself in the security of having a hand to hold. I just never felt this before, like somebody is invading my space. I didn't realize how independent I've become.

Therapist: On the one hand you need your space and want people to let you alone and not to invade your space and on the other hand you want to be close to someone to talk to, to turn to. You want both of them and yet you sense that one is in conflict with the other.

Reflection of a Commitment to Change

Client: The person did not show up for the party. I'm trying real hard to be tough. I put on this exterior and not let it hurt. I said to myself, "I'm not going to let myself hurt again. If I just keep filling in the space [hurt] with anger, then I won't get hurt because there won't be any room for the hurt to seep in."

Therapist: You are determined not to allow yourself to get hurt by what others do or do not do and to protect yourself by being angry.

Levels of Accurate Empathy

Both Egan and Carkhuff differentiate two types of empathic responding. Egan (1982) distinguishes between primary-level accurate empathy and advanced-level accurate empathy, whereas Carkhuff (1969) differentiates between interchangeable (similar to that of the client) and additive (adds to what client said) levels of empathy. Egan's two levels of accurate empathy are presented here.

Primary-Level Accurate Empathy

This level of empathy "means communicating basic understanding of what the client is feeling and of the experiences and behaviours underlying these feelings" (Egan, 1982, p. 87). The therapist merely tries to let the client know that she understands what the client *explicitly* said about herself. Empathic responses indicate that the counsellor has understood those themes that are readily apparent from the client's statements. Nonverbal communication and interchangeable responses are important modes of communicating primary empathy (Welfel & Patterson, 2005). Empathic statements help clients to explore and clarify their problem situation from their frame of reference. Counsellors do not try to probe deeper into what the client might be implicitly or half saying (Egan, 1982). The primary level of empathy is used mostly during the first stage of therapy to help clients explore themselves.

Example

Client: I really think that things couldn't be going better. I have a new job and my husband is not just putting up with it. He thinks it's great. He and I are getting along better than ever, even sexually, and I never expected that. I guess I'm just waiting for the bubble to burst.

Therapist: Things are going so well between you and your husband that it seems almost too good to be true (Egan, 1982, pp. 87–88).

Advanced-Level Accurate Empathy

This form of empathy "gets at not only what clients clearly state but also what they imply or leave only half stated or half expressed" (Egan, 1982, p. 89). At this level the therapist gets at a client's feelings that are hidden or buried and only hinted at and are outside of the client's immediate awareness (Thwaites & Bennett-Levy, 2007) and gives voice to the deeper meanings of the client's experience (Truax, 1967/1976). Advanced empathy is not to be confused with interpretation in that advanced empathy is always based on the client's frame of reference. In interpretation, the therapist is the source of meaning and feeling, not the client. Advanced-level empathy is designed to help clients develop new perspectives on themselves – increase self-understanding – and on their problem situation and to bring about client action. As such, advanced empathy is mostly used in the middle and later stages of helping.

Example

Peter: I find biology really tough. I get through it, but I don't think I'm good enough to be in premed. I'm not going to make it into med school. It's not that I get distracted like some other guys – girls and drink and stuff like that. I frankly don't think I'm smart enough for premed. There's too much competition and it's not the only occupation in the world.

Therapist: It sounds like you know the decision you want to make about studies and are ready to accept it. But in the last two sessions you've referred briefly to other concerns, perhaps some concerns with relationships with others or some sexual concerns. I may be hearing things that aren't there, but I thought I'd check it out with you (Egan, 1982, p. 89).

Measuring Accurate Empathy

Several measures have been developed to assess the quality of therapists's empathic responding. These measures view the quality of empathic responding as being on a continuum with one pole indicating that the therapist is not empathic and the other pole indicating that the therapist is empathic. The therapist can use these measures to assess her level of empathic responding and to improve it.

Carkhuff (1969) developed a five-level measure of empathy called *Empathic understanding in interpersonal processes: A scale for measurement (EUIP)*. Carkhuff provides a brief description of each level of empathic response and a typical therapist's response. The therapist's response at the first level shows no understanding of the client's feelings. At the third level, the therapist's responses are interchangeable with those of the client, whereas at the fifth level, the therapist responds to the client's deeper-level feelings.

Carkhuff and Pierce (1975) added a second dimension to the empathic scale, that is, whether the therapist gives *direction* to the client. This was called the *Discrimination Inventory (DI)* and comprised five levels. In the first three levels the therapist provides no direction to the client, and in the last dimensions the therapist offers direction to the client. The five levels of empathic responding with the corresponding action provided by the therapist are summarized in Table 2.1.

The Technique of Empathic Responding

The Empathic Cycle

Barrett-Lennard (1962, 1981) viewed the empathic response in terms of a process which contains steps and phases. The combined steps and phases form the empathic cycle, referred to as an attentional/experiential/communicational sequence. Responding to individual client statements is "a process of listening and observing, resonating, discriminating, communicating and checking your understanding" (Nelson-Jones, 2005, p. 52). Barrett-Lennard (1981) identifies five steps and three phases in the empathic cycle.

Steps of the Empathic Response

Step 1: The therapist actively attends (with an empathic set) to the client who is in some way expressive of his own experiencing and concomitantly expects, hopes, or trusts that the therapist is receptive.

Step 2: The therapist reads or resonates with the client in such a way that directly or indirectly expressed aspects of the client's experience become experientially alive, vivid, and known to the therapist.

Step 3: The therapist expresses or shows in some communicative way a quality of felt awareness of the client's experiencing.

Step 4: The client attends to the therapist's response sufficiently at least to form a sense of perception of the extent of the therapist's immediate personal understanding.

Step 5: The client then continues or resumes visible self-expression in a way that also carries feedback elements for the therapist, potentially of two kinds. One kind is confirming or corrective in respect to the content of the therapist's just-shared view or sense of the client's

Table 2.1   Level of empathic response and direction given

	Level of empathic response*	Nature of direction given**
Level 1	The therapist either does not attend to or detracts significantly from the client's verbal and behavioural expressions and communicates significantly less than what the client communicated.	The therapist provides no direction to the client; therapist may ask questions or provide empty reassurance or advice.
Level 2	The therapist responds to the expressed feelings of the client, but subtracts noticeable affect from the client's communications.	The therapist provides no direction to the client; therapist typically responds to the content of the client's statement and offers some form of advice.
Level 3	The therapist's responses are essentially interchangeable with the client's statements in that they express essentially the same affect and meaning.	The therapist provides no direction to the client.
Level 4	The therapist's responses add noticeably to the expressions of the client by expressing feelings a level deeper than the client was able to express.	The therapist offers some direction by identifying the client's deficit, the reason for the deficit, and the emerging desired change. The therapist's statement takes the form of "You feel ... because you are not able to ... and you want to ..."
Level 5	The therapist's responses add significantly to the feeling and meaning of the client's expressions in that they accurately express feeling levels below what the client was able to express or the therapist is able to be fully with the client in her deeper self-exploration.	The therapist's response provides specific direction. It takes the form of "You feel ... because you can't ... and want to ... . One step is ..."

*Summary of Empathic understanding in interpersonal processes: A scale for measurement, from Carkhuff (1969).
**Summary of the Discrimination Inventory from Carkhuff & Pierce (1975).

felt experience (expressed in Step 3). The other possible kind is informative regarding the extent to which the client generally perceives a relationship of personal understanding with the therapist. The cycle begins over at Step 1.

Phases of the Empathic Response

Phase 1: Awareness: The inner process of empathic listening, resonation, and personal understanding.

Phase 2: Vocabulary to symbolize it: Expressed empathic understanding.

Phase 3: Express it: Received empathy, or empathy based on the experience of the person empathized with. The steps and phases of the empathic cycle are summarized in Figure 2.1.

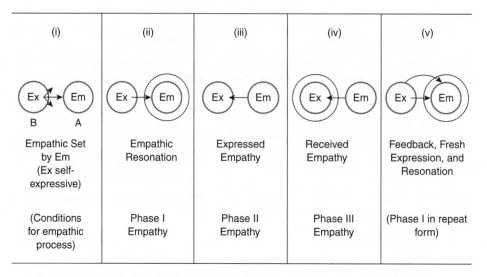

Figure 2.1 Schematic outline of the empathy cycle. (Ex = person engaged in primary *expression* and exploration; Em = responding, *em*pathizing person. Lower-case Roman numeral i–v represent Steps 1–5, respectively; outer circles in ii, iv, & v mark peaks of impact/arousal/involvement in hearing or being heard empathically; solid lines represent principal communicative expression)

Source: Barrett-Lennard, 1981, p. 94 (© American Psychological Association, Washington DC; reprinted with permission)

Guidelines for Formulating and Communicating Empathic Responses

Carkhuff (1969) presents guidelines to be considered when formulating and communicating empathic responses. He contends that therapists will find that they are most effective in communicating an empathic understanding when they:

1. Concentrate with intensity upon the client's verbal and nonverbal expressions (e.g., voice, face, bodily movements) and read between the lines.

2. Concentrate upon responses that are interchangeable with those of the client, particularly in the early stages of therapy.

3. Formulate their responses in language that are most attuned to that of the clients.

4. Respond with the same feeling tone as that communicated by the client.

5. Move tentatively toward expanding and clarifying the clients' experiences at higher levels.

6. Concentrate upon what is not being expressed by the client and fill in what is missing.

7. Use the clients' behaviours as a guideline to assess the effectiveness of their responses.

In summary, the use of empathic responses shows to the client that the therapist understands and cares for her; helps the client to focus on the important feelings and other deep-seated emotions and to explore them more deeply; and helps the client to integrate her perceptions and feelings in a more complete self-awareness. Empathic responses also serve as a check for the therapist to determine if she understands the client.

Common Problems and Empathic Inhibitors

Common Problems

The use of empathic responding does come with its problems (MentalHelp.net, 2005). One of the problems is that clients are invited to enter deeply into their feelings and pour them out. It is important that therapists be open to their own feelings and genuinely interested in and willing to help the clients deal with their problems. Second, clients might misread empathic responses as the therapist agreeing with them or making a judgment about them. In both cases it is important for the therapist to correct the clients' perception. Third, in talking about their feelings, the clients might feel worse rather than feel better in working towards a solution. It is important for the therapist to assess the clients' resources to work through feelings. Fourth, inexperienced therapists might confuse being empathic with being sympathetic and think that they need only to identify with and support the clients' experiences. The empathic therapist uncovers unspoken feelings, communicates this understanding to the clients, and provides new insights. Fifth, inexperienced therapists might feel very uncomfortable in providing empathic responses and feel the need to be more active. It is important for the therapist to remain patient and observe the clients' reactions in being with a therapist who cares, is nonjudgmental, and attunes herself to the clients' subjective experiences.

With regards to advanced-level empathic responses that border on interpretations, it is important to attune them to the readiness of the client to accept them because otherwise they could interfere with the flow of the therapy session. One could make the mistake of prematurely inviting the client to address the deeper underlying issues when the client has no sense of them or is not ready to go there. One should put off formulating an advanced-level empathic response until the client has almost arrived at formulating it for herself.

Empathic Inhibitors

Inhibitors to achieving a shared understanding of a client's inner experiences include personal biases, prejudices, assumptions, preconceived ideas, and stereotyped notions. An example of an empathic inhibitor is when a counsellor believes that a client is not getting better because she is not making sufficient effort. With this attitude, it is difficult to empathize with a depressed client, for example, who appears to make minimal effort to get better. Further empathic inhibitors consist of the overuse of questions, making judgments, giving advice, and interruptions. Such interventions stem from the therapist's rather than the client's agenda and inhibit the client from entering her experience and speaking from it.

Illustration: Tania

The following transcript is that of a young adult female client, Tania (pseudonym), who worked through issues related to obsessive-compulsive disorder. Below is a summary of a session, excerpts from a session transcript, its conceptualization, and a description of the therapist's interventions.

Summary

Tania was brought up in a home where the expression of feelings were viewed negatively and suppressed. She was led to believe that only facts mattered. During this session, she became aware of an incongruence between what she was hearing (self-image) within herself and her true sense regarding the place of feelings in her life. This awareness brought about feelings of sadness and anger in not being free to express feelings. The session took a turn at T25 where the therapist picked up on Tania's desire to be free and explored with her the obstacles which kept her from realizing this. The session ended with Tania expressing a commitment to take charge of her life and how she is to live it.

Transcript

(The client (C) began the session by stating to the therapist (T) how her attitude towards the place of feelings in one's life changed because of a book she read. The significance of the asterisks is explained below. Some parts of the transcript are omitted.)

*T5:   You are able, now, to say that feelings matter?

C5:   Yeah, I think they do. This has partly to do with something I read this week and I got a more rounded out picture. You see, before, I looked upon everything as facts. You know, this is a fact, that's a fact, it doesn't give a damn to what you feel about it, it's still the fact of the thing. But now I think your experience must have something to do with it too.

*T6:   The reading of a book gave you a new perspective in how to look at feelings and facts and how the two work together?

C6:   You know, I told myself your feelings matter as much as anything else, but deep down inside there is something saying, you can't trust your feelings.

T7:   Could you say more about not being able to trust your feelings?

C7:   It's just that it's something that was drilled into me and it's safer to keep it than contradict it. At least it feels a lot safer.

*T8:   It's better, for you, to put feelings aside rather than to acknowledge them and to make them part of you.

C8:   Well, I used to think that, but I'm not so sure any more. I think that feelings might have a place of their own. Actually, I'm sure they have.

*T10:   You are still debating as to whether they do or do not have a place.

C10:   They do have a part to play, but I also have to be careful.

T11:   Don't give them too much room.

C11:   Right. Just in case, just to be sure.

T12:   What does it mean to you to allow feelings to become part of the way you respond and interact and go about doing things and the way you are?

C12:   It seems that it is more natural than always to be on your back.

**T13:   It's like letting the water flow rather than trying to dam it up?

C13:   (Long pause.) There's always a big, "Well, what if?" in the background.

T15:   How do you sense that "What if?" What is it about?

C15:   It just seems like one big black cloud and it's very scary, and it seems that there is somebody who has a lot more authority than I have.

T16:   There's something ominous about it?

C16:   Yeah (long pause).

T17:   (Therapist senses sadness in her eyes and change in her face.) Are you in touch with any sad feeling now?

C17:   Yeah.

T18:   I would like you to stay with it and try to feel all of it and see what it's like and as you become aware of a part of it, see what it is saying. Allow it to speak to you about something new that comes up and see what the whole of it is about. Do not analyze it. Do not force it, let it be, let it surface until you can recognize some aspect of it.

C18:   (Long pause.)

T19:   Where are you at with all of it?

C19:   (Long pause.) (Sigh.) I just feel sort of crushed, and I feel very angry, but as soon as I start to feel very angry, I don't let myself.

T20:   What are your feelings of anger about?

C20:   (Sigh.) I'm angry because I feel I'm not free, I also think, I don't have any right to be free.

T21:   And when you hear that "You have no right to be free," what is it that you experience at that moment?

C21:   Sort of hopelessness, and then I say, "Well, okay, I don't have any right to be free."

T22:   Any other feeling?

C22:   Well, "Why don't I have a right to be free?"

T23:   And what does the other side (of the debate) say?

C23:   The other side doesn't have to give answers. It's only got to give orders.

**T25:   You experience, in a sense, wanting to be free and yet, you also sense something that prevents you from being free.

C25:   You know, I must be right. (Sigh.)

**T26:   The image I have is something wanting to come through the ground, and yet at the same time, there's something on top keeping it down, stepping on it.

C26:   But maybe it's supposed to stay in the ground.

T27:   Did you hear yourself saying that? What do you experience inside?

C27:   It might sound funny, but it makes me feel more secure. Maybe safe in another – world.

**T28:   It might be dangerous to be yourself, to come out and to be different?

C28:   Yeah, cause maybe I'm not supposed to be different.

T29:   Do you worry when you are out there?

C29:   (Long pause.) Maybe I'm just wasting energy, you know.

T30:   How do you mean that?

C30:   Well, maybe working so hard to change things, I should just stay where I am.

*T31:   (Being facetious.) Let good enough alone and let the feelings be an insignificant part of you and just look at facts. Live that way and learn how to live with them.

C31:   No, my God. I can't do that, I'll smother.

**T32:   I get the feeling that you're beginning to see in greater perspective the role that feelings play. You're quite convinced that they are a significant part and you're not able to go to where you were before. Things have to be different.

C32:   (Long pause.) Okay, so I know all of that and you know all of that.

T33:   To pull a few things together. You mentioned that you're aware of feelings and how in the past you have suppressed them. You also experienced feelings of anger within you, but the minute you were able to allow these to come to the surface, and you were able to put a name on them, you sensed something pushing them away and not allowing them to surface prominently and clearly. You see yourself in a struggle, wanting to feel, and then not allowing yourself to feel.

C33:   Well, sometimes I do let myself experience feelings. I get very angry and then when I get very angry, I feel guilty because I'm angry. So, it's useless.

T34:   What is the guilt about?

C34:   Just because I'm angry.

T35:   Is there someone saying that it's not proper for you to be angry? What does this person mean in saying that it's not proper for you to be angry?

C35:   I don't know if it has to be one person, but I think it's one person.

T37:   Who is that person?

C37:   Sometimes it's my mother. I don't think she ever said it in words, but it still seems that's where it's coming from.

T38:   You receive that message in other ways?

C38:   (Long pause.) You know what makes me so mad? I'm the same way.

T39:   You see your mother in you?

C39:   I don't mind sometimes. Only for some things, like a fussy attitude with rules and regulation. I really think you got no right to be angry with somebody else. Well, somebody who means well. I heard that before.

*T42:   They can step all over your feet, as long as they mean well, it's okay?

C42:   Well, I don't know how they can mean well by stepping all over your feet? So, how do you get to the point where you can say, "Well, it damn well does matter!" How do you get there? That it matters. That they haven't got any right to overpower you.

T44:   That's the question you ask yourself or are wondering about.

C45:   I just wish someone would tell me, without having to think about it.

T46:   You're wondering then how to make the next move? How to shift things?

C46:   I'm wondering that and on the other hand I'm saying, well maybe I have no right to even consider it let alone want it. God, I could be hearing it when I'm 180, you know. I mean, what does it all matter?

T47:   Even as I hear you say that, I don't think that you believe it.

C47:   No, I really don't believe that it matters.

**T48:   What's new for you, is that feelings do matter, and secondly, that you can no longer allow other people to put you down; you want to figure out for yourself how you can make this change so that the old way of relating will stop.

C48:   Cause, it's kind of childish when you think of it, to always depend on somebody else to tell you what you can do and what you can't do.

**T51:   You want to take charge for what you can and can't do?

C51:   Yes, to do what I would like to do.

Conceptualization

Tania's tendency towards self-actualization and autonomy and the organismic valuing process were supplanted, at a very young age, by the pursuit of a self-image shaped by conditional positive regard and by conditions of worth. Unknown to her, she was influenced (subception) by an ominous internalized voice that shaped attitudes towards the expressions of feelings such as anger. Tania experienced incongruence between the person she felt she wanted to be and a deeper inner ominous "voice" prescribing how she should be. In the process, Tania became alienated from herself. The goal of therapy was to help Tania enter into her phenomenal world (subjective reality) and to respond from her internal frame of reference regarding the place of feelings in her life. By this process, Tania reactivated the self-actualizing tendency and the valuing process, developed a sense of positive self-regard, undid the conditions of worth, and moved towards greater autonomy.

Therapist Interventions

To achieve the therapeutic goals, the therapist used a variety of interventions including exploratory and clarifying questions, minimal encouragers, paraphrases, empathic responding, summaries, and focusing. Tania set the agenda for each of the sessions. The therapist used *primary-level accurate empathy*, indicated by a single asterisk [*] preceding a therapist response, and *advanced accurate empathy*, indicated by two asterisks [**] preceding a therapist response. It is noted that primary-level accurate empathic responses were used more frequently at the beginning of the session whereas advanced accurate empathic responses were used more frequently at the middle and end of the session. When viewed more closely, the earlier therapist responses related to affect (T13, T28, and T42) and the later responses related to wanting to change (T25, T26, and T32) and to a determination to take charge of her life and make changes (T32, T46, T48, and T51).

Something to Think About

1. What is meant by the "as if" quality in empathy?
2. How do primary and advanced levels of accurate empathy differ?
3. Is it legitimate to broaden empathic responding to include desires, yearnings, and commitment to change?
4. What is meant by the empathic cycle?
5. How did the therapist's reflection of her wishes help Tania to assume responsibility for her life?

References

Adler, A. (1931). *What life should mean to you*. New York: Little, Brown.

Allport, G.W. (1937). *Personality: A psychological interpretation*. New York: Holt, Rinehart, and Winston.

Arlow, J.A. (1979). Psychoanalysis. In R. Corsini (Ed.), *Current psychotherapies* (pp. 1–43). Itasca, IL: F.E. Peacock Publishers.

Barrett-Lennard, G.T. (1962). Dimensions of therapist response as causal factors in therapeutic change. *Psychological Monographs, 76*(43, Whole No. 562).

Barrett-Lennard, G.T. (1981). The empathy cycle: Refinement of a nuclear concept. *Journal of Counselling Psychology, 28*(2), 91–100.

Carkuff, R.R. (1969). *Helping and human relations: A primer for lay and professional helpers* (Vol. 1). New York: Holt, Rinehart, and Winston.

Carkhuff, R., & Pierce, R. (1975). *The art of helping: Trainer's guide*. Amherst, MA: Human Resource and Development Press.

Egan, R. (1982). *The skilled helper: Model, skills and methods for effective helping* (2nd Ed.). Monterey, CA: Brooks/Cole Publishing Co.

Fliess, R. (1942). The metapsychology of the analyst. *Psychological Quarterly, 11*, 211–227.

Kohut, H. (1977). *The restoration of the self*. New York: International Universities Press.

Lipps, T. (1897). *Raumästhetik und geometrisch-optische Täuschungen*. Leipzig: JA Barth.

Lipps, T. (1903). *Ästhetik: Psychologie des Schönen und der Kunst: Grundlegung der Ästhetik, Ester Teil*. Hamburg, Germany: L Voss.

Mahler, M., Pine, F., & Bergman, A. (1975). *The psychological birth of the human infant*. New York: Basic Books.

Meador, B., & Rogers, C.R. (1979). Person-centreed therapy. In R. Corsini (Ed.), *Current psychotherapies* (pp. 131–184). Itasca, IL: Peacock.

Meier, A., & Boivin, M. (2001). Conflict resolution: The interplay of affects, cognitions and needs in the resolution of intrapersonal conflicts. *Pastoral Sciences, 20*(1), 93–119.

MentalHelp.net (2005). http://www.mentalhelp.net/psychhelp/chap13/chap13d.htm

Nelson-Jones, R. (2005). *Introduction to counselling skills: Texts and activities* (2nd Ed.). London: Sage.

Nichols, M.P. (1995). *The lost art of listening*. New York: Guilford Press.

Raskin, N.J., & Rogers, C.R. (1989). Person-centreed therapy. In R. Corsini & D. Wedding (Eds.), *Current psychotherapies* (pp. 155–194). Itasca, IL: Peacock.

Rogers, C.R. (1959). A theory of therapy, personality, and interpersonal relationships as developed in the client-centreed framework. In S. Koch (Ed.), *Psychology: A study of a science* (Vol. 3) (pp. 184–256). New York: McGraw-Hill.

Rogers, C.R. (1966). Client-centreed therapy. In C.H. Patterson, *Theories of counselling and psychotherapy* (pp. 403–439). New York: Harper & Row.

Rogers, C.R., Gendlin, E.T., Kiesler, D.J., & Truax, C.B. (Eds.) (1967). *The therapeutic relationship and its impact: A study of psychotherapy with schizophrenics*. Madison: University of Wisconsin Press.

Strean, H.S. (1994). *Essentials of psychoanalysis*. New York: Brunner/Mazel.

Thwaites, R., & Bennett-Levy, J. (2007). Conceptualizing empathy in cognitive behaviour therapy: Making the implicit explicit. *Behavioural and Cognitive Therapy*, *35*, 591–612.

Titchner, E.B. (1909). *Experimental Psychology of the Thought Processes*. New York: Macmillan.

Truax, C. (1967/1976). A scale for the measurement of accurate empathy. In C. Rogers, E. Gendlin, D. Kiesler, & C. Truax (Eds.), *The therapeutic relationship and its impact: A study of psychotherapy with schizophrenics* (pp. 555–568). Madison: University of Wisconsin Press.

Welfel, E.R., & Patterson, L.E. (2005). *The counselling process: A multitheoretical integrative approach* (6th Ed.). Toronto: Thomson.

3 The Experiential Focusing Technique

Chapter Summary

The technique of focusing takes empathic responding from a cognitive, affective, and intuitive process to a process that also engages bodily sensing and assumes that the body knows. In empathic responding, it is the therapist who brings his understanding to the session, but in focusing it is the client who finds his own understanding of the problem by connecting the implicit with the symbolic or with an image. Experiential focusing invites both the psychotherapist and client to enter deeply, through bodily sensing, into the client's subjective experience with the purpose of the client finding there the solution to his problems. This chapter presents the essential components of the experiential focusing technique, outlines its basic steps, and demonstrates its use by providing excerpts from an actual therapy session. Experiential focusing is particularly helpful to keep the clients focused in the here-and-now, to shift from intellectualizing about their problems to experiencing what lies beneath them, and to allow change to be guided from these inner experiences.

Introduction

Eugene Gendlin (1964/1973) developed focusing-oriented psychotherapy partly from his philosophy and theory of experiencing and partly from his research on the process and outcome of psychotherapy. In collaboration with Carl Rogers and his colleagues at the University of Chicago, Gendlin (1981) studied why some clients improved in psychotherapy while others did not. They observed that successful therapy was not determined by the therapist's orientation or technique or the type of problem being worked on; rather, what the client did internally made the difference. Successful clients spoke from their own experiencing process; they regularly checked inside themselves for a whole bodily felt sense of their situation. Successful clients were able to connect with a conceptually vague but bodily felt sense, were able to stay with it while it came into focus and let that which was there emerge from it and guide the change process. These discoveries led to further research on understanding how this inner checking can be discovered and how it effects psychotherapy change (Gendlin, 1996).

This chapter, divided into three parts, presents Gendlin's experiential focusing technique. The first part presents the theoretical aspects of focusing, the second part addresses the practice of experiential focusing, and the third illustrates the use of focusing by providing excerpts from a transcribed therapy session.

Theoretical Aspects

This part begins with Gendlin's critique of contemporary personality theories and their inability to explain change. It then presents his theory of change, which is organized according to three broad topics, namely experiencing, focusing and its phases, and the role of the personal relationship.

Gendlin's Critique of Personality Theory

Gendlin (1964/1973) observed that contemporary personality theories were not able to conceptually explain change. The theories postulated that personality maintained its character (e.g., being likeable) despite circumstances and that personality involved identity and continuity through time. Personality was viewed as a structured entity with defined contents (e.g., traits) and patterns. Far from explaining personality change, personality theories endeavoured to define personality as tending not to change when change is expected. On the other hand, Gendlin observed that personality theories asserted that change does actually occur. However, since structure and content tend to maintain themselves and distort present experience, personality change can be accounted for only if it can be shown how resistance to change yields to change.

Gendlin (1964/1973) noted two problems that inhibit change and two observations that facilitate personality change. The two main problems of personality theories that made change theoretically impossible are ascribing to the "repression paradigm" and to the "content paradigm" (Gendlin, 1964/1973, p. 441). The repression paradigm supposes that a child, in its development, represses from consciousness those feelings, urges, or behaviours which are not seen as affecting a positive regard from others. This paradigm explains the development of personality, but it does not explain change of personality, because the person will continue to repress his unwanted feelings, urges, etc. To explain personality change as the uncovering of repressions is theoretically not consistent. The content paradigm assumes that personality is composed of content such as traits which are constant, and yet this paradigm does not have a vocabulary to describe how these contents can change. A personality theory is needed which has the vocabulary to explain how content changes in therapy.

Gendlin (1964/1973) observed that theories of personality subscribed to two universal observations of circumstances under which change takes place. The first of these observations is that change occurs when the person is engaged in some intense feeling process by which a person's concepts and structures become modified. The second observation is that significant personality change occurs within the context of an ongoing relationship where the person becomes aware of things that he could not otherwise have become aware of and where the person works through therapeutic relational problems.

Gendlin (1964/1973) states that the two problems (repressive and content paradigms) and the two observations (change is associated with an intense feeling process and takes place within the context of a personal relationship) are related. It is observed that clients do become aware of what is repressed and do modify their personality contents. Since the traditional personality theories are not able to explain this phenomenon, a new theory which reformulates repression and the definitions of personality constituents is needed so that observed changes can be theoretically formulated.

Gendlin's Theory of Change

In a published article, Gendlin (1964/1973) offered a theory of personality that describes the process by which change occurs. A major factor in personality change is the ability to attend to one's inner experiencing. The process entails a back-and-forth movement between the pre-symbolic and symbols. The constituents of this feeling process (focusing) include the concepts of direct referent, unfolding, global application, and referent movement. Before presenting these concepts, we present his notion of experiencing with its characteristics. This is followed by a presentation of focusing (the feeling process) and of the role that an effective therapeutic relationship plays in focusing and change.

Experiencing

The central concept in Gendlin's (1964/1973) personality theory is that of experiencing. In psychology, experience refers to all concrete psychological events. Gendlin defines experiencing as "a process of concrete, ongoing events" (p. 447), as a felt process, that is, inwardly sensed, bodily felt events that constitute "the basic matter of psychological and personality phenomena" (p. 448). Major characteristics of experiencing are the direct referent, implicit meaning, and carrying forward.

Direct referent: A direct referent refers to "an inward bodily feeling or sense" (Gendlin, 1964/1973, p. 448) to which a person can turn at any time to resolve problems. Experiencing is termed the "direct referent." This mode of experiencing differs from other modes of experiencing, such as external events or symbols interacting with our feeling process without reflective attention paid to the direct referent. It is also distinct from external objects and the logic to which we can refer to resolve emotional difficulties.

Implicit meaning: The direct referent contains implicit meaning; it embodies the meanings of what we say and think. Without the direct referent or the feel of the meaning, verbal symbols and words are only noises. Although implicit meanings differ from explicit meanings, both are in awareness (Gendlin, 1964/1973). Explicit meanings are when felt meanings occur in interaction with verbal symbols and we feel what the symbols mean. Implicit meanings are just the felt meanings without a verbal symbolization. Most of our perceptions, thinking, and behaviours proceed on implicit meanings and rarely on explicit meanings such as symbols, words, and logic.

Completion: carrying forward and interaction: Implicit meanings, in themselves, are incomplete and await interaction with symbols (e.g., words, pictures) to be brought forward and to be made explicit. The implicit bodily feeling is preconceptual and only when it interacts with verbal symbols (or events) does it become explicit (Gendlin, 1964/1973). Thus, to carry forward, a bodily felt process requires that an implicit meaning be made explicit through some symbolized form.

Focusing and its Phases

Change takes place through attending to the direct referent, that is, through focusing (Gendlin, 1964/1973). Focusing is the whole process that evolves when the person attends to the direct referent of experiencing. Focusing entails attending to a bodily felt sense that at first is unclear and so that something new emerges. Focusing comprises four phases described below.

Phase 1: Direct Referent in Psychotherapy

Focusing begins with the client presenting some vague, puzzling, troublesome experience out of which emerges a definitely felt, but conceptually vague, referent (e.g., feeling agitated). As the client continues to focus his attention on the direct referent, he might be able to conceptualize some rough aspects of it. In doing so, he feels the felt meaning more strongly and vividly, becomes more hopeful of focusing within him, and is less likely to settle for conceptual explanations and apologies. Nothing is vague about the referent; the person can turn to it with his inward attention. It is vague only conceptually.

As the person attends to the direct referent or the felt meanings, the original fears or emotions decrease. However, if he momentarily loses track of it, the anxiety flares up again, and the vague feeling returns. As the person refers to and correctly symbolizes the felt meaning, the felt meaning becomes sharper and more distinct. The symbolizing of the felt meaning carries the "organismic process a step forward" and at such times the person's experiencing is "ahead of" and "guides" his concepts (Gendlin, 1964/1973, p. 453). The person forms concepts and checks them against his direct felt meaning and decides their correctness; if they are not correct or if inadequate, he replaces these formulations with one that is more correct.

Phase 2: Unfolding

In focusing on a directly felt referent, there usually is a gradual step-by-step process of coming to know it better, and in some instances there is a very noticeable opening up (Gendlin, 1964/1973). With the sudden dawning and physical relief, the person suddenly knows. He might just sit there nodding or saying words such as "yes, I've got it" without finding words or concepts to say precisely what he "has got" (p. 454). It is possible that if the person is interrupted, he might lose it, only to say later that he felt what it was at that moment, but that they lost it.

The unfolding of a direct referent involves a deeply emotional and surprising recognition of the good sense of one's own feelings. The person feels them to be right and may repeatedly say this to himself. Because the feelings feel right and make sense, the resolution of problems can occur at this phase. However, it might also happen that after the unfolding the person still sees no way out. The person at least knows it now.

Phase 3: Global Application

The process of direct reference and unfolding affects many aspects of the person in a global way, which the person might experience immediately after the unfolding of a felt referent or which he might experience days later. The person is flooded by many different memories, feelings, and situations, all in reference to the felt referent. During this period of wide application the person might sit in silence recognizing and voicing some of the pieces of this flood. Many changes occur in the person because of this unfolding, whether the person thinks or does not think about the difference that the unfolding has made. The unfolding, itself, changes the person in all of these respects; the change is not limited to the particular problem, but there is a change in many areas (Gendlin, 1964/1973).

Phase 4: Referent Step

Following the three previous phases, the person experiences a definite movement in the direct referent. He experiences the direct referent differently and in a new way. The focusing process and the person's symbolizing and attention take direction from the direct-referent movement. Without referent movement, all that which is spoken about is merely talk, intellectualization, or reporting. In reference movement, there is the experience that something more than logic and verbalization have taken place. Referent movement, in brief, is a "change in the felt meaning which functions in symbolizing" (Gendlin, 1964/1973, p. 458).

The Self-Propelled Feeling Process

When the person begins to focus and connect with a bodily felt feeling, a referent, he finds himself pulled along by the force of the referent. This feeling process has "a very striking, concretely felt, self-propelled quality" (Gendlin, 1964/1973, p. 459). It is important not to distract the client from this self-propelling process by too much talk, analysis, etc. The person needs silence to remain immersed in something felt and to process the experience. This overall feeling process gives verbalization to the underlying flow of events of change. The "self-propelled feeling process is the essential motor of personality change" and "the motor of therapy" (Gendlin, 1996, pp.459, 297).

The Role of the Therapeutic Relationship

Gendlin's (1996) second observation is that change takes place within the context of an effective or therapeutic relationship. The manner of experiencing is affected by the responses of the therapist. A client's manner of experiencing will be constricted if the other interrupts with his own ideas and concerns before he understands what is said. In such a situation, the client will think and feel less than when he is alone. On the other hand, the manner of experiencing is very different when the client senses that the therapist is there for him and the client feels comfortable, safe, and secure.

Manner of Experiencing

In an effective or therapeutic relationship, the person's manner of experiencing is characterized by immediacy, presentness, and richness of fresh detail (Gendlin, 1964/1973). Experiencing is "a changing flow of feeling which makes it possible for every individual to feel something in any given moment" (Gendlin, 1961. p. 234). Immediacy of experience refers to the person being in touch with whatever is going on inside of him. Presentness refers to the person experiencing something now. Experiencing is what a person feels at this moment. Richness of fresh detail refers to the host of details that a person experiences implicitly, some of which he could symbolize or differentiate.

In structure-bound experiencing, where, for example, a psychologist is inclined to notice only the content (e.g., anger) of a stale pattern, the person's experience is constricted and consists only of a few emotions and meanings and is lacking the myriad of fresh details of the present. Structure-bound experience prevents a client from experiencing something new. Such structured experience is described as a "frozen whole" (Gendlin, 1964/1973, p. 462). One cannot experience something outside of frozen-whole experiences and nor can one experience anything new. Since structured frozen-whole experiencing does not function in interaction with present detail, the structure is not modified by present circumstances. Gendlin (1964/1973) says that "experiencing is process and always functions implicitly" (p. 462).

As mentioned earlier, symbols or events carry forward the process of experiencing. Therefore, it can be said that experiencing essentially is an interaction between an implicit feeling and symbols (or an outside person or event). Experiencing takes place at the juncture of the interaction between awareness (symbolization) and an implicit feeling. This explains why the responses of the other affect a person's manner of experiencing. If there is a response there will be ongoing interaction, and because of this interaction certain aspects of the personality will also be in process and change (Gendlin, 1964/1973).

To explain how experience which has been variously called "unconscious," "repressed," and "covert" is brought into process, Gendlin (1964/1973, p. 463) uses the term "reconstituted." By this he means that the experiencing process, which was interrupted, is begun anew.

Contents as Process Aspects

Gendlin (1964/1973) reformulates the notion of content (e.g., personality traits) in terms of process aspects. He defines content as an implicit felt meaning that has been symbolized. That is, when implicit meanings interact with symbols, content is formed. The content is a symbolized unit that points to an experience. Therefore some aspect of implicit functioning must be ongoing in interaction with symbols and experience in order for content to be generated and to exist.

Gendlin (1964/1973) distinguishes between to "carry forward" and to "reconstitute." To carry forward means "that symbols (or events) occur to interact with already implicitly functioning aspects of ongoing experiencing," and to reconstitute "means that the process has become ongoing and implicitly functions in respects in which it previously was not ongoing" (p. 464). Continued carrying forward into ongoing interaction is necessary to reconstitute the experience long enough for the individual himself to obtain the ability to carry it forward as self-process.

Gendlin (1996) provides eight characteristics of a felt sense or referent. The characteristics of the felt sense are viewed from the perspective of the client's process and not from the perspective of the therapist's interventions. The eight characteristics are summarized in Table 3.1.

The Practice of Experiential Focusing

Gendlin (1981) translated his concepts of the feeling process into practical strategies that are encompassed in his experiential focusing technique. This section presents the basic steps and indicators of focusing.

Table 3.1   Characteristics of a felt sense (Gendlin, 1996)

1. A felt sense forms at the border zone between the conscious and unconscious. The source of a felt sense can be felt directly.
2. The felt sense has at first only an unclear, vague, and fuzzy quality and is not recognized as a distinct emotion.
3. The felt sense is experienced bodily and occurs inwardly as a physical and somatic sensation; the felt sense is a distinct feeling that has not yet opened to reveal what it contained.
4. The felt sense is experienced as a whole, a single datum that is internally complex and includes many.
5. The felt sense moves through steps; it shifts and opens step by step; a step that arises from the felt sense transforms the nature of the whole experience.
6. A step brings one closer to being oneself; one senses oneself differently.
7. The process steps are in the direction of growth.
8. Theoretical explanations of a step can be devised only retrospectively.

The Basic Steps of the Focusing Process

The basic steps of the focusing process were published by Gendlin (1981, 1996) and were elaborated and expanded by some of his followers (Friedman, 1986; McGuire, 1991; Greenberg, Rice, & Elliott, 1993; Hendricks, 2007). The names that Gendlin gave to these steps were retained. The authors of this book have modified the description of these steps for application to individual psychotherapy. Knowing these steps and being able to conceptualize them provides the therapist with invaluable tools for creative work. The seven steps outlined below represent Gendlin's model of change.

Clearing a Space

When used for individual therapy, focusing begins with the problem or feelings that the client presents at the outset and agrees to address. As the client engages in the focusing exercise, he is asked to set aside immediate problems and extraneous worries of the day and to pay attention to the feeling or problem at hand. To clear a space means to create an internal environment that is receptive and open to fully experience the problem or feeling. This step is completed when he arrives at an accepting and friendly internal space where he feels separate from and yet connected to the problem (Greenberg, Rice, & Elliott, 1993).

Felt Sense of the Problem

In this step, the client attempts to get at the broader felt sense of the problem or feeling by placing his attention to the bodily sense of the problem in order to allow a "holistic felt sense to form" (Greenberg et al., 1993, p. 171). The felt sense has a vague and unresolved edge and implicit richness (Gendlin, 1996). In arriving at the felt sense, the client connects with a bodily felt feeling of the problem. The person scans inside the body to locate the felt sense which might reside in the stomach, chest, neck, or shoulders. As the person scans the body and locates the felt sense, he also tries to sense the whole of the problem. This step, therefore, involves two substeps. The first is to identify where in the body the person feels the problem (*body sensing*), and the second is to sense the whole of the problem as if standing outside of it and distant from it (*whole sensing*) (Greenberg et al., 1993). This step has been successfully accomplished when the client has located a place in the body where the experience resides and is in contact with the wholeness of the felt sense.

Finding a Handle

The third step is to symbolize the global sense of the problem. The client searches for and finds a word, phrase, symbol, or image that captures the quality of the bodily felt sense. The client searches inwardly for a descriptive label for the nonverbal felt sense and waits for it to emerge spontaneously. The symbols that emerge often take the form of qualities such as "a balloon in my stomach" and "a weight on my shoulders." This step of finding a handle is completed when a phrase, picture, symbol, label, etc., emerges.

Resonating Handle and Felt Sense

As the therapist reflects the client's symbolization, the client resonates with the symbols, checks them out against the felt sense, and refines them until they are just right in capturing the felt sense. This entails going back and forth between the felt sense and the word, phrase, or image, to see if they fit with each other (Gendlin, 1981). When the person identifies a correct word, phrase, or image, he will feel a bodily shift – a "little relief" (Gendlin, 1996, p.73). The person allows the felt sense to speak so that he can dialogue with it and can fine-tune it with the word, phrase, and/or image that is connected to it. This step completes the experiential process task by integrating the verbal conceptual and nonverbal experiential elements (Greenberg et al., 1993).

Asking

In the next step, the client asks questions inwardly to his bodily felt feeling and waits to see what arises spontaneously (Gendlin, 1996). This step has two substeps. The first is getting the crux of the issue, that is, finding out what it is about. A client asks questions such as "What is it really about?" "What is the worst thing about this whole thing?" The second step is moving forward. That is, a client asks questions such as "What would it need to feel okay?" "How can it be made better?" This step can't be rushed; it requires time and practice. This step is fully resolved when the client verbally and nonverbally expresses experiences of physical relief, freedom, and satisfaction, and demonstrates happy facial expressions (Leijssen, 1990).

Receiving

This step entails the client being honest with himself, being open and friendly, and welcoming the new understanding, the changed feeling, or whatever comes. That which is new is not always pleasant, as it can point to a client's disliked behaviours or characteristics. However, it is important for the client to savour, taste, appreciate, and dwell on that which is new and different. This helps the client to consolidate the experience and to appreciate the shift that has taken place. It is also a time for the client to see if he has edited anything out and to identify what he has been afraid to deal with. The answer or solution is not the final one; it is only the first step (Gendlin, 1996).

Recentring and Carrying Forward

Once the exercise has been completed, the person reacquaints himself with his body, the room, and surroundings. This is followed by the therapist asking the client a simple question: "What was the experience like for you?" The focus is on the process; it is not a time to rehash the content of the exercise or to discuss how this might impact on the client's out-of-therapy actions.

When Focusing is Indicated

Gendlin (1996) clearly states that focusing in and of itself is not sufficient for psychotherapy but is one essential element. The focusing procedure specifies what is valuable and eliminates what makes for failure in the essential process. These techniques are beneficial when they are done experientially. Effective therapy entails experiential or verbal-symbolic elements in a person's processing of his emotional experience. The following situations provide opportunities for focusing.

Unclear Felt Sense

A prototypical marker for focusing is an unclear felt sense, that is, a sense that something is amiss or not right or out of "whack." The felt sense is not recognized as a distinct emotion or familiar feeling but remains vague and fuzzy. The unclear felt sense differs from familiar feelings and from experiencing an emotion, such as anger, where the person knows the source of the feelings. In the case of an unclear felt sense, it remains unclear and one does not know how to describe or characterize it, and yet one knows that it has its own particular quality (Gendlin, 1996).

Dead-End Discussions

Focusing may be used to help clients to disengage from "dead-end discussions" that take place, for example, when the therapy consists of interpretations and inferences without an experiential focus or when the person in his talk does not connect thoughts with a bodily felt sense (Gendlin, 1996). Gendlin says that "a real change is a shift in the concrete bodily way you have the problem, and not only a new way of thinking" (p. 9). He further adds that "a concrete experience must occur in response to an interpretation: otherwise nothing has been achieved by the interpretation and it should be at least temporarily discarded" (p. 10).

Dead-End Unchanging Feelings

Focusing can be used when a client expresses feelings of being overwhelmed, disorganized, angry, scattered, confused, anxious, or empty. The client might be unable to proceed in the therapy session because they have so much going on that they feel frozen or paralyzed. They continue to emote and feel the same feelings over and over again, and yet do not move on. Such feelings are referred to as "dead-end feelings" because they arise and remain unchanged and seem quite clear and final. Such feelings do not have a "murky edge to them that asks to be explored" (Gendlin, 1996, p. 12). For example, a client does not say "I feel afraid, but I don't know why." Rather, the client says, "I am afraid and that is it." For such feelings to move forward, the client must sense their unclear edge. Focusing helps a client to move beyond the emotion and become enabled by discovering the implicit meaning of the emotions.

Being Conflicted

Focusing can also be used to resolve human conditions such as intrapsychic conflicts where a person has two states of mind, needs, or attitudes with regard to the same thing, or is torn within regarding a decision to be made. With a special adaptation, focusing can be used to resolve intrapsychic conflicts. In such cases, one wants to make sure that the two parts of the conflict are both highly energized and differentiated even though they are part of the same person. A key phrase that one could use after the client presents the conflict is something like this: "I wonder what is in the middle of this." Such an expression encourages the client to attend to a bodily felt feeling and thereby go beyond the conflict and to what is supporting it.

Illustration: Simone

Simone (pseudonym), in her late twenties and a recent graduate in the mental health profession, sought counselling because she was concerned how her own sexual abuse affected her feelings and views about lesbian relationships. Below are a summary of the therapy session, a conceptualization of the case, a description of the steps of the therapy process, and excerpts from a transcript of an actual session.

Summary

Simone began the session asking whether her childhood sexual abuse by her sister affected her sexual orientation and her feelings and thoughts about lesbian relationships. Simone has very close, supportive, caring, and intimate relationships with her female friends, and yet she has no desire for a sexual relationship with them. This bewilders her, since in working with lesbian couples she observed that they had similar emotional needs and yet their relationship became sexual. A focusing exercise was introduced to help Simone sort out her confusion regarding her feelings towards women and her sexual orientation. In the exercise, Simone pictured herself being in a dark hole, like in a prison, sitting naked with her arms clasped around her legs. She sensed that she was sent there because she did something wrong, but she could not understand why this was so. A light from floor level appeared that allowed her to see herself. Then a woman from behind her arrived, threw a blanket around her, then took her hand and led her out of the hole towards where she was meant to be. The woman was caring and accepting of her. Simone linked the focusing experience to her relationship with women, saying that she wants to be accepted, supported, and acknowledged by women but not have a sexual relationship. With this her confusion regarding her sexual and affectional needs with women and her sexual orientation were resolved.

Conceptualization

Simone's confusion about the meaning of her sexual and affectional feelings for women and her sexual orientation, is related to her not having been affirmed for her growth-oriented strivings and in not having been provided guidance regarding her affectional and sexual needs. This failure leads to her being out of touch with the "direct referent" that nevertheless impacted her conscious thoughts and feelings and brought about a state of confusion regarding her sexual and affectional needs and sexual orientation. The focusing exercise helped Simone to access her "direct referent" and to take the lead from it to resolve her confusion.

Therapy Process

The therapy process followed the steps of the focusing exercise, namely clearing a space, getting in touch with a felt sense of her problem, getting a handle on the underlying problem, checking back and resonating with the handle, asking what was needed to make it better, and receiving and accepting support, love, and safety. These steps are indicated in the transcript. The session ended with Simone recentring herself and providing feedback.

Transcript

Simone began the session by describing her childhood sexual abuse at the hands of her sister. She expressed her confusion that her own emotionally intimate relationships with women do not lead to lesbian relationships of the sort she observed in her work with lesbian couples. She wondered whether her own childhood abuse affected her sexual orientation. Having checked her readiness to enter into a focusing exercise, the therapist, with Simone's permission, proceeded with the exercise. In the transcript, C = Client, T = Therapist, and the numbering following the letter is the response number. Some parts of the transcript have been omitted.

Clearing a Space

T04:   I would like you to take a moment, get in touch with all of your confusion, and bring it together to form one package. As you get in touch with the confusion, clear your mind so that you can be wholly present to it. Experience all of it. Let me know when you are able to experience all of that.

C04:   I have this image of – like a Christmas tree, it is spiky, and it got needles and there are like question marks and exclamation marks, like saps of lightening coming out of this mess. It is a very vivid image.

T05:   You have a vivid image of . . .

C05:   Yes, it came suddenly. It represents all of the questions and the confusion. It looks like a Christmas tree in the shape of an egg.

Bodily Felt Feeling

T06:   Do you have a bodily felt sense of this image? Where do you experience this in your body?

C06:   (Pause: 20 secs.) It is gone.

T07:   Are you in touch with anything else now?

C07:   It is like it went up – and it is stuck at the top – I feel a slight tension in my stomach and my abdomen and there is tightness in my chest and shortness in my breath.

T08:   Stay with all of that – the tension in your stomach, the tightness in your chest, and shortness of breath – and if it shifts, move with it.

C08:   (Pause 60 secs.) I am no longer in my body. There is a lot of pressure in my head.

T09:   In what part of your head do you feel the pressure?

C09:   Here, in my temples. It is like somebody is squishing my head.

T10:   Stay with all of that. If it moves, move with it. If something else comes up, be open to that experience.

C10:   (Silence 55 secs.) Everything is calm now, my heartbeat, my stomach.

T11:   How are you with all of that?

C11:   I am beginning to feel so sad.

T12:   Stay with the sadness, and embrace it. Let it take you where it will.

Finding a Handle or Label

C12:   It is so dark inside and quiet. It is like I am all alone.

T15:   You feel sad, it is dark and quiet. Stay with your feelings and if they move, move with them.

C15:   I think that I am naked and I am sitting with my arms wrapped around my knees. I have my knees pulled up to my chest and I am rocking, I am a child.

T16:   As you are there, how do you feel?

C16:   Like in a prison. I am so confused.

T17:   Stay with the feelings. Get in touch with the whole of the experience.

C17:   I don't know why I am here. I don't know what I did wrong. (Begins to sob; silence 15 secs.). I am so scared. (Therapist hands her tissues.)

T18:   Stay with your feelings of being sad, alone, and not knowing what you did wrong.

C18:   I keep rocking myself to soothe myself, trying to convince myself that it will be okay, and trying to be brave. I don't know why I am in the hole. I know that I am not bad. I know that I tried so hard. It doesn't make sense.

T19:   Remain with your feeling of sadness, with you rocking to comfort yourself. Stay with the whole of it for a little while longer. Let the feelings guide you and take you to where they will.

C19:   There is this light at the bottom of the floor on the right. It looks like a projector light coming from a hole. It is very distracting.

T20:   What feelings are associated with it?

C20:   Just confusion. I don't understand. With the light, I can see me. What am I doing here?

Asking

T21:   What is needed to make all of this better? Go slowly and let it come from the experience of it as to what it needs to make it better.

C21:   (Silence 45 secs.). I just had this image – somebody comes from behind me and lays a blanket over me, wraps it around me, and then takes me by the hand and leads me away from the dark.

T22:   Someone is there to embrace you, to comfort you.

C22:   The blanket is nurturing and loving and it is meant to take away my cold and to comfort me.

T23:   Remain with all of that – with the blanket wrapped around you, someone taking your hand and leading you out of the darkness and out of the sad feelings. Stay with all of that and experience it, take in and taste how good it feels.

Receiving

C23:   (Silence, 95 secs.) It is a woman that came to get me, she has a cloth veil over her head, and I can see her face. She reminds me of Mary and she has a long robe and takes me into the light.

T24:   How is that experience for you?

C24:   I know and I feel that everything is going to be okay, that I am going to be safe but I don't know where I am going because I don't know who she is but whatever she represents is good and pure and I am safe.

T26:   In being with her, you feel safe, secure, and loved, nurtured; you trust that wherever she takes you, it will be okay for you.

C26:   Yeah, not totally. I am curious who she is but my gut feeling tells me that it is okay and that it will be okay. I see us walking away.

Recentring

T28:   Take a few minutes, now, to pull yourself together. When you are ready we can talk about this experience.

C28:   (Silence, 90 secs.) Okay.

Describing Experience

Simone found the exercise to be very powerful and quickly brought up a vivid image of the girl overwhelmed with the sense of sadness and aloneness, a feeling that Simone was not aware of. At the beginning of the exercise she found it hard to stay with the bodily sensations that shifted from the abdomen to tension in her head. When the bodily sensations subsided, everything went dark except a little ray of light at the bottom that allowed her to see herself. She felt that she was not a bad person and that the woman accepted, acknowledged, affirmed, and embraced her goodness. The exercise helped Simone to consolidate her intuitive goodness, to sort out her confusion, and to discover herself in relation to others. In applying the insight from this exercise to her relationship with women, Simone said "I liken this to my experience with women in that with my intimate girlfriends who I perceive to be emotional, supportive, caring, and affectionate, my intimacy needs are met and therefore the relationship is complete without sexual engagement, whereas with men, I feel incomplete without sexual intimacy which is connected to me emotionally. This would explain my confusion because if I have the foundation for an intimate relationship with women, why would the natural progression not be toward sexual intimacy. This speaks to my curiosity about the meaning of the sexual relationship for lesbian couples."

Something to Think About

1. How do the "repression paradigm" and "content paradigm" fail to explain personality change?
2. What is meant by the direct referent?
3. How does the direct referent implicitly influence our actions and thoughts?
4. How does the therapeutic relationship affects clients' experiences?
5. How did the use of focusing help Simone to clarify her confusion about her sexual orientation?

References

Friedman, N. (1986). On focusing. *Journal of Humanistic Psychology*, *26*(1), 103–116.

Gendlin, E.T. (1961). Experiencing: A variable in the process of therapeutic change. *American Journal of Psychotherapy*, *15*, 233–245.

Gendlin, E.T. (1964/1973). A theory of personality change. In P. Worchel & D. Bryne (Eds.), *Personality change* (pp. 439–489). New York: Wiley. Reprinted in A.R. Mahrer & L. Pearson (Eds.) (1973). *Creative developments in psychotherapy* (pp. 439–489). New York: Jason Aronson.

Gendlin, E.T. (1981). *Focusing* (2nd Ed.). New York: Bantam Books.

Gendlin, E.T. (1996). *Focusing-oriented psychotherapy: A manual of the experiential method.* New York: Guilford Press.

Greenberg, L.S., Rice, L.N., & Elliott, R. (1993). Experiential focusing for an unclear felt sense. In Greenberg, Rice, & Elliott, *Facilitating emotional change: The moment-by-moment process* (pp. 165–185). New York: Guilford Press.

Hendricks, M.N. (2007). Focusing-oriented experiential psychotherapy. *American Journal of Psychotherapy*, *61*(3), 271–284.

Leijssen, M. (1990). On focusing and the necessary conditions for therapeutic personality change. In G. Lietaer, J. Rombauts, & R. Van Balen (Eds.), *Client-centered and experiential psychotherapy in the nineties* (pp. 225–250). Leuven, Belgium: Leuven University Press.

McGuire, K. (1991). Affect in focusing and experiential psychotherapy. In J.D. Safran & L.S. Greenberg (Eds.), *Emotion, psychotherapy and change* (pp. 227–251). New York: Guilford Press.

4   The Gestalt Empty-Chair and Two-Chair Techniques

Chapter Summary

This chapter presents the core concepts of Gestalt therapy and outlines the procedures for using the Gestalt Empty-Chair and Gestalt Two-Chair techniques to work through unfinished business and internal conflicts, respectively. The techniques are most effective when problems are conceptualized using a psychodynamic approach such as Gestalt therapy. The techniques are illustrated by their application to the problems of two different clients. The effectiveness of these techniques is demonstrated with both clients increasing their awareness of their problem, reclaiming agency over their lives, assuming responsibility for their actions, and living more authentically. These two techniques are particularly helpful for clients who experience intense pent-up emotions, bear grudges about hurt in past relationships, and experience internal conflicts. When compared to empathic responding and focusing, the two Gestalt techniques work with emotions and feelings more actively by inviting the client to express them directly to a person made present by imagination.

Introduction

This chapter presents the Gestalt Empty-Chair and the Gestalt Two-Chair techniques derived from the Gestalt therapy co-founded by Fritz and Laura Posner Perls. Fritz and Laura were influenced by social-oriented psychoanalysis, Gestalt psychology, phenomenology, existentialism, field theory, and dialogical theory (Yontef & Simkin, 1989).

Fritz Perls, trained in classical psychoanalysis, was influenced by Karen Horney and Wilhelm Reich, both post-Freudian social psychoanalysts who emphasized social and interpersonal influences on personality development. Gestalt psychology views human phenomena in terms of a dynamic and integrated whole rather than as individual parts that can be studied and understood in isolation. Phenomenology is a method that helps persons to stand aside from their usual way of thinking so that they can differentiate between what is actually perceived at the moment (e.g., anger at a supervisor) and what is a residue from the past (e.g., anger towards a childhood abuser). Existentialists focus on people's existence, relations with others, joys, sufferings, etc., as directly experienced in the here-and-now. Field theory contends that a person's life space constitutes a whole where the parts are in immediate relationship with each other and influence all other parts of the field. Dialogical theory postulates that relationships grow out of contact between two differentiated persons where the boundary between "me" and "not me" is clearly established. It is from these influences that Gestalt therapy emerged (Woldt & Toman, 2005).

The goal of Gestalt therapy is to help persons to gain greater self-awareness, and thus to become authentic and meaningfully responsible to themselves so as to choose and organize their existence in a meaningful manner (Yontef & Simkin, 1989). To facilitate this process, Gestalt therapists design experiments and techniques. Two of the more popular techniques are the Gestalt Empty-Chair and the Gestalt Two-Chair techniques typically used to resolve unfinished business and intrapersonal conflicts, respectively. These two techniques are the focus of this chapter.

This chapter is divided into three parts. The first part presents the Gestalt view of personality and its organization and the processes that guide the practice of the two Gestalt techniques. The second part presents the Gestalt Empty-Chair technique (GECT) and the third part presents the Gestalt Two-Chair technique (GTCT).

Part 1: Personality Organization and Processes

The application of GECT and GTCT is guided by theoretical concepts, principles, and processes derived from Gestalt therapy. Included among these interrelated concepts are primary motivating factor, contact boundary, stages of personality development and its subsystems, processes of personality development, organismic self-regulation, and boundary disturbances. A description of the therapeutic goals, the role of the therapist, and Gestalt techniques completes this section.

Primary Motivating Factor

Self-actualization is the primary motivation and the inherent goal in human development and in the pursuit of relationships (Perls, 1969). Self-actualization is present-oriented and is understood as "the process of being what one is and not a process of striving to become" (Kempler, 1973, p. 262). All of the other human needs are part of this overriding need to actualize self. A person's human needs are construed in terms of a figure–ground relationship where at a given moment one need may emerge and direct a person's behaviours while the other needs recede into the background. Needs therefore move from ground to figure and when satiated back to ground and a new need (figure) then captures and directs the individual's behaviour. This process of moving in and out of the figure and ground field is flexible and fluid, and for each individual the need that dominates (becomes a figure) in a particular situation may be different in another setting (Passons, 1975).

Contact and Contact Boundary

The terms contact and contact boundary are fundamental to Gestalt theory. Contact is the meeting between one person and another or between one person and her environment. Contact is the point at which I experience "me" in relation to whatever is "not me" and where I experience "me" as distinct from "you." Contact can take place only between two separate and independent persons. Contact involves both a sense of self and a sense of the other with whom contact is made (Clarkson & Mackewn, 1993). The point in the contact at which something transpires and happens (e.g., loving) is called the contact boundary. It is at this contact boundary that the person actively takes something across the contact boundary which is rendered usable (e.g., being loved).

People are defined by their personal boundaries, called I-boundaries, that are determined by a whole range of life experiences and by the person's innate capacities to assimilate the experiences (Polster & Polster, 1980). The person's I-boundary determines the type of contacts that she will have and that will govern her life. I-boundaries may include body boundaries (e.g., not experiencing sensation below the neck), value boundaries (e.g., rigid values), familiarity boundaries (e.g., unwillingness to venture forth), expressive boundaries (e.g., not wanting to be touched lovingly), and exposure boundaries (e.g., being private) .

Stages of Personality Development

In virtue of her contact boundaries, a person passes through three stages of development, namely, the *social, psychophysical*, and *spiritual* stages (Kempler, 1973). The stages are seen as sequential and representative of the individual's potential level of awareness. Major personality development occurs during the psychophysical stage. At this stage, the child becomes aware of her self, responds psychologically to stimuli from the environment, and becomes capable of differentiation. There is a shift from organic sensory sensing (e.g., coldness) to psychic sensing (e.g., sadness). This stage is characterized by being one's own person and is described in terms of personality that is divided into three subsystems: being, self, self-image (Kempler, 1973, p. 262).

Subsystems of the Personality

During the psychophysical stage, the three subsystems of personality develop, namely, *being*, *self*, and *self-image* (Kempler, 1973). *Being* is present from birth and is the essential existence of the organism. The human organism begins life as a rapidly differentiating bundle of growing potentials. This needy growing composite of processes is called a human and its activity is called being. It is organically rooted and universally oriented with no awareness of an insideness versus an outsideness, no me versus you. *Self* develops as the individual interacts with her environment. It is the creative process which leads the individual to actualizing behaviours. It represents that part of personality concerned with wants. *Self-image* is that part of personality that says what we should do and which hinders creative growth. In a fully functioning person moving towards growth and expansion, the three subsystems are in harmony with each other. When the subsystems are not in harmony, unfinished business and internal conflicts, among other experiences, can occur.

Processes of Personality Development

Three major processes occur at the contact boundary that influence the development of personality, particularly the development of the *self* and *self-image*. These processes are *adaptation*, *acknowledgment*, and *approbation* (Kempler, 1973, 1977). *Adaptation* is the process whereby the individual discovers and defines the boundaries within which she exists. This is the process of becoming aware of what is self and what is nonself. It is becoming aware of the world in which one exists and adapting one's behaviour to it. Adaptation leads to a growing differentiation and appreciation of the boundaries in which one exists. *Acknowledgment* is the affirmation or validation of the child's self-directed actions, behaviours, and thoughts. The acknowledgment is in service of the child and leads her to develop a sense of self, an appreciation of her own existence, and a personal valuing system for her own behaviours (Korb, Gorrell, & Van De Riet, 1989). "Watch me" is the child's password to her parents as she plays. "In his innocent wisdom he knows that he must be acknowledged" (Kempler, 1973, p. 263). *Approbation* connotes approval or disapproval. A child receives approval if it acts in accordance with the adults' expectations and receives disapproval if it acts contrary to the parents' expectations. Whereas acknowledgment leads to awareness of self, approbation creates a self-image. Approbation is the process whereby people develop internal conflicts and experience unfinished business. A child who receives approbation in place of acknowledgment soon learns to seek approval from others rather than acknowledgment. Instead of "watch me," she now asks, "Didn't I do well?" Once this process is instituted, the individual develops a polarization in her personality. Approbation acts to interfere with the development of a sound and healthy notion of self. The self acts to move the individual to actualize herself. The self-image acts to hinder that process.

Organismic Self-Regulation

Perls (1973) conceptualized personality development as a product of the individual's striving to maintain a balance between conflicting forces. At every moment the individual is confronted with either an external demand or an internal need, either one of which activates action to restore the balance. This striving for balance is designed to reduce tension within the individual, a process referred to as "organismic self-regulation" (p. 246); that is, regulation of self based on bodily awareness. Since the person's needs are many, this process continues all the time. When the organismic self-regulation fails to some degree or the person remains in a state of disequilibrium for too long a time, the person develops emotional problems such as "boundary disturbances" and unfinished business (p. 4).

Boundary Disturbances

Boundary disturbances can be understood as disturbances in relationships where a person may merge with another, may incorporate the other, or may exclude the other. The person may also assume responsibility for what transpires, blame the other for what transpires, or assume shared responsibility. These changes, which are at the basis of emotional problems, are referred to as boundary disturbances. Perls (1973) identified five boundary disturbances, namely, *introjection*, *projection*, *confluence*, *retroflection*, and *deflection*. Introjection refers to the incorporation of standards, attitudes, and ways of acting and thinking which are not ours. In this process, the person tends to take responsibility for what actually is part of the environment. In projection, the person perceives the environment as being responsible for what originates within oneself. The person disavows and disowns those aspects of her personality that are difficult, offensive, or unattractive. In confluence, the person merges with the environment and is not able to tell what belongs to her and what belongs to the environment. Being unaware of the boundary, she is not able to make good contact with others or with the environment. In retroflection, the person turns the energy to be used for adaptation inward upon herself. The person treats self as she wanted to be treated by others (e.g., caresses self). Deflection is a blunting of the impact of interaction either with self or from the self. An example is smiling to mitigate the expression of criticism or anger.

Therapeutic Goals, the Role of the Therapist, and Techniques

The overriding objective of Gestalt therapy is to bring about an integration of the individual by increasing self-awareness and enabling the individual to be self-regulating (Perls, 1969). Helping the client achieve self-regulation means helping the client discover that they can do many things for themselves and do not have to depend on others. The ability to regulate self helps clients to complete unfinished business and resolve internal conflicts caused by the formation of self-images. Increasing a person's awareness also facilitates integration. Perls (1973) believes that awareness by itself is "curative" (p. 73). Given awareness, the individual will be able to deal with any unfinished business that will always emerge. Perls (1969) states that "integration is never completed; maturation is never completed. It's an ongoing process forever and ever" (p. 69).

The role of a Gestalt therapist is to create an atmosphere conducive to growth and to act as a catalyst for growth. This atmosphere is brought about by the therapist facilitating the clients' awareness of themselves in the here-and-now (Perls, 1969). The now is the present, it is what the person is aware of, it is that moment in which they carry their so-called memories and expectations with them (Perls, 1947). As a catalyst, the therapist offers the clients opportunities to discover their own needs, to discover those parts of themselves that they have given up because of environmental demands, to provide a place in which the client can experience growth and increase their own awareness. For a more detailed description of Gestalt therapy, the reader is referred to Joyce and Sills (2007).

The general goal of Gestalt techniques is to challenge clients to take responsibility for themselves, work in the present, and work through impasses (e.g., unfinished business). The techniques designed to help clients get in touch with their inner experiences are experiential in nature (Perls, 1969). Two of the specific techniques are GECT and GTCT, presented separately below in Parts 2 and 3 of this chapter.

Part 2: The Gestalt Empty-Chair Technique

This part first addresses the topic of unfinished business in terms of its description, dynamics, identifying markers, and resolution. Next, the procedures for using GECT to resolve unfinished business are presented and illustrated by providing excerpts from a transcript of an actual session.

Unfinished Business

Description

Unfinished business refers to nagging, unresolved, unexpressed, or withheld feelings, memories, and events of hurt, anger, and resentment towards another person. By holding on to the unfinished business or avoiding their closure, the person invests available emotional energy in sustaining the incompleteness, thereby leaving little emotional energy available for encountering situations in a new way. Unfinished business is primarily a product of the warring subsystems of the personality (self and self-image) brought about by a failure in self-regulation.

Dynamics

Unfinished business emerges when a person does not feel validated or heard, when a person does not have a voice or authority over her own life, or when interpersonal needs are not met. Due to the overpowering influence of the self-image or the fear to express itself because of anticipated emotional hurt, the needs of the self go unmet, and this leads to frustration, anger, and hurt. The blocking of the expression of feelings and needs and the holding back of the feelings do not fully disappear but are encoded in memory and remain as unfinished business that interfere with the person's ability to respond creatively and adaptively to new and current situations (Perls, Hefferline, & Goodman, 1951).

Indicators of Unfinished Business

One indicator of unfinished business is a long-standing bitterness and resentment towards a significant other for the way one was treated (Greenberg, Rice, & Elliott, 1993). For example, a client may feel resentful towards her mother for not having protected her from her abusive father. A second indicator are longings, sadness, and hopelessness that are the signs of interruption of expression of feelings evoked in relation to a significant other. An example is that of a client, divorced for ten years, still yearning to be with his ex-wife and not finding fulfilment in any other relationship. A third indicator is unresolvable guilt for harm caused to others. For example, a 35-year-old single male was haunted by the feelings of guilt for the way he treated his women dates during his twenties and early thirties.

Process in Working Through Unfinished Business

The process in resolving unfinished business consists of four shifts. These shifts are briefly described and illustrated for a young female client, Belinda (pseudonym), who, in a monologue with her mother sitting in an empty chair next to her, expressed her resentment to her mother for being too negative and inhibiting her lifestyle.

Expression of a Lingering Feeling

The process of resolving unfinished business begins with the client expressing some lingering feeling such as anger and regret. The therapist helps the client to access the feeling as fully as possible and to express the feelings in a direct, concrete, and responsible manner to the other.

Belinda: "I feel intensely angry towards you for being too demanding, shaming me in front of my friends and putting me down as not being good enough nor smart enough."

Expression of Longings, Unmet Needs/Desires

As the client expresses her feelings, the therapist listens for the client's longings and unmet needs and desires and makes these explicit. The movement from the expression of feelings to the articulation of desires and needs represents a client shift in the process.

Belinda: "I want you to value me as a person, to respect my choices and decisions even though you might not agree with them."

Empathic Understanding

By an empathic understanding, the client becomes aware of the motive underlying the unfinished business and accepts it without condoning the events that led up to it. The client might invite the other to be part of her life or might forgive the other for the hurtful actions and behaviours caused.

Belinda: "I know that you love me and mean well, I forgive you for it, but I don't accept what you did."

Resolution and Closure

The successful completion of the aforementioned shifts might lead to a sense of relief, peace, empowerment, and mastery over the unfinished business. The client is ready to integrate the unfinished business as part of her life experience and to move on.

Belinda: "I will do what I need to do even if it is without your support. I am not leaving you behind. I invite you to join me in my journey where we can love each other and be separate persons and still be together."

Gestalt Empty-Chair in Action

The office set-up and the procedures for conducting the GECT will now be presented. Excerpts from a transcribed therapy session illustrate how GECT can be used to complete unfinished business. It is important to conceptualize the client's unfinished business in terms of the impoverished self, the power of the self-image, and the failure to negotiate business at the contact boundary.

Office Arrangement

The use of GECT requires that the office have available a third chair to be used to seat an imaginary person. A third chair is placed distant from the other two chairs and brought in only for the exercise. Bringing in the chair at the beginning of the exercise and then removing it when the exercise is completed symbolizes bringing in and removing the person towards whom the client has unfinished business.

Procedures

At the beginning of a session, one listens for cues to determine whether the client is harbouring current or past unfinished business. After identifying unfinished business and its target (e.g., father), one assesses its intensity and the client's readiness to work through the unfinished business. One can assess readiness by asking a simple question, "How deeply do you experience this feeling?" If one senses a moderate to a high intensity of feeling (e.g., intense anger) towards the targeted person, one can anticipate the client is ready for GECT.

The therapist introduces GECT, and if the client agrees to engage in this experience, the therapist outlines the procedure, saying "For this technique I typically use a chair in which we place the targeted person. You will then be asked to express all of your feelings towards the other person. I will help you to express your feelings. Are you comfortable with this?" If the client responds positively, the therapist proceeds to bring in the chair and asks the client where she would like to have it positioned. The client is asked to imagine the targeted person sitting in the empty chair.

Before beginning the monologue, the client is instructed to take a moment to get in touch with all of her feelings towards the targeted person. The client is then invited to face the chair and to express her feelings towards the person. As the client expresses herself, the therapist carefully tracks the client's feelings and unmet needs and keeps the monologue focused on the unfinished business. It is important for the client to maintain contact with the other and to speak from her voice, that is, from the self. The therapist carefully guides the client through the resolution process according to the four shifts mentioned earlier.

When the client has reached a resolution, one terminates the exercise by asking the client something like, "Is there something you would like to add before we end this exercise?" If no more needs to be said, one removes the chair and proceeds to the debriefing, at which time the client is asked "What was the experience like for you?" or something similar. The focus is not on rehashing the monologue but on the client's experience in using this exercise to resolve unfinished business.

Illustration: Robert

Robert (pseudonym), 22, single and caucasian, sought therapy to help him to understand why he was not able to maintain relationships with women. Below are a summary of the session, its conceptualization, a description of the therapy process, excerpts from a transcript of a therapy session, and a description of the experience following the session.

Summary

At the beginning of the session, Robert expressed his desire to understand the cycle of breaking up and then reconnecting with his girlfriend. In exploring this pattern and his feelings of anger, the image of his mother emerged. He felt she was at the heart of his difficulty in relating to women. To help him vent his anger towards his mother and to complete the unfinished business, GECT was introduced. The use of GECT helped Robert to tell his mother that he was tired of pleasing her, making her happy, and doing the right thing for her, and that he resented her for having been mean and hostile towards him when he did not comply with her wishes. He wanted her out of his life, and when she refused to leave, he picked up the chair and symbolically removed her from the office. In removing her, he felt empowered and enabled to take charge of his life.

Conceptualization

Robert's relational difficulties with his girlfriend, particularly his feeling that she is too demanding and invasive and that he not able to assert his needs towards her, appear to be related to his relationship with his mother, who did not affirm his pursuit of self-actualization and failed to establish clear contact boundaries between herself and Robert. In terms of boundary disturbance, he used his energy to develop a self-image that was responsible for his mother's happiness rather than to invest his energy in the development of a sense of self. He managed intimate relationships by giving into the needs of others to maintain the peace, and when he could no longer bear it, ending the relationship and getting some distance, only to repeat the cycle again and again. Robert failed to develop the skills required to regulate self-needs with self-image needs in a harmonious way, and consequently when in a relationship he felt a discrepancy between his innate striving for self-actualization and the pull towards living out his self-image.

Therapy Process

The therapy session began by identifying the unfinished business, assessing its intensity, and determining Robert's readiness to engage in GECT (C1–C25). In the use of GECT, Robert was able to identify and express his unresolved feelings towards his mother (*expression of a lingering feeling*) (C25). This was followed by Robert asking his mother to let him be free to be his own person (*expression of longings, unmet needs, wishes*) (C34). In the process Robert developed a sense of empathy for his mother in wanting to have heard what she had to say (*empathic understanding*) (C47). The session ended with Robert feeling empowered and taking charge of his life (C36–C37; C42–C45) (*resolution and closure*). Throughout the exercise, the therapist encouraged Robert to speak in terms of "I" and "You" and to repeatedly check whether his words fitted well with his feelings as experienced. The purpose was to validate and affirm the new emerging self, to differentiate himself from his mother, to activate the self-actualization process, and to reinstate the organismic self-regulation system.

Transcript

(After having explored his ambivalent feelings towards his girlfriend and their cyclical relational pattern, he began to feel anxious and associated these feelings with his mother. He expressed his readiness to monologue with his mother.)

C25:   She's (mother) got something to do with my relationship to women. Something comes to an awareness and fades away. It has something to do with pleasing others.

T29:   Try out a few statements and see if they fit with what you're feeling. Use "you" and "I" statements.

C29:   I'm tired of trying to please you, to make you happy. I carried that for too long. I'm tired of you being a bitch. I'm tired of trying to do the right thing for you. I feel as if you've been standing on my shoulder all my life and every time I do something that doesn't fit to what you want, you let me know.

T34:   Um-hum.

C34:   If you don't want to be happy that's your responsibility. I want to be happy and I'm not going to let you ruin my life. Now get off my back and get out. Out! You hard-headed woman, go away. Go away. I'll call you when I want to be with you. Until then go away. (Pause, 52 secs.) She doesn't want to leave.

T35:   You want her to leave.

C35:   Why don't you pick up your bags and leave. Come on lady you're moving. (Robert picks up the chair and moves it to the hallway.)

Describing Experience

In describing his experience, Robert mentioned that he felt empowered in placing his mother in the hallway, and in doing so he put her out of his mind and removed her influence over him. He added that he would like to have heard his mother reply to his comments, which indicates that Robert wants to establish clear boundaries with her, since it is within the context of these boundaries that both he and his mother can grow and become independent and autonomous persons. Robert was ready for an authentic encounter with his mother. Robert stated that the exercise helped him to get in touch with feelings that he was unaware of. He felt empowered in articulating his feelings towards his mother.

Part 3: The Gestalt Two-Chair Technique

The Gestalt Two-Chair Technique (GTCT) was designed to resolve intrapersonal (internal) conflicts. In using GTCT, it is imperative to conceptualize the client's conflict in terms of Gestalt theory in order to clearly identify the conflict, name its two dimensions (e.g., voices), assess the readiness of the client to resolve the conflict, set up the exercise, and then carefully and firmly lead her through the resolution process.

The first part of this section presents theoretical aspects related to conflicts and their resolution, namely, defining and identifying conflicts, naming their voices, and identifying the stages in resolving conflicts. The second part presents the procedures for using GTCT, and the third part illustrates the use of GTCT to resolve a conflict.

Theoretical Aspects

Definition of Conflict

Gestalt therapists view conflicts in terms of intrapersonal (internal) rather than interpersonal conflicts. Internal conflicts represent the self's failure to mediate the needs of *being* and *self-image* that results in a conflict between the two (Perls, Hefferline, & Goodman, 1951). A conflict, therefore, represents a person being split into warring camps with the self-image dominating the self and with the self resisting the self-image.

Identifying Conflicts

To identify conflicts one listens for words such as "but," "should," "must," "torn," and so on. An internal conflict is expressed in statements such as, "I would like to but I am afraid." Instead of a single clear preference arising, the person is torn between alternatives. There is an experience of two parts of the self in opposition, rather than the experience of a single integrated self in process.

Naming the Voices and the Chairs

In his chair work, Perls (1969) named the two empty chairs the *Topdog*, representing the self-image, and the *Underdog*, representing the self. These parts have unique voices that utter both explicit and implicit messages. The Topdog speaks in terms of should, ought, or must and is the controlling and bullying part of the personality. The Underdog typically complains, is angry, unhappy, and sad, speaks in terms of wants and desires, and is the victim part of the personality. Names that are derivatives of Topdog and Underdog can be given to the parts of the conflict and to the chairs. For example, a derivative of Topdog might be "Master," "Mean," or "Bulldozer," whereas a derivative of Underdog might be "Slave," "Victim," or "Powerless" (Polster & Polster, 1973). The client's collaboration is requested to name the parts. It is best to use abstract words (e.g., Wall) rather than real names (e.g., Harry).

Stages of Conflict Resolution

The process of conflict resolution can be viewed in terms of four progressive stages that have been clinically derived and empirically supported (Meier and Boivin, 1986, 1988, 2001). The stages are differentiated by the client's changing experiences expressed in terms of affects, cognitions, and needs/wants as the conflict is resolved. These stages are: (a) Opposition stage – characterized by the two voices being in opposition and engaged in the expression of negative affect (e.g., anger) and critical judgments (e.g., blaming). Both voices demonstrate intensive negative energies. (b) Empathic stage – marked by a decrease in the expression of criticisms, judgments, and negative affect and an increase in positive affect and the beginning of the expression of desires and wishes. One voice (usually the Topdog) becomes aware how she has hurt the Underdog and becomes empathic towards her. The Underdog expresses pleasure in knowing that the Topdog actually cared. Both openly and honestly express what they want from the other. (c) Collaboration stage – the number of criticisms, negative judgments, and negative affects decreases and the number of positive affect and want/desire statements increase, one voice offers to collaborate and the other voice accepts the offer. Both voices are willing to assume their responsibility to make a difference in their life. (d) Resolution stage – the voices express their comfort in being able to work together to improve their lives and express their appreciation for the dialogue and for being mutually open, honest, and respectful with each other.

Procedures in Using GTCT

The therapist begins the session in the typical manner. If the client presents an internal conflict, the therapist assesses whether or not to use GTCT and the client's readiness to engage in its use. When both parties agree to use GTCT, the therapist introduces the exercise, sets up the chairs, and structures and fosters a productive dialogue.

Assessing Readiness for Gestalt-Two Chair Work

After identifying a conflict, the therapist assesses the intensity of the conflict and the readiness of the client to engage in a process leading to the resolution of the conflict. This can be accomplished by asking a simple question such as, "How angry are you at the other for always controlling you?" If the client expresses moderate to strong anger, the client is assumed to be ready to engage in the GTCT.

Introducing the Technique and Setting Up the Chairs

The therapist and client proceed to collaboratively identify the conflict and its voices. The therapist asks the client if she is ready to engage in a dialogue while playing the role of the two voices. If the client agrees, the therapist might add, "For this technique I typically use two chairs in which I place the voices. Would you be comfortable with this?" If the client responds positively, the therapist describes the dialoguing procedure. The client is informed that she will move from chair to chair as she speaks from the respective voices. This dialogue will continue until the conflict is resolved. After this explanation, the therapist brings in a third chair and asks the client where she would like it to be positioned. The therapist then asks the client how she would like to name the two chairs.

Structuring and Fostering a Productive Dialogue

GTCT begins with the therapist asking the client from which chair she would like to begin to speak. Typically the client begins in her chair (Underdog). The client is then instructed to take a minute to get in touch with her feelings towards the other voice, and, when ready, to share these. When the client has expressed all that she wants to say from the chair, she is invited to take the other chair and to respond to what was said.

As the client begins to speak from the new chair, the therapist might summarize what the previous voice said, use empathic statements to highlight the emotional quality of the statement, and use instructions to move the client from one chair to the other and to heighten an experience. The process of moving back and forth continues until the conflict has been resolved.

As the dialogue progresses, the therapist ensures that the two voices remain in constant contact with each other, assume responsibility to speak authentically from their experience, and speak concretely and practically rather than abstractly. The therapist might ask the client to pay attention to a particular aspect of her experience (e.g., sadness) or to repeat a statement (e.g., "I hate you") with greater volume to heighten the experience (Greenberg, 1979). The therapist uses the conflict resolution stages explained earlier to monitor the progression of the process.

Illustration: Rick

Rick, 26 years old, single, and caucasian, requested therapy to help him to understand why he was not able to make commitments. What follows is a summary of the session, its conceptualization, a description of the therapy process, and excerpts from a transcript of the one-hour therapy session.

Summary

Rick began the session saying that he felt that there was something stopping him from being happy, committed, and being who and what he would like to be. He pictured that which was stopping him as an invisible wall. There were two voices within him, that of the Wall and that of the Self. To help Rick engage in a dialogue with the two voices and bring about a solution, GTCT was used. The Self was tired of the Wall telling him what to do, how to be, and to be cautious of people. In his defence, the Wall said that the Self was just a kid and needed to be protected. The Self expressed his need to be cared for and to care for others, to take risks, to be spontaneous, and to have more space. The Wall began to understand the feelings and needs of the Self and agreed that he was too rigid and stifling. Both agreed to work together to take risks and learn.

Conceptualization

Rick's internal conflict appears to be a product of having been approved for complying to his parents' wishes and desires and for having been disapproved in pursuing his own natural tendency towards personal growth and development. The result was the development of an impoverished self and an overdeveloped and domineering self-image. Without an integrated sense of self, Rick found it difficult to commit himself and to make personal decisions in the interest of himself for fear of reprimand. The goal of therapy is to establish the self-regulating process.

Therapy Process

The process progressed from the Wall and the Self being in *opposition* with each other (C20–C36) to the Wall becoming *empathically* aware of how he was stifling the Self (C37–C44). Both agreed to *collaborate*, take risks, and learn from the experience (C45). The two voices reached a *resolution* by the end of the session (C56). During the exercise, the therapist helped the two voices to remain in contact with each other and to work towards an agreeable resolution.

Transcript

Upon having determined that the client was ready to engage in GTCT, the therapist and client named the two voices and chairs (Wall and Self), the therapist explained the GTCT procedures, brought in the third chair, and the client determined from which chair he wanted to begin the dialogue. The client responses are named according to the two voices, Wall and Self. The therapist's interventions, which comprise mostly summaries and giving instructions for the client to move from chair to chair and to respond to the gist (e.g., needs) of what was said, are omitted here because of limited space. In the transcript, C = Client, T = Therapist, and the number following the letter is the response number.

Opposition Phase

C22: (Self) I'm tired of fighting you, Wall. I'm tired of being alone. Why don't you just get lost and leave me alone. Tired of you saying don't risk, don't get close, carry your pride, don't be foolish. I'm just tired of all the DON'TS.

C29: (Wall) You're just a kid. Somebody's got to protect you and that's my job.

C30: (Self) If you keep going that way I don't want to stick around. I can't hold up much longer under your pressure, tired of hurting. You know one day the hurt is going to be too much, I'm going to pull the plug and say good-bye world, then where are you going to be?

C31: (Wall) I'm a little dumbfounded about what you said. I can see that you have the possibility of pulling the plug. My first reaction is I'm in charge. Yet I see you have ways of pulling the plug. Sure you can go ahead and pull the plug. What's it going to give us? What do you want? I'm just trying to do my job.

C33:   (Self) I'm telling you that parts of your job are in the way. You're treating me like a kid. But I'm not just a kid. And there are some things I need to survive. I need to be close to people. I need to feel wanted.

Empathic Response

C37:   (Wall) I agree what you need, and the question I have is how do I protect you in that. I get the impression that I've been a mother hen and that I don't want to let go of the apron strings. All of a sudden I am asked to let go of that; I don't know if I should. I'd like to know what you have in mind before I let go of the strings. Sure I'd like to see you happy and at the same time I don't know at what price.

C40:   (Self) Got a few things to learn don't you. I can't say, neither can you nor anybody else say, what the next moment's going to be like, if we risk a little, there's no sure bet about what's going to turn out of it. You know if there is a sure bet, life becomes rather dull doesn't it. I want to get rid of the dullness. I want to learn to risk a little and be more spontaneous. Like to trust myself a little more. Could you please let go a bit. I'm not asking you to disappear. I need protection and I don't need as much protection as you're giving me now. Right now it's stifling. I want to live.

C43:   (Wall) I hear your need for spontaneity and I see how important it is and yet I'd like a little variety myself. I'm tired of protecting you the way I've been protecting you. I know I've been stifling and I think I can protect you in a different way. I've thought a lot about it, and I know that I need to let go, but what do I let go of? How do I let go? In fact I've started letting go and I'm ready to let go more. It's still the "How" and I guess that we can work out the "How" as we go along. If I let you risk a little then I can learn a little more about how to let go and when to let go. How does that sound to you?

Collaboration and Resolution Phases

C46:   (Self) I'm glad to hear that. I'd like you to let me risk and let me learn.

C49:   (Wall) I get the feeling you don't want me around any more. I can't just let go, disappear. I'd like to be around as an overseer of the whole thing and generally agree with what you're saying. I'm going to let you risk as long as you agree to let me learn. I am willing to make changes. But be patient with me.

C54:   (Self) I'm glad to hear that you're willing to make changes. I'd like to know when this is going to start and how we can proceed. I'm eager to get on with it. How does that sound?

C55:   (Wall) Well that sounds okay to me. I stress, be patient with me.

Describing Experience

Rick reported that he was surprised how at the beginning of the exercise he was quickly struck by intense emotions. In the dialogue with the wall, he felt relief in the sense that he was given a ticket to risk and to learn. He senses that because of the exercise there is an opportunity to be different and do things differently. He is willing to trust, risk, and learn.

Something to Think About

1. How can interactions at the contact boundary lead to emotional disorders?
2. What is the relationship of approbation to the development of the self-image?
3. Distinguish between indicators of unfinished business.
4. How do the personality subsystems participate in an internal conflict?
5. How did empathy contribute to the resolution of Rick's internal conflicts?

References

Clarkson, P., & Mackewn, J. (1993). *Fritz Perls*. London: Sage Publications.

Fagan, J., & Shepherd, I.L. (Eds.) (1970). *Gestalt therapy now: Theory, techniques, applications*. New York: Harper & Row.

Greenberg, L. (1979). Resolving splits: Use of the two chair technique. *Psychotherapy: Theory, Research, Practice, Training, 16*(3) 316–324.

Greenberg, L.S., Rice, L.N., & Elliott, R. (1993). *Facilitating emotional change: The moment-by-moment process*. New York: Guilford Press.

Joyce, P., & Sills, C. (2007). *Skills in Gestalt counselling and psychotherapy*. London: Sage Publications.

Kempler, W. (1973). Gestalt Therapy. In R. Corsini (Ed.), *Current psychotherapies* (pp. 251–286). Itasca, IL: F.E. Peacock Publishers.

Korb, M.P., Gorrell, J., & Van De Riet, V. (1989). *Gestalt therapy: Practice and theory*. New York: Pergamon Press.

Latner, J. (1973). *The gestalt therapy book*. New York: Bantam Books.

Meier, A., & Boivin, M. (1986). Client verbal response category system: Preliminary data. *Journal of Consulting and Clinical Psychology, 54*, 877–879.

Meier, A., & Boivin, M. (1988). *The resolution of conflicts and the client verbal response category system*. Ottawa, Ontario: St. Paul University. Unpublished MS.

Meier, A., & Boivin, M. (2001). Conflict resolution: The interplay of affects, cognitions and needs in the resolution of intrapersonal conflicts. *Pastoral Sciences, 20*(1), 93–119.

Passons, W.R. (1975). *Gestalt approaches in counseling*. New York: Holt, Rinehart, & Winston.

Perls, F.S. (1947). *Ego, hunger, and aggression: The beginnings of Gestalt therapy*. New York: Random House.

Perls, F.S. (1969). *Gestalt therapy verbatim*. Toronto: Bantam Books.

Perls, F.S. (1973). *Gestalt approach, and eye witness to therapy*. New York: Bantam.

Perls, F.S., Hefferline, R.F., & Goodman, P. (1951). *Gestalt therapy: Excitement and growth in the human personality*. New York: Delta Books.

Polster, E., & Polster, M. (1973). *Gestalt therapy integrated: Contours of theory and practice*. New York: Brunner/Mazel.

Woldt, A., & Toman, S.M. (2005). *Gestalt therapy: History, theory and practice*. Thousand Oaks, CA: Sage Publications.

Yontef, G.M., & Simkin, J.S. (1989). Gestalt therapy. In R. Corsini & D. Wedding (Eds.), *Current psychotherapies* (pp. 323–361). Itasca, IL: F.E. Peacock Publishers.

5 The Use of Metaphors in Therapy

Chapter Summary

People often use metaphors to describe experiences that are new and unique to them or that words seem inadequate to grasp and convey. Metaphors are encoded with affective, cognitive, and motivational aspects of one's experience. Often a person uses a metaphor to describe his current image of others and self. Exploring the metaphor brings to light a deeper understanding of one's current problem, and the transformation of the metaphor brings about a sense of empowerment and deeply rooted changes. This chapter presents a definition of metaphor, explains its power for change, distinguishes between client-generated and therapist-generated metaphors, and outlines procedures for exploring and transforming client-generated metaphors. The use of metaphors is similar to focusing in that both help clients to surface implicit meanings by connecting them to a symbol, image, or event. However, metaphor work differs from focusing in that it asks the client to transform the metaphor to engender empowerment and bring about the desired change. The case of Karen demonstrates how to proceed to explore and transform a metaphor, and at the same time demonstrates the power of metaphors to bring about change.

Introduction

Metaphors have been an essential feature of human communication throughout all of history. The use of stories, parables, anecdotes, fairy tales, mythologies, and rituals with a metaphorical content is widespread, and these have long been used to convey specific messages (Barker, 1985). These metaphoric modes of communication convey a meaning which transcends their literal meanings. They contain a deeper message which the teller intends to convey and the receiver has the challenge to decipher.

Four prominent approaches to the use of metaphors in psychotherapy are those by Barker (1985), Siegelman (1990), Kopp (1995), and Grove (1996). All of these are linguistic approaches in that they try to bring about change by either telling a story, providing an anecdote, constructing a metaphor, or asking the person to transform their metaphors. This chapter integrates concepts and techniques derived from the approaches by Kopp, Grove, Siegelman, and Barker in working with client metaphors. The chapter is divided into two parts. The first part presents the definition, structure, power, and types of metaphor. The second part presents client-generated metaphors. The chapter ends by illustrating the use of metaphors in an actual therapy session.

Metaphor: Definition, Structure, and Power

Metaphor Defined

The literature on metaphors suggests that this word has two origins. First, the word *metaphor* is derived from the Greek *meta*, meaning "above," "over," or "across," and *pherein*, meaning "to carry or bear from one place to another" (Kopp & Craw, 1998, p. 307). Second, the word metaphor has the same root as *amphora*, an ancient Greek vessel for carrying and storing precious liquids (Tompkins & Lawley, 1996). Aristotle (*Poetics*, 1457) defined metaphor (*meta-phora*), to mean "giving the thing a name that belongs to something else; the transference (epi-phora) being either from genus to species or from species to species or on the grounds of analogy" (cited in Turbayne, 1971, p. 11). Elsewhere Aristotle (*Rhetoric*, 1410b) states that "ordinary words convey only what we know already; it is from metaphor that we can best get hold of something fresh" (cited in Lakoff & Johnson, 1980, p. 190).

Metaphors therefore have two aspects. One aspect is transferring a meaning from a previous experience, event, object, or action to a current experience, event, object, or action. A metaphor thus "carries meaning over from one domain to another" (Kopp, 1995, p. 92) and links "domains by connecting insight and feelings and what is known with what is only guessed at" (Siegelman, 1990, p. 3). Kopp states that a metaphor is a "bridge between the domain of internal imagery and the domain of external life in which an image is used to convey meaning about a situation" (p. 141). The second aspect is that a metaphor embodies meaning and information in symbolic form (Tompkins & Lawley, 1996, p. 3). Metaphors are "mirrors reflecting our inner images of self, life and others" (Kopp, 1995, p. xiii). The task is to decipher the symbolic meaning embedded within the image, phrase, word, etc. A metaphor can be taken literally at the conscious level; however, at the unconscious level it embodies symbolic meaning which must be deciphered (Turbayne, 1971).

The clinical use of metaphors is based on their symbolic meaning. To illustrate, Kopp (1995) presents the example of Carol, whose metaphoric image of her husband is "He barges into the house like a locomotive" and whose metaphoric image of herself, in relation to her husband, is "I am a tunnel" (pp. xvi–xvii). When translated into interpersonal language, Carol experiences her husband as a bulldozer who rolls over her, as having the power in the relationship, and she feels helpless and at his mercy. The metaphor has affective, cognitive, and motivational components or meanings. From an affective point of view, Carol feels overpowered, ignored, and taken advantage of, to name a few. From a cognitive perspective, Carol contains her feelings of being overpowered, etc., by describing her husband's behaviour as being similar to that of a locomotive. This concept provides an explanation for her husband's behaviour and a means by which she can control her feelings. From a motivational (e.g., desire, wish, need) perspective, Carol desires a relationship where there is equality, mutual respect and caring, acceptance, empathy, etc. The latter are less accessible and less evident and therefore require greater work to decipher. The richness of a metaphor, therefore, rests with deciphering its full meaning in terms of affective, cognitive, and motivational meanings.

Structures of Metaphors

Metaphors have an internal structure, referred to as metaphoric structure, that elucidates the pattern that links two different things (Kopp, 1995). The structure of a metaphor can best be understood by comparing linear to nonlinear correspondence (Kopp, 1995). Linear correspondence describes relationship of items characterized by linear, logical, cause-and-effect relationships. Linear correspondence involves a logical "if–then" relationship (e.g., if $a = b$, and $b = c$, then $a = c$, or if Socrates is a man, and men will die, Socrates will die). Nonlinear correspondence describes correspondence of pattern and organization characterized by nonlinear causal chains. This is represented by Kant's four-part analogy "a is to b as c is to d," pointing not to a resemblance between two things but between two relationships between quite dissimilar things. Using the four-part analogy, Carol's metaphor for her husband and herself, as mentioned earlier, reads as follows: my husband (a) is to me (b) as a locomotive (c) is to a tunnel (d). A metaphoric image, when explored, will bring forth novel ways of looking at things and responding to them.

People metaphorically structure their social and individual realities, that is, they structure how they perceive, think, feel, and behave verbally and nonverbally. An example of a metaphoric structure of individual reality is, "I am a tea kettle that can't let the steam out" (Kopp, 1995, p. 102). The author proposes that a metaphoric structure of reality is comprised of six substructures (called metaphorms) representing self, others, life, and the relationship of the self to these elements (e.g., self–self, self–others, self–life) (Kopp, 1995).

The Power of Metaphors

The power that metaphors exercise when used in psychotherapy is similar to the power that metaphors have in the development of language. Within the field of linguistics, metaphors are considered to have played a key role in the evolution of language and in the construction of symbolic meaning. For example, "where a precise word is lacking, a speaker resorts to the powers of logical analogy (metaphor) to designate novelty by using a word denoting something else that is a symbol for the thing the speaker means" (Kopp, 1995, p. 94). In the same way that metaphors can be a source of novelty and change in language, so too exploring and transforming metaphors can be a source of novelty and change in psychotherapy.

Metaphors are considered to be powerful vehicles for change because they combine two modes of cognition, logical and imaginal, into a distinct third form: metaphoric cognition (Kopp, 1995). Logical cognition proceeds logically from premise to conclusion. Imaginal cognition, on the other hand, paints a global-synthetic pictorial representation of a phenomenon. A metaphor combines both image and word, that is, it integrates both propositional/syllogistic and imaginal cognition. From a psychoanalytic perspective, metaphors are seen as lying at the interface between primary and secondary process thinking. Freud (1923) stated that "thinking in pictures is ... only a very incomplete form of becoming conscious. In some way, too, it stands nearer to unconscious processes than does thinking in words, and it is unquestionably older than the latter both ontologically and phylogenetically" (p. 14). If one considers that primary process thinking is expressed mainly through the language of imagery and secondary process thinking is expressed mainly through words, then metaphors may be seen as the integration of primary and secondary process thinking.

The power of metaphors, therefore, resides in the integration of two ways of knowing self and reality, the logical and imaginal, and in the integration of the primary and secondary processes. Metaphors simultaneously "tap into many sensory modalities and several levels of cognition from the sensorimotor to the concrete to the more abstract" (Siegelman, 1990, p. 104). Papp (1982) points out that "explanatory language tends to isolate and fragment" whereas "figurative language tends to synthesize and combine" (cited by Barker, 1985, p. 36). Metaphors, with their multidimensional and inexact nature, leave room for the random while at the same time allowing psychotherapy to be purposive (Combs & Freedman, 1990). Metaphors therefore are powerful because they carry a lot of extra meaning and suggest many options for clients and therapists to pursue.

Client-Generated Metaphors

Broadly speaking, psychotherapeutic metaphors can be classified as being either client-generated or therapist-generated (Loue, 2008). The focus of this chapter is on client-generated metaphors, a recent development in the practice of psychotherapy. Two of the main leaders in this area are Kopp (1995) and Grove (1996). The material that follows draws in large part on the writing of Kopp.

Client-Generated Metaphor Defined

Client-generated metaphors come entirely from within the client's experience, are represented as an internal construct within visual, auditory, and kinesthetic modalities and submodalities, and are coded with symbolic attributes which contain meaning and significance for the client (Tompkins & Lawley, 2003). Client-generated metaphors are idiosyncratic and very personal, and transformed within the world view of the client.

Theoretical Influences

Kopp (1995) was significantly influenced by Freudian, Jungian, and Adlerian concepts in the identification, understanding, and working through of metaphors in psychotherapy. These influences will be briefly described.

Psychoanalytic Concepts

Freudian concepts of primary and secondary process thinking, censorship or repression, and transference had an impact on Kopp's therapeutic work with metaphors. Primary process thinking uses primarily visual or other sense impressions, that is, it "thinks in pictures" (Freud, 1923, p. 14) and is similar to imaginal cognition. Secondary process thinking is primarily verbal and follows the laws of syntax and logic. Freud observed that "thinking in pictures" is an incomplete form of becoming conscious, that it stands nearer to unconscious processes and is older than secondary process thinking both ontologically and phylogenetically (p. 14). The unconscious, because of censorship or repression, reveals itself in metaphors or symbols. The concept of "transference" resembles that of metaphor. The German word for transference is *übertragung,* which means to "carry something from one place to another" (Kopp, 1995, p. 116). Metaphors are seen as lying at the interface between primary and secondary process thinking and embrace both ways of thinking.

Jungian Ideas

In Jung's (1916/1960) analytical psychology, sensory imagery plays a central role. The emotionally infused image is the primary organizer of the human psyche. In this system, archetypes and myths are universal metaphoric images. These universal images point to a universal dimension of human experiences – the metaphoric structure of transcultural reality and to its interconnecting patterns (Kopp, 1995).

Adlerian Notions

Adlerian analytic psychology (1956) holds that one's thoughts, opinions, and assumptions, not facts, are the primary determinants of behaviour. The perspective that emphasizes facts is based on linear/logical/rational thinking. Adler goes beyond linear and syllogistic cognition and includes nonlinear and imaginal cognition. This is best illustrated in his concept of *lifestyle* which comprises one's basic assumptions, beliefs, images, expectations, goals, and coping strategies. While lifestyle dynamics are usually interpreted as using syllogistic and propositional cognition, one's lifestyle is also represented in imaginal and metaphoric cognitive modalities. This is exemplified by Adler's (1956) concept of the *schema of apperception* which is associated with analogical processes in contrast to logical processes. According to Adler, all cognition is the apperception of one thing through another, that is, all conception is based upon analogical apperception. In addition, Adlerians use early childhood memory images to identify lifestyle themes and to interpret current behaviours. Metaphor therapy, in contrast, uses early recollections as a direct representational image of current issues and subjective meaning (Kopp, 1995).

Types of Client-Generated Metaphors

Kopp (1995) identified two forms of client-generated metaphors, linguistic metaphors and early memory metaphors.

Linguistic Metaphors

Linguistic or spoken metaphors are typically "word-pictures that create a resemblance between an image and a referent situation" (Kopp, 1995, p. 94). A linguistic metaphor uses an image as a means to convey meaning of the situation to which it refers. For example, in the metaphor, "I am a tea kettle that can't let the steam out" (Kopp, 1995, p. 102), the client uses the image of a "tea kettle that cannot let the steam out" to describe his own inability to express his emotions. In generating a linguistic metaphor, the person paints a picture with words and integrates the two forms of communication, namely nonlinear/imaginal communication with linear/verbal communication.

Early Memory Metaphors

These are metaphors, for a current problem situation, which on a bodily feeling level are associated with an early memory image. For example, a man who snored so loudly was troubled because it disturbed his wife's sleep and she spent part of the night in the living room. This event was associated with an early childhood experience when he had pneumonia and coughed and was noisy. His brother threatened to leave the bedroom and sleep elsewhere. The metaphor for these events could be "the noisy sleeper" (Kopp, 1995, p. 46).

Unlike spoken metaphors which are always metaphors, early recollection metaphors, to be called metaphors, must carry meaning over "from the domain of imagery [coughing in the above case] to a referent situation in one's current life [snoring]" (Kopp, 1995, p. 39). Further, if a person at the time that he is experiencing strong feelings or symptoms recalls an early recollection in relation to the feeling or symptom, it can be said that the early recollection is a metaphor for that feeling or symptom (Kopp, 1995).

Techniques to Unravel Metaphors

Three common techniques used to unravel the meaning of a metaphor are active imagination, creative imagination, and clean language. All three forms are pertinent for work with client-generated metaphors.

Active Imagination

Active imagination refers to the ability to let go of secondary process thinking and engage in primary process thinking that allows what is present to take form and shape, regardless of whether it is socially acceptable or unacceptable. Active imagination refers to the ability to think in a global-synthetic, symbolic, and pictorial form. Active imagination differs from passive imagination such as in dreaming.

The term active imagination was used by Jung (1916/1960) when discussing the creation of symbols of which metaphor is one subclass. Siegelman (1990) defines active imagination as "a process by which a person loosens his conscious focus, puts himself in a state of reverie, and allows psychological contents, such as a dream image, to emerge and to become elaborated. This embellished product of the unconscious then becomes a partner in a dialogue with the patient's ego in which neither dominates. What results is a 'symbolic product ... that contains elements of both'" (pp. 158–159). The concept of active imagination was foreshadowed by Kris's (1952) concept of "regression in the service of the ego," that assumes that temporary regression can lead to better integration, and to Winnicott's (1978) definition of transitional phenomena that mediate subjective and objective realities (Siegelman, 1990).

Imagination is a potent tool used to create something new – a third thing – that transcends two domains when there is a dialogue between them. In metaphor therapy the "third thing" is the metaphor itself. It emerges from a dialogue between sensorial awareness and the unconscious.

Creative Imagination

Creative imagination is a special form of active imagination. In active imagination, one allows what is present to emerge, to make itself present in terms of pictures, images, etc. In creative imagination, the person actually creates something new from that which is metaphorically presented.

Creative imagination is a quality required on the part of both therapist and client when working with metaphors. In therapist-generated metaphors, the therapist must possess the quality of creative imagination to create the metaphors, and in client-generated metaphors, the client must possess the capacity to explore and elaborate the metaphors.

The metaphor-maker, in entering the domain of creative imagination, draws out an image that resembles a pattern of meaning present in a specific situation to which the metaphoric image refers (e.g., "I'm just spinning my wheels at this job"). The starting point for this creative imaginative process is the client's metaphoric language or early childhood memory. From this metaphor or early childhood memory, the client is encouraged to create a scenario which has potency for change (Kopp, 1995). The client is encouraged to stay within his own metaphor, to expand and elaborate it, and ultimately to transform it. The meaning and insights that a client gains can be more profound than if the metaphor is talked about or analyzed (Kopp, 1995). The methods used to explore and transform metaphors seek to create a shift in the client's cognitive mode of processing information, "from primarily verbal-logical to imaginal-analogical cognition" (Kopp, 1995, p. 132).

Clean Language

Grove (2003) developed a linguistic tool which he calls "clean language" to help the client unfold the *metaphor landscape*, that is, the client's scenario or story that emerges as the dialogue proceeds (Tompkins & Lawley, 2003). Clean language is content-free and refers to using interventions, particularly questions that are open-ended, not leading, and allow the client to speak from his experience (Grove, 2003). This allows the therapist to enter into the client's unique subjective world. Grove presents guidelines on how to use clean language to help clients explore their metaphors. In using clean language one works from the internal frame of reference of the client and not from the external frame of the therapist. That is, one carefully listens to the client's description of the metaphor and one works with what is described. In using clean language, there is no interpretation or explanation, there is observation and description.

Eliciting and Exploring Client-Generated Metaphors

Kopp (1995) presents two types of client-generated metaphors, *client's metaphoric (linguistic) language* and *client's early memory metaphors*. Two of the techniques used in exploring these metaphors are creative imagination and clean language. Most of the material in this section draws on Kopp. The phases and the steps for the two forms of client-generated metaphors are treated separately.

Eliciting and Exploring Client-Generated Linguistic Metaphors

The process of eliciting and exploring linguistic metaphors entails four phases and six steps. The six steps are: (a) listen for client metaphors, (b) invite client explanations of the metaphor, (c) explore the metaphor as a sensory image, (d) invite the client to explore associated images, (e) invite the client to transform or change the metaphor, and (f) invite the client to draw parallels between the metaphor and the current situation. The phases and steps are summarized in Table 5.1.

Table 5.1   Eliciting and exploring client-generated linguistic metaphors

Phase	Description/Task
1. Identify and explore client's metaphoric image	Step 1: Identify and recognize the client's metaphor. Step 2A: Therapist invites the client to explore the metaphoric image by asking questions such as: "When you say [the metaphor] what image/picture comes to mind?" or "Could you describe the [metaphor]?" Step 2B: If the client does not understand the instructions, the therapist can say, "If I were seeing it [the metaphoric image] the way you see it [in your mind's eye] what would I see?"
2. Client describes metaphor and associated feelings	Step 3: Therapist invites the client to explore the metaphor as a sensory image (e.g., its setting, action, time). Step 4: Therapist invites the client to describe his feelings and experience associated with the metaphoric image; therapist guides the client through this process using nonleading questions.
3. Client transforms metaphoric image	Step 5A: Therapist invites the client to change the metaphoric image by asking a question, such as, "If you could change the image, how would you change it?" Step 5B: Or, the therapist invites the client to consider a change suggested by the therapist by saying, "What if the [part of metaphor to be changed] were [the suggested change]?" When the client has explored the original metaphor and transformed the image, the therapist leads him out of the domain of metaphoric imagination "to the domain of logical discourse and the external world of everyday life and literal meanings."
4. Client makes parallels between metaphor and original situation	Step 6: The client is asked a question such as: "What parallels do you see between your image [the metaphoric image] and [the original situation]?" or "How might the way you changed the image apply to your current situation?"

Source: Summarized From Kopp, 1995.

Eliciting and Exploring Early Memory Metaphors

Kopp (1995) presents an eight-step approach to guide clients in eliciting and exploring early recollections or early memory metaphors. Early recollections are a form of autobiographical memory representing a one-time childhood incident that one can picture in one's mind. Kopp (1995) gives the following as an example of early memory:

> I remember one night when my father came into my bedroom to calm me down. I told him I was afraid because I thought I heard something in my closet. He said, "Let's see if there is anything there, you stay in bed and I'll look in to the closet." He went to the closet and opened the door and looked inside. Then he sat on the bed and sang "You are my sunshine" and I fell asleep. What I remember most clearly is the soothing sound of his voice. (p. 37)

The above recollection describes a specific and one-time incident, the actions and interactions are clearly described, and it is a clear memory image involving sensory imagery. It is these qualities that render an early recollection as a metaphoric image for a current life situation or problem (Kopp, 1995). As mentioned above, an early recollection qualifies as a metaphor if it is recalled at the time that a client is experiencing or describing strong feelings or symptoms in relation to a problem, and if it carries meaning over from the recalled early recollection to the present experience. Other forms of autobiographical memory such as autobiographical facts (e.g., I remember flying to Chicago with my father) and generic personal memories (e.g., I remember what it felt like to walk from my apartment to the University of Chicago campus in winter) do not qualify as metaphoric imagery.

Kopp (1995) presented the process of eliciting, exploring, and transforming early recollections in terms of eight steps rather than in terms of phases, as he did for client-generated metaphors. However, the steps can be grouped according to phases, as we have done here. Each phase comprises one or more steps (Table 5.2).

Pitfalls in Using Metaphors

Siegelman (1990) points out three pitfalls in the use of metaphors, namely, overvaluing, undervaluing, and literalizing (freezing) metaphors. Milioni (2007) suggests two more pitfalls, namely, using metaphors as a silencing device and hijacking a metaphor by putting a different meaning on it.

Overvaluing Metaphors

One of the pitfalls is overreliance on metaphors and excessive zealousness in pursuit of them (Siegelman, 1990). The danger is that if a therapist becomes preoccupied with metaphors and gives them preferential treatment, he can become blinded to other important therapeutic processes. To be productive, metaphors must be seen in context, that is, as a part of a larger picture. Failure to do this has the potential to lead one to pursue an unjustified path. Pursuit of a metaphor needs to follow the agenda of the client, or at best be a collaboration between therapist and client.

Table 5.2   Eliciting and exploring early memory metaphors

Phase	Description/Task
1. Eliciting an image of an early experience	Step 1: Therapist asks client to focus on a central issue and to elicit a sensory experience of it. Then asks, "Where in all of this are you most stuck?" or "Which part of this is the biggest problem for you?" Step 2: Therapist asks the client if he can remember a recent time when he felt this way (stuck), to form an image of the situation so that he begins to get the same feelings that he had then, to begin to feel these feelings in his body in the same way he felt them then.
2. Eliciting early memory metaphors and exploring them	Step 3A: Therapist asks the client to recall the first early childhood memory that comes to mind; something specific that happened only once and preferably before the age 7. Step 3B: If the client offers a report instead of an early recollection, the therapist can ask the client to describe a specific example of it or to indicate a specific time this occurred. Step 3C: If the client is unable to recall an early recollection, the therapist asks for an early recollection from later years. Step 4: After an early recollection has been elicited the therapist explores the metaphor in asking the details of the memory. Step 5: Therapist asks what stands out most vividly in that memory. Step 6A: Therapist asks how the client felt at the moment. Step 6B: Therapist asks client why he felt that way or reacted that way.
3. Transforming early metaphors	Step 7: Therapist asks the client how he would change the memory if indeed he could change it; if the client is not able to change it, the therapist stops the process.
4. Exploring connections between current situation and early memory metaphor	Step 8A: If the early memory metaphor has been transformed, the therapist invites the client to explore the connections or parallels between the current situation and the early memory metaphor. Step 8B: Therapist might share connections that he might see.

Source: extracted from Kopp, 1995.

The exploration of metaphors cannot be forced upon the client, and particularly on clients who cannot imagine.

Undervaluing Metaphors

A second pitfall is the failure of the therapist to recognize the implicit metaphors embedded in the patient's everyday experience and in the experience of the therapeutic interaction.

The more "concrete" therapies of the conscious focus on changing specific behaviours or specific cognitions and tend to overlook a more metaphoric or symbolic way of looking at the world. The tendency is to look at a behaviour for what it is and not at its symbolic meaning. Siegelman (1990) states that "our inability to see the hidden or implicit metaphors can prevent patients from enlarging the meaning of their experience" (p. 128). Patients cannot be helped to reconstructively play with their own narrative unless therapists themselves know how to play.

Literalizing or Freezing Theoretical Metaphors

The third pitfall is the literalizing of metaphors in theory and in practice. A metaphor is a lens through which we look at reality, it is an approximation of the reality, it is not the reality. Problems arise when metaphors become frozen, reified, or literalized. That is, when metaphors are thought of as the truth rather than as an approximation of the reality. Summarizing Spence (1987), Siegelman (1990) states that "metaphor is most useful when dealing with the unknown and the complex in a tentative way. And it is useful to the extent we are conscious of speaking or thinking in metaphors" (p. 131). Carveth (1984) states that we literalize a metaphor when we literalize the figurative statement "A equals B." We treat this statement as if A intrinsically means B rather than treating it as a way of speaking. To indicate that A and B are similar and at the same time recognize that it is only an approximation, we put quotation marks around the equals sign so that the statement reads: A "equals" B. This makes it a tentative statement; it is not literalized (Siegelman, 1990).

In her research on therapist- and client-generated metaphors, Milioni (2007) pointed out the danger of therapists using a client-generated metaphor as a silencing device. In such cases, the client's world view is closed down and denied in favour of the therapist's interpretation. Milioni pointed to a second danger that is hijacking the metaphor. This refers to the therapist snatching away from a client a metaphor like an object and putting a different meaning to it. The client's implicit response to the therapist is "that's mine, give it back."

Ethical Considerations

Therapists using metaphors subscribe to the position that change can take place without recourse to client insight, client experiences, and the client describing real events (Tompkins & Lawley, 2003). It is their contention that these can be bypassed in bringing about significant and lasting changes. As with all potentially powerful therapeutic interventions, therapists using metaphors must exercise sound clinical judgment that is informed by an understanding of psychodynamic theory and psychopathology (Kopp, 1995). Being aware of the limitations of metaphors, Freud (1900/1953) warned in *The Interpretation of Dreams*, that we "should not mistake the scaffolding for the building" (p. 536).

Siegelman (1990) cautions against the indiscriminate use of metaphors and advocates that they be used when the time is right. In his view, metaphors are like interpretations. Similar to interpretations, it is important that the timing be right for the therapist to offer a metaphor to the client. According to Freud (1940/1949), interpretations are made when the client has already arrived at the insight himself (p. 43). In this sense, interpretations are therapist–client shared interpretations. In the same way, Siegelman advocates that metaphors too be therapist–client co-constructed and co-shared.

Illustration: Karen

Karen (pseudonym), in her early thirties, and a helping professional, sought counselling because of an interpersonal problem with her sister. Below is a summary of the therapy session, a conceptualization of the case, a description of the steps of the therapy process, and an excerpt from the session.

Summary

Karen began the session by reporting an interpersonal problem with her sister who forcefully and heartlessly imposes her expectations, values, and opinions on Karen. She saw her sister as a boulder and herself as a tired and worn out mattress. The therapist used this metaphor to empower her by transforming it. In transforming the metaphor of the mattress, Karen visualized the mattress as standing on its end and letting the boulders bounce off it and fall to the ground. When this idea was transferred to her relationship with her sister, Karen saw herself as standing tall, strong, and firm, and letting her sister's criticisms and harsh thinking fall by the wayside.

Conceptualization

The problem was conceptualized in terms of helping Karen move from a position of disempowerment to a position of empowerment and acquiring the courage to stand up to the negative impositions of her sister.

Therapy Process

In the therapy session Karen articulated the interpersonal problem, formed a metaphor regarding her sister and herself, explored the metaphor with regards to the affective, motivational, and meaning aspects, transformed the metaphor, and then applied it to her relationship with her sister. The therapist, at T20, explored whether Karen's relational difficulties were related to an early memory. Since it appeared that the problem was not related to an early memory, the therapist followed the procedures for transforming a linguistic metaphor.

Transcript

In the transcript, C = Client, T = Therapist, and the number following the letter is the response number.

T01:   Where would you like to begin this session?

C01:   I would like to talk about the tense relationship that I have with my sister.

T02:   Could you tell me more about your tense relationship.

C02:   We have this ongoing relationship that leaves me feeling a lot of dread, weighted, resentful, angry, defensive, and on guard.

T03:   Feeling weighed down by your sister, angry at her for what has happened, resentful towards her, and on guard.

C03:   The feelings are heavy and preoccupying.

Phases 1 & 2: Formation and Exploration of a Metaphor of Herself and of her Sister

T04:   If you were to paint a picture or form an image, how do you visualize this heaviness?

C04:   I see it as a heavy old spring mattress, just tired, weary, and worn.

T05:   Feeling weighed down is like a mattress that is tired, worn, and weary.

C05:   But keeps trying to spring back, so it is like a back-and-forth motion, being weighed down and trying to spring back up. The more it is weighed down, the less able it is to spring back up. It is becoming old and worn out.

T06:   Do you have any other sensations, feelings, or thoughts in being this mattress?

C06:   I sense that there must be another way, a better way, to manage this relationship. I feel conflicted between wanting to push back and wanting to pull away for peace sake. I don't think either is the solution.

T07:   Relationally then, you feel conflicted, tense, and you make efforts to try to get the relationship back on course.

C07:   Yes, just manageable.

T08:   You feel like the mattress, weighed down, worn, and weary. What is the image of your sister relative to the weighed down and worn out mattress?

C08:   A boulder. A heavy, large, imposing boulder.

T09:   What is the feeling?

C09:   The feeling is of being squashed, intensely imposed upon. A heavy boulder being repeatedly dropped on me.

T10:   The mattress takes the impact and after the impact it tries to push it off.

C10:   Push it off, to regain its form.

Exploring Whether this is a Linguistic or Early Memory Metaphor

T11:   I am wondering whether you have experienced something like this recently.

C11:   Not that I am aware of.

T12:   Nothing comes to mind.

C12:   Other than the relationship with her.

Phase 3: Transforming the Metaphor

T13:   Let us come back to the image of the mattress. If you were to change the image of the mattress and the impact on it, how would you change that image?

C13:   I would change the mattress from being worn to being firm. And I would move the mattress from a laying down position to an upright position so that it would stand upright and be firm.

T14:   You being the mattress relative to the boulder – to your sister – you would stand up and be firm.

C14:   I would be firm enough to sustain the impact of her blows but not allow her to penetrate me or squash me or knock me over. When she attempts to impose her comments or criticisms on me I would be able to let them roll off. So I would be able to stand tall, be firm, and allow things to roll off.

T15:   Seeing yourself then as this mattress, that is standing upright, you see yourself as letting things roll off; things might hit you but they would fall by the wayside.

C15:   Bounce off or roll off, not penetrate or squash.

Phase 4: Application of Transformed Metaphor to Presented Problem

T16:   How do you see this changed image connect to the problem that you mentioned at the beginning of this session, that is, to your relationship with your sister?

C16:   I don't see the boulder changing. I can't imagine that things would be different. So I see that I need to change in the sense that I need to stand on my own two feet and be firm and not allow things to penetrate me. I need to let things roll off.

T17:   In the initial image, the mattress was laying flat and things were falling on it and you had to struggle to get back to shape. In the new image, you are standing upright, are firm, and things that are hitting you are dropping by the wayside.

C17:   It is not knocking me over, it is not squashing me. It is coming to me, but then I am able to let it roll off.

T18:   You are able, then, to stand up to your sister, let her say whatever she wants to, but what she says will not have an impact on you, you will let it roll off just like water rolls off from a duck's back.

C18:   I am going to let it go.

T19:   You see yourself as being more capable to manage whatever your sister throws your way.

C19:   Keeping the boundaries with her firm and in place and standing firm.

T20:   Do you have any other feelings associated in being this way with your sister?

C20:   To see me that way, to see the mattress – and the boulder coming at it and the mattress standing erect, standing tall, standing firm and staying in place. I feel empowered. I feel hopeful.

T21:   If you were to speak of you being the mattress and your sister the boulder, how would you describe how you are relative to her?

C21:   I would be firm, I would be true to myself, I would stand on my own two feet, and I would not allow her impositions or imposing ways to penetrate me, to affect me, to weigh me down. I would be able to roll them off. I would be able to let them go and I would be at peace within myself, not have a need to defend myself but just stand tall and proud and firm.

T22:   You would not let things get to you. Is there anything else that you would like to add?

C22:   No.

Describing the Experience

Karen stated that she found the exercise "very empowering to be able to imagine a realistic different way of being in a relationship." At the same time she found it freeing to experience "this upright and firm way of being in a relationship as opposed to a tired, worn mattress." In connecting the transformed metaphor to her relationship with her sister, Karen felt that she could stand tall, and be strong and firm with her sister.

Something to Think About

1.   How do metaphors differ from facts?
2.   What makes for the potency of metaphors?
3.   How does a metaphor represent a nonlinear correspondence?
4.   How is overvaluing metaphors a limitation?
5.   How did Karen's transformed metaphor help to resolve the relational problem?

References

Adler, A. (1956). *The individual psychology of Alfred Adler: A systematic presentation in selections from his writings*. H. & R. Ansbacher (Eds.). New York: Basic Books.

Barker, P. (1985). *Using Metaphors in Psychotherapy*. New York: Brunner/Mazel Publishers.

Carveth, D. (1984). The analyst's metaphors: A deconstructionist perspective. *Psychoanalysis and Contemporary Thought, 7*, 491–560.

Combs, G.N., & Freedman, J. (1990). *Symbol, story and ceremony: Using metaphor in individual and family therapy*. New York: W.W. Norton & Co.

Freud, S. (1900/1953). *The interpretation of dreams. Standard edition* (Vol. 5). London: Hogarth Press.

Freud, S. (1923). *The ego and the id. Standard edition* (Vol. 19, pp. 12–63). London: Hogarth Press.

Freud, S. (1940/1949). *An outline of psycho-analysis. Standard edition* (Vol. 23). London: Hogarth Press.

Grove, D. (1996). And ... what kind of man is David Grove? Interview with P. Tompkins & J. Lawley, *Rapport Magazine, 33.*

Grove, D. (2003). *Problem domains and non-traumatic resolution through metaphor therapy.* http://www.devco.demon.co.uk/problemdomains.html, pp. 1–15.

Jung, C.G. (1916/1960). The transcendent function. In H. Read, M. Fordham, G. Adler, & W. McGuire (Eds.), *The collected works of C.G. Jung* (Vol. 8, Bollingen Series 20) (pp. 67–92). Princeton: Princeton University Press.

Kopp, R.R. (1995). *Metaphor therapy: Using client-generated metaphors in psychotherapy.* New York: Brunner/Mazel Publishers.

Kopp, R.R., & Craw, M.J. (1998). Metaphoric language, metaphoric cognition, and cognitive therapy. *Psychotherapy: Theory, Research, Practice, Training, 35*(3), 306–311.

Kris, E. (1952). On preconscious mental processes. *In Psychoanalytic explorations in art* (pp. 303–318). New York: International Universities Press.

Lakoff, G., & Johnson, M. (1980). *Metaphors we live by.* Chicago: University of Chicago Press.

Loue, S. (2008). *The transformative power of metaphor in therapy.* New York: Springer.

Milioni, D. (2007). 'Oh, Jo! You can't see that real life is not like riding a horse!': Clients' constructions of power and metaphor in therapy. *Radical Psychology, 6*(1).

Papp, P. (1982). Staging reciprocal metaphors in a couples group. *Family Process, 21,* 453–467.

Siegelman, E.Y. (1990). *Metaphor and meaning in psychotherapy.* New York: Guilford Press.

Spence, D.P. (1987). *The Freudian metaphor: Toward paradigm change in psychoanalysis.* New York: W.W. Norton.

Tompkins, P., & Lawley, J. (1996). Meta, Milton and metaphor: Models of subjective experience. *Rapport Magazine, 36,* August.

Tompkins, P., & Lawley, J. (2003). *Clean space: Modelling human perception through emergence.* Anchor Point, *17*(8).

Turbayne, C.M. (1971). *The myth of metaphor.* Columbia, SC: University of South Carolina Press.

Winnicott, C. (1978). D.W.W.: A reflection. In S.A. Grolnick & L. Barkin (Eds.), *Between reality and fantasy: Transitional objects and phenomena* (pp. 15–34). New York: Jason Aronson.

Task-Directed Imagery

Chapter Summary

The last two decades have seen a renewed interest in the use of imagery in psychotherapy to manage and resolve numerous personal and relational problems and to address physical ailments and diseases. Many of the images used are spontaneous, therapist-suggested and guided images. The use of imagery in a psychotherapeutic setting has often been questioned because very little research has examined its effectiveness. This chapter presents a novel form of imagery, task-directed imagery, that has been designed to enable persons to cope with a wide variety of personal and relational problems. Task-directed imagery begins by helping a person to feel empowered to confront a specific personal or relational problem, and then, from this empowered position, the person attempts to face and resolve the problem. Maylyn, in the illustration, was able to negotiate the developmental task of separating and individuating by asserting her need for psychological space without feeling guilty about it. Empirical studies have demonstrated that task-directed imagery is effective to resolve personal and relational problems such as improving trust in intimate relationships, letting go of control over others, and being able to self-soothe and self-comfort.

Introduction

The concept of imagery was introduced in psychotherapy by Janet (1898) a century ago to treat hysteria and obsessions and it has been used in psychotherapy ever since. However, imagery has not been held in the same regard among American psychologists as it has been among its European counterparts. European psychologists have for a "long time demonstrated a deep sensitivity and involvement in the realm of imagination" (Sheikh & Jordan, 1983, p. 396). American psychologists have, by and large, tended to regard imagination as unproductive, impractical, and unempirical (Shorr, 1995). With the introduction of behaviourism in North America there was a moratorium on inner experience including imagery. These positions, combined with the traditional psychoanalytic view which held that fantasy and images were defence mechanisms and manifestations of regression or resistance, led to a history of negativity towards and an avoidance of imagery in psychotherapy. Gradually, however, through the influence of humanistic psychology, the study of imagery regained its respectability and credibility. In this regard the behaviourists provided a strong impetus to its reexamination and use in therapy (Sheikh, Kunzendorf, & Sheikh, 2003).

To enhance personal growth and treat emotional problems and physical diseases, many forms of imagery have been designed, including spontaneous imagery, therapist-suggested imagery, guided imagery, and client-generated imagery (Singer, 2006). This chapter presents a specific form of imagery, called task-directed imagery (Meier & Boivin, 1993), which emerged from the therapy of a client to help her to let go of her obsessions and compulsions. Task-directed imagery has been extended to enable people to cope with a wide variety of personal and relational difficulties. The first part of this chapter presents the theoretical context of task-directed imagery. The second part presents task-directed imagery under the topics of theory, designing imagery exercises, and uses of task-directed imagery. The last part demonstrates how task-directed imagery was used to enable Maylyn to resolve an interpersonal problem. The chapter concludes with a summary.

Imagery in Context

This section presents four related concepts – namely, fantasy, memory, visualization, and imagery – presents the characteristics of imagery, and concludes with a brief description of the major types of imagery.

Fantasy, Memory, Visualization, and Imagery

Fantasy is a mental creation which has little or no connection with reality (e.g., a person with bird-like wings). Jung (1935/1976) states that "a fantasy is more or less your own invention, and remains on the surface of personal things and conscious expectations" (p. 171). Retrieval of stored memory more or less conforms to reality while imagery need not respect reality, nor is it inhibited in its creative process (Achterberg & Lawlis, 1981). Visualization, on the other hand, is imagery that employs the visual sense. This powerful form of image is primarily used in healing imagery. In creative visualization one uses one's imagination to create a clear image of something one wishes to manifest (e.g., destroying cancerous cells) (Achterberg, Dossey, & Kolkmeier, 1994). There are two different modes in creative visualization. One is the receptive mode, where the client simply relaxes and allows images or impressions to come to her without choosing the details of them; she takes what comes. The other is the active mode, where a person consciously chooses and creates what she wishes to see or imagine.

Imagery differs from fantasy, retrieved memory, and visualization. Imagery is plausible and has a link with reality. It is the "mental invention or recreation of an experience that in at least some respects resembles the experience of actually perceiving an object or an event, either in conjunction with, or in the absence of, direct sensory stimulation" (Finke, 1989, p. 2). In imagery, the "images have a life of their own and ... the symbolic events develop according to their logic" (Jung, 1935/1976, p. 171). Imagery, unlike visualization, may employ any one of the five sensory modalities, that is, sight, sound, smell, taste, or a sense of movement. In the task-directed imagery, a person is actively engaged in the creation of an image, not a fantasy, visualization, or memory of a previous event. In forming the image, the person draws on each of the five sensory modalities.

Components of Imagery

Images have three components, namely a visual, somatic (sensory), and a cognitive or experiential meaning component (Ahsen, 1968). The visual component is the image itself. This is an awareness or attention component, with some of the attention being conscious and clear and some of it possibly outside of awareness and remaining vague. The somatic component comprises a set of bodily feelings and tensions that include some correlations of emotions. The cognitive or experiential meaning component comprises meaning that arises spontaneously in the mind or later when the person attempts to understand the event (Nucho, 1995). An image, therefore, is a unit that comprises an awareness, a bodily response and an interpretation. This triadic unity "is considered to display certain lawful tendencies towards change that are meaningfully related to psychological processes" (Sheikh, Kunzendorf, & Sheikh, 2003, p. 20). These three components are inseparable and may appear in any of the five sensory modalities (e.g., seeing, hearing). However, depending on the specific experience, one of the three modalities may be more dominant than the other two.

Characteristics of Imagery

Various characteristics of imagery have been noted that make it a very effective and valuable tool for psychotherapy (Sheikh et al., 2003). First, experiencing something in imagery can be considered to be in many ways psychologically equivalent to experiencing the thing in actuality (Klinger, 1980). Second, images permit the spanning of the conscious and unconscious more easily than language (Panagiotou & Sheikh, 1977). Often where words fail to open the door to deeper-lying experiences, images are able to evoke not only memories but also the affect and motives associated with the memories. Images bring to the level of awareness that which was hidden in the unconscious and unlocks suppressed emotions and stimulates natural healing in the person (Sheikh & Jordan, 1983). Third, images act as the source of action and guide behaviour by representing the goal to be attained. Images which emerge from the felt sense of one's own reality not only provide underlying meanings and deeper feelings, but also act as signposts for future development of attitudes, perceptions, and behaviours (McMahon, 1976). Fourth, mental imagery is a means of avoiding the snares of rational thinking and sterile ruminations. It can be practiced with people who are incapable of systematic reflection and is oriented directly toward the individual's affective experience. Fifth, imagery is a direct experience of the inner world. Releasing an image from the unconscious and bringing it to awareness appears to be a basic growth process in the inner world. In experiencing such an image, the person is changed by that experience (Samuels & Samuels, 1975). Applying these characteristics to task-directed imagery, it is assumed that a person experiencing, in imagination, positive personal qualities (e.g., confidence, courage) is empowered and enabled to achieve a task (e.g., being assertive with a supervisor) in keeping with the inherent qualities of the image. The person, at the same time, is changed by this experience.

Types of Imagery

Task-directed imagery represents a particular type of imagery that will be compared to and contrasted with spontaneous imagery, therapist-suggested imagery, guided imagery, and client-generated imagery.

Spontaneous imagery refers to an image that is freely evoked while the client is relaxing, listening to music, or looking at an object or a painting. The therapist does not present the image to the client but it is freely and spontaneously elicited. For example, while relaxing, a client became aware of tightness in the abdomen which was visualized as a balloon filled with air.

Therapist-suggested imageries are imageries that have been selected, in advance, for their therapeutic value and the client is asked to focus on the image and report what is experienced. These are also referred to as starting images or imagery prompts (Nucho, 1995). Examples of starting images include imagining being in a meadow or in a cavern, and climbing a mountain (Leuner, 1984). It is expected that the different starting images will lead the person to focus on different parts of her life and therefore generate a broad spectrum of experiences, feelings, etc. A starting image used by Shorr (1995) is that of a rose. For example, a client might be asked to "Imagine yourself being a rose." A person might imagine a rose as not yet open, and is then asked to imagine it being open. She is asked to describe the experience which is then explored and discussed.

Guided imageries are prerecorded specific imagery scripts (Nucho, 1995). The client is asked to journey through the script and then at the end of the script to share her experience. Examples of guided imageries are Antique Object (Ferrucci, 1982) and the Inner Child Exercise (Rainwater, 1979). An example of a short guided imagery is the Well (Shorr, 1974, p. 116). Shorr gives the following instruction to the client: "Now I want you to imagine that you are standing on top of a dry well – then I want you to imagine another identical you that ... is in the bottom of the well – but the one at the top has a rope that is lowered to the bottom. Now tell me what happens – what would happen?"

In client-generated imagery, minimal structuring is provided by the therapist. These images are at times referred to as induced images (Korn & Johnson, 1983). Client-generated images are created with some element of conscious or preconscious activity. For example, the therapist might instruct the client to "Go to a place where you feel good in your body and master of your life, and when you are there, describe what is there."

Task-directed imagery is designed to help a client to achieve a personal or relational goal by first empowering the client and then asking the client to proceed from this empowered position to confront and resolve a current personal or relational problem. The empowered position is akin to a helpful or healthy ego state from which a client proceeds to deal with a problem generated by a troubled or hidden ego state (Watkins & Watkins, 1997).

Task-Directed Imagery

The theoretical concepts underlying the development and use of task-directed imagery are presented first. This is followed by a description of the procedure in designing a task-directed imagery session. The last section briefly presents some of the uses of task-directed imagery.

Theoretical Aspects

In its development, task-directed imagery was guided by a psychodynamic, experiential, developmental, and phenomenological/discovery-oriented psychotherapy approach. This approach postulates, in part, that: (a) psychic organizations (e.g., ego states) influence personal and relational behaviours, (b) clients, when in a safe, protective, nurturing, and challenging therapeutic environment, are able to discover the inner resources to change and transform their personal and interpersonal behaviours, and (c) psychotherapy is a process that entails the exploration of the problem, insight into the roots of the problem, and the implementation of the insight in personal and relational behaviours (This approach is detailed in Chapter 11.) The theoretical aspects of task-directed imagery are summarized under four topics: psychic organization, client inner resources, the self-discovery therapy approach, and therapy process.

Psychic Organization

The goal of task-directed imagery is to transform psychic organizations that in turn enable persons to change overt behaviours. For a task-directed imagery therapist, understanding a person's psychic organization is extremely important because it is assumed that this influences a person's attitudes, behaviours, and relationships. In a great number of problematic behaviours and relationships, there is something amiss at the level of psychic organization.

One's psychic organization is the product of one's experiences, particularly infant and childhood experiences. These early experiences regarding self, other, and the world, become organized to form, for example, schemas (Young, 2005), ego states (Watkins & Watkins, 1997), and internal representations (Klein, 1961). For the purpose of this chapter we will refer to these organized experiences as ego states (The concept is detailed in Chapter 7). The psychic organization has many ego states each of which comprise feelings, cognitions, memories, yearnings, and sensations. Typically, a person has one or more unique ego states for each significant person, such as a father, mother, brother, and sister. For example, when the word father is mentioned, a person will conjure up specific memories, feelings, thoughts, sensations, and yearnings. Generally ego states readily become available through association with a word such as father. However, some ego states, because of the painful experiences that constitute them, are not readily available and can be brought to awareness only through techniques such as hypnosis or imagery. The ego states not readily available are called hidden and problematic ego states.

Task-directed imagery works with ego states in two ways. First, it attempts to understand the person's problem in terms of a hidden and problematic ego state that needs to be transformed. Second, at the beginning of an imagery exercise, the therapist helps the client to create an ego state where the person feels empowered, wholesome, and good about self. Task-directed imagery uses this ego state to help the person to deal with a difficult personal or relational problem. In the process, the hidden problematic ego state is uncovered and transformed and the person becomes enabled to cope with the presenting problem.

Client Resources

Task-directed imagery takes the position that the majority of clients have the inner resources and the capacities to cope with the challenges of daily living and with their emotional problems. As well, clients have a sense of where, within themselves, they need to look to cope with the realities of their life, including emotional problems. This place can be expressed in terms of relational, self, sexual, and/or noetic (meaning-making, transcendent) needs that are often embedded within an image. The harsh reality is that for some clients, because of life circumstances and situations (e.g., trauma, abuse), these needs became deeply buried within their psyche and are consciously unknown. Yet, these various needs cry out to be heard and at times find themselves expressed in ways that are not helpful to the person. To bring lasting resolution to the client's presenting problems, it is important that the hidden needs be uncovered, acknowledged, and expressed in genuine and authentic ways.

The Self-Discovery Therapy Approach

To uncover the hidden needs and bring them to awareness, task-directed imagery subscribes to a self-discovery and phenomenological approach to therapy. This approach often uses bodily-oriented and semi-hypnotic (e.g., focusing) (Gendlin, 1996) techniques to access the deeper layers of experience that include hidden needs. In using this approach, the hidden needs are often expressed in terms of images, symbols, and metaphors that are to be deciphered. It is important that therapy help a client to discover the meaning of a particular image, symbol, or metaphor and use the meaning to reorient her life. A self-discovery approach helps clients to discover not only themselves, but also their relational style and patterns when relating to others.

Task-directed imagery has as its goal to help people become enabled to secure for themselves what is needed in life. To help a client become enabled, it is crucial to understand the significant part of their lives the person is not living and yet yearns to live without consciously knowing it. The use of a self-discovery approach to therapy ensures, as much as this is possible, that the fundamental issues are presented and addressed. With this understanding, the therapist is able to determine the skills, competencies, and/or capacities that need to be developed so that the person becomes enabled to cope with the challenges of daily living and with emotional problems.

The Therapy Process

Practically every aspect of human growth and development can be construed as an unfolding of potentials according to identifiable phases or stages. The same is true for the psychotherapy process that entails a number of phases with each having specific tasks to accomplish. Three of these phases are the *exploratory phase, awareness phase,* and *action phase* (Meier & Boivin, 1998). Task-directed imagery can be used to further each of these phases but it has been designed particularly for the *action phase*.

In the *exploratory phase*, the client explores the feelings, thoughts, needs (self and relational), meanings, and values that underlie and negatively influence her behaviours, actions, and interactions. The client might also explore her style of relating with others. For example, a client who becomes involved with unavailable partners might explore this pattern of relating.

In the *awareness phase,* the client begins to realize how her feelings, thoughts, needs, meanings, and values are linked to earlier experiences and negatively impact on her behaviours and interpersonal interactions. The person gains a new insight and a new perspective on the problem. The client sees the old with new eyes. The awareness is a powerful experience and may in itself be a curative or corrective or lead to new actions and behavioural patterns.

The client, in the *action phase*, begins to live from the new awareness, tries it out in new actions and new interpersonal behaviours. The client experiments with new behaviours and actions and retains those that are consistent with how she feels about herself. At times, clients might not know how to translate new awareness into new actions. In these situations the therapist can design imagery exercises to help the client become enabled and to act in a new way in her imagined behaviour. Acting in different and new ways is part of every therapeutic approach and the hallmark of all therapies.

Designing Task-Directed Imagery: Procedures

Task-directed imagery has been designed to help clients become enabled to achieve, in imagination, a personal or interpersonal goal. To achieve the goal the client needs to possess similar feelings, attitudes, and personal dispositions that were demonstrated in other situations. For example, to be assertive with a supervisor, it is important for the client to feel confident and courageous in asserting herself with a nonsupervisor. Therefore prior to undertaking task-directed imagery, the client is asked to experience the qualities associated with being assertive. Through this, a helpful ego state is established from which the client functions to resolve a problem. The client is then asked to imagine being somewhere (e.g., on the beach, in the park) where she experiences being in this helpful ego state. The client then describes where she imagines herself to be, what she senses and feels. The client is instructed to stay with all of these feelings and imagine approaching the supervisor. When this task is completed the client describes how she feels now that the task has been completed. This in brief summarizes the task-directed imagery procedure.

Designing an imagery exercise to enable a client to resolve a personal or relational problem comprises four parts, namely, conceptually understanding the client's difficulties, defining the imagery task, designing the imagery exercise, and obtaining client feedback following the exercise. All four parts, in the order presented, are included in all task-directed imagery; none of the parts are skipped. The four parts of task-directed imagery are now presented with reference to a client having difficulty trusting in a (trustworthy) intimate relationship.

Part 1: Understanding the Difficulty in the Context of the Client's Dynamics

The first step in using task-directed imagery is to help a person to identify the problem and to understand it in terms of the client's underlying dynamics, that is, in terms of a hidden and problematic ego state. It is imperative to understand the dynamics of the difficulty to trust, for example, in order to design a task which specifically and directly addresses the problem. A psychodynamic and relational understanding of the difficulty to trust is extremely helpful as it determines the nature of the imagined task and the goal for the imagery exercise. For example, for the case of Maylyn, illustrated at the end of this chapter, it is important to understand her difficulty to set limits and feel good about it in terms of the developmental task of separating and individuating (Mahler, Pine, & Bergman, 1975).

Part 2: Defining the Imagery Task

Using the clinical material, the therapist assesses whether an imagery exercise will help her resolve the difficulty to trust in intimate relationships. This assessment is usually made within the first 10 to 15 minutes of a session. It is helpful, perhaps imperative, to view the problem in terms of a polarity with the one pole representing the problem end on a continuum and the second pole representing the solution towards-which-to-strive end on the continuum. The former represents an inability to trust and the latter the ability to trust in intimate relationships.

When it is decided that task-directed imagery will be used and it has been assessed that the client has the necessary personal capacities and resources to deal with a presenting trust issue, the client's inner struggles and dynamics are translated into a theme which is treated using task-directed imagery. That is, the therapist offers the theme (trusting) to the client, who is asked to imagine this image and feeling. The therapist does not suggest an image to the client but invites the client to formulate an image which embodies the experience of trusting someone. The therapist uses this image in helping the client to work through the problem by designing a task-directed imagery exercise according to the four steps described below.

Part 3: Designing Task-Directed Imagery

Most task-directed imagery exercises will comprise four steps that are described and illustrated using the example of helping a person to develop trust in an intimate relationship. If a person is not able to negotiate Step 3, one terminates the exercise and explores with the client what she is experiencing at that moment.

Step 1: Concretizing a situation in which one feels empowered (is able to trust): In this first step the client is asked to imagine being in some concrete setting or situation where she can trust easily. The client is asked to describe the setting in terms of what is seen, heard, smelled, tasted, etc. The client is to be as sensorial in description as befits the setting. At this point the client is discouraged from describing feelings. To help the client with this step, the therapist might offer the following instructions.

1. I would like you to make yourself comfortable in your chair, close your eyes if you wish, and allow yourself to become relaxed. Take a few minutes to become settled.

2. Now, in your mind, imagine being some place where you are able to be comfortable in being with a person and able to trust the person. It can be a place you have already been to. It could also be at a new place, a place you have never been at before. Let me know when you have formed such an image.

3. (When the client indicates that she has formed an image, say:) I would like you to describe the image for me. What do you see? Feel? Smell? Hear? Are you alone? Who are you with? (At this point, proceed slowly and obtain all relevant information.)

Step 2: Describing feelings in the imagined setting: When the client has presented a sensorial description of the setting, ask how it is for her to feel able to trust in this imagined setting. The client is asked to describe her state of mind, thoughts, feelings, etc., in that place where she is able to trust. This state of mind represents a helpful ego state. (Pay attention to words such as feeling strong, relieved, free, at peace, etc., as these words complete the description of the helpful ego state and will be used to set up the task for Step 3.)

Step 3: Carrying feelings and attitudes from the imagined setting to the difficult task: In the third step the client is asked to stay connected to the good feelings and attitudes experienced in the imagined setting and to carry them to a real but often difficult setting, that is, to trust in an intimate relationship. This task is usually difficult to execute and the client is encouraged to proceed slowly and take the time needed. At times the client might meet an obstacle; if so, she is asked to circumvent or surmount the obstacle. Even if the client says that she cannot surmount it, encourage the client to continue a little while longer. The carrying forth of these good feelings and experiences can be either geographical or intrapsychical. For example, a person might be asked to transport herself from a log cabin to a brook, or from a state of fearing to love to loving, or from being dependent to being independent. To help the client negotiate this task, the therapist might provide the following instructions.

4. I would like you to hold on to all of these experiences of being strong, courageous, calm, and being able to trust and at the same time imagine being with the painful situation that you described earlier (name the painful incident). As you are with the painful situation, do not lose the feeling of being able to trust and its associated feelings and thoughts. Go slowly. Take your time. If you feel that you are losing your good feelings and thoughts, go back to the image of trusting. Proceed gradually and go back and forth between the two if you have to. Let me know when you have been able to imagine being with the painful moment and at the same time feel good with yourself and are able to trust the person.

5. (When the client has indicated that she has completed the task to trust when facing the painful situation, continue as follows:) What image do you have in mind? Where do you find yourself? Describe the setting for me.

Step 4: Client feedback: When the client has completed Step 3, she is asked to describe how she achieved the task and to describe her feelings in having been able to achieve it. To guide this process, the therapist might ask the following questions. (If the client's eyes are closed, invite the client to open them and be present.)

6. What is it like for you to have faced the painful situation and be able to trust? (Ask the person to describe her feelings, thoughts, etc.)

7. How did you manage to bring it around so that you were able to trust the person? (Listen carefully and explore the experience.) Is there anything else that you would like to say about this experience? (If the client says no, then bring the session to an end.)   ·

Usually all of the four steps are carried out in one and the same session. However, with some clients who are less resourceful, one may want to proceed more slowly. In this case, one could proceed with Steps 1 and 2 and then terminate the exercise when they have been completed. In the following session, one would begin with Step 1 and then proceed to Steps 2, 3, and 4. The purpose of using this graded approach is to give the client time to become aware of the moments in her life when she was able to trust others. Another purpose is to consolidate this experience, which will become a resource for working through future painful situations.

Part 4: The Client Describes Her Experience

Following the completion of Step 4, the client is asked to report on her experience and provide feedback on the use of the imagery exercise. The goal of the feedback is to assess how task-directed imagery works dynamically to bring about change, and to understand the process. The therapist is interested in two aspects of the experience, namely, how the client managed to bring about the trusting relationship and how the client feels having achieved the task. This is explored in great depth to assess the process and dynamics in using task-directed imagery to bring about change. To obtain this information, the therapist might ask the following questions.

1. How did you manage to bring it about so that you were able to hold on to the feeling of trust and confront the painful situation? (Listen carefully to how the client proceeded to achieve the task. Do not rehash the exercise but focus on the process and dynamics of the imagery exercise.)

2. What was this experience like for you? (Listen to what the client has to say, summarize it, and ask for clarification if needed. Then bring the session to a close.)

Uses of Task-Directed Imagery

Task-directed imagery has been used therapeutically to enable persons to resolve a variety of personal and relational problems (Meier & Boivin, 1993). It has been used to resolve intra-psychic conflicts, negotiate developmental tasks, cope with pressure at the workplace, acquire skills to compromise, resolve fear of intimacy, and acquire the ability to self-comfort and self-soothe. Research that supports the effectiveness of task-directed imagery will be presented in a forthcoming book on *Task-directed imagery in psychotherapy: theory, practice and research,* by Augustine Meier and Micheline Boivin.

Illustration: Maylyn

Maylyn (pseudonym), a married woman with three children, sought therapy to learn how to cope with a clinging, demanding, and competitive neighbour, Eve. Below are a summary of the therapy session, a conceptualization of the problem, a description of the therapy process, and excerpts from a transcript illustrating the use of task-directed imagery.

Summary

The therapy began with Maylyn describing her relationship with Eve, who has become very demanding, clinging, smothering, needy, and competitive. Maylyn has made attempts to push back and distance herself from the relationship that were exacerbated by a recent incident between their children which Eve did not handle well. This led to a rupture in their communication, with neither speaking to the other since the incident. Maylyn finds this state of affairs unsettling since in any other relationship, if something like this transpired, she would have talked to her friends about what happened and they would have reconciled and maintained a relationship.

The description of the problem indicated the possibility of using imagery to help Maylyn set limits with a needy person and feel that she is not judged or punished for it. To assess her ability to perform the task, the therapist explored with Maylyn her past relationships where she was able to set limits. She indeed has friends with whom she has a mutual understanding of what they can give and take, and they are able to negotiate the lines in their relationship without judgment and punishment.

Having established that Maylyn has the capacity to set limits in a relationship, a task-directed imagery session was designed according to the four steps. *Step 1*: She imagined being in her home and calling a friend who she has not seen in a very long time. Both understand and accept that they have busy lives and demands that do not allow them to connect as often as they would like. *Step 2*: Being with her friend in this imaginary setting felt freeing, reassuring, and comforting because she knows that the relationship will be there in spite of their not being able to give to the relationship all of the time. They felt no need to justify or make excuses for this. *Step 3*: In this step Maylyn imagined setting limits with Eve by being able to go about her life doing her own thing, having the distance that she needs, and feeling okay with that. She felt at ease in giving herself permission to set limits without the need to justify or defend them. She felt settled and at peace with her decision and actions. *Step 4*: Maylyn was able to achieve this task, in large part, by being able to put her needs in the relationship first and not have to defend her need for distance, knowing that the distance is healthy for her. She observed that the need for distance is different from pulling away.

Conceptualization

In her relationship with Eve, Maylyn struggled with the developmental task of stepping back from unwarranted demands in a relationship, living her life according to her needs, and setting limits to her giving without having to justify it and fearing being punished. When she relates to individuated persons she finds it easier to speak to them about relational issues since the hurt and anger, if and when present, would be more circumscribed in the situation, whereas if there is an issue with a person who is needy and wants enmeshment, such as Eve, Maylyn is prone to become angry about the situation, fearing being drawn into an enmeshed relationship and needing to defend her independence and autonomy. Maylyn's task is to resist the unwarranted demands of others and pursue her own life according to her relational and self needs and not feel that she has to justify her behaviours.

Therapy Process

The session began with the therapist exploring the nature of the problem to determine the task to be addressed, namely, to feel comfortable setting limits with a needy neighbour and not allow herself to be drawn into an enmeshed relationship. Maylyn's ability to set limits in relationships with other friends indicated that she had the capacity to set limits in the current problematic relationship. In the first two steps of the imagery exercise, Maylyn developed a helpful ego state from which to work to resolve the relational problem. In the third step, Maylyn imagined being with Eve and at the same time maintaining her sense of individuality and setting limits without fear of being punished for her behaviour. In the fourth step, Maylyn expressed her confidence that she is able to maintain her space without having to justify or defend herself.

Transcript

In the excerpts from the transcripts that follow, the therapist's responses, namely empathic responses, summaries, or open-ended questions, are in large part omitted for lack of space. In the transcript, C = Client, T = Therapist and the number following the letter represents the response number.

Step 1: Concretizing a Situation in which Maylyn is Able to Set Limits and Feel Good About it

T09: I would like you to imagine being someplace where you are in a relationship, where you are able to know how much of yourself you are going to give to the relationship and feel good in your own skin about it. If the other person reacts to this, you know how to deal with her reaction and the two of you are able to work it out. (Pause.) Let me know when you imagine this situation.

C09: (Silence 25 secs.) Okay.

T10:   Where do you see yourself being that way?

C10:   I am in my own home and I call up my good friend who I have not seen in a very long time. We talk and catch up on each other's lives. There has been a long lapse of time since we talked. There is a sense of shared excitement to reconnect and to catch up and understanding that we both have busy lives and demands that don't allow us to connect as often as we would like. There is understanding and empathy in the relationship.

Step 2: Describing the Feeling of Being in the Imagined Setting

T11:   What is it like for you to be this way in the relationship?

C11:   It is freeing. There is an easiness about being in this relationship in spite of being limited by circumstance and by distance.

T12:   Any other feelings in being in this relationship?

C12:   It is reassuring and comforting to feel that we can just pick up where we left off and not have to justify or defend or make excuses for why we distanced.

C14:   There is a sense of security knowing that the relationship will still be there in spite of the distance or the lack of energy invested in it.

C15:   And a mutual respect and understanding that we cannot give to the relationship all of the time.

Step 3: Carrying (Transporting) Feelings and Attitudes from the Imagined Setting to the Difficult Task

T16:   I would like you now to remain in touch with the feeling that your relationship has its limitations and both of you are able to accept the limitations and you do not have to justify how much of yourself you give to the relationship. I want you to stay with these feelings and imagine being in the relationship with Eve without having to justify setting limits in the relationship. I would like you to stay in touch with these feelings, hold on to them, and imagine being with Eve in the way you freely want to be with her. Work with this in your imagination so that you can be that way with her. Let me know when you have been able to do this. (Silence 15 secs.) Go at your own pace with the task and if you sense that you are losing the feelings, go back to feelings in being with your friend in your home and pick up the feelings, and then continue to imagine being with Eve and giving of yourself to the relationship how much you want to give and feeling okay with that.

C16:   (Silence, 90 secs.) Okay.

T17:   Where do you see yourself . . .

C17:   I see myself as being able to go about my life and do my own thing without feeling unsettled and being able to take the distance that I need to take and feel okay with that.

T18:   Do you have any other feelings?

C18:   I feel confident that I need to take space for myself and take distance from her to be true to me. I feel more at ease to give myself permission to do that without the need of having to justify or defend what I am doing. I feel more settled. More at peace with my decision and actions.

Step 4: Client Feedback

T20: How were you able to bring it around in your imagination so that you were able to take the distance you needed and not have to justify it but feel settled with it?

C20: I think that in large part just being able to put my needs in the relationship first and not have to defend or justify my need for space or for distance and also to know that distance is healthy for me. Also to see that taking space, taking distance is different from pulling away.

Describing the Experience

In describing her experience, Maylyn mentioned that she gained an insight into how this situation paralleled the relationship with her family, when she was growing up, where taking distance from relationships within her family was never encouraged or supported. As an adult, when she began to live her own life, she felt punished and judged for that or love was withheld when she tried to move away to become her own person. In her relationship with Eve, she feels that she is being punished when she attempts to take distance. She feels angry about that and also fears that if she attempts to enter into a discussion about the incident and her decision to take distance, she will not be respected and she may then become defensive and question her right to assert her needs. Maylyn felt a need to push back from Eve's clinging, demanding, and impositional behaviours in order to take distance from her. For her this was a familiar but unsettling feeling.

Something to Think About

1. How does visualization differ from imagery?
2. Wherein lies imagery's potency to effect personal and interpersonal change?
3. What is meant by spontaneous imagery?
4. How is the third step in task-directed imagery crucial to bring about change?
5. What was the turning point in the therapy with Maylyn?

References

Achterberg, J., Dossey, B., & Kolkmeier, L. (1994). *Rituals of healing: Using imagery for health and wellness.* Toronto: Bantam Books.

Achterberg, J., & Lawlis, G.F. (1981). *Bridges of the body/mind.* Champaign, IL: Institute for Personality and Ability Testing.

Ahsen, A. (1968). *Basic concepts in eidetic psychotherapy.* New York: Brandon House.

Desoille, R. (1961). *Théorie et pratique du rêve éveillé dirigé.* Suisse: Éditions du Mont-Blanc.

Ferrucci, P. (1982). *What may be: Techniques for psychological and spiritual growth.* Northamptonshire: Turnstone Press Ltd.

Finke, R.A. (1989). *Principles of mental imagery*. Cambridge, MA: The MIT Press.

Gendlin, E.T. (1996). *Focusing-oriented psychotherapy: A manual of the experiential method*. New York: Guilford Press.

Janet, P. (1898). *Névroses et idées fixes*. Paris: Masson.

Jung, C.G. (1935/1976). The symbolic life. *Collected Works* (Vol. 18). Princeton: Princeton University Press.

Klein, M. (1961). *Narrative of a child analysis* (Vol. 4). London: Hogarth Press.

Klinger, E. (1980). Therapy and the flow of thoughts. In J.E. Shorr, G.E. Sobel, P. Robin, & J.A. Connella (Eds.), *Imagery: Its many dimensions and applications*. New York: Plenum.

Korn, E.R., & Johnson, K. (1983). *Visualization: The uses of imagery in the health professions*. Homewood, IL: Don Jones–Irwin.

Leuner, H. (1984). *Guided affective imagery: Mental imagery in short-term psychotherapy*. New York: Thieme Stratton Inc.

Mahler, M., Pine, F., & Bergman, A. (1975). *The psychological birth of the human infant*. New York: Basic Books.

McMahon, C.E. (1976). The role of imagination in the disease process: Pre-Cartesian history. *Psychological Medicine, 6*, 179–184.

Meichenbaum, D. (1977). *Cognitive-behavioral modification: An integrative approach*. New York: Plenum.

Meier, A., & Boivin, M. (1993). Task-directed imagery compared to behavior rehearsal to produce "letting-go" behavior. Paper presented at the 1993 Annual International Meeting of the Society for Psychotherapy Research, Pittsburgh, Pennsylvannia, June 22–26.

Meier, A., & Boivin, M. (1998). *The seven-phase model of the change process: Theoretical foundation, definitions, coding guidelines, training procedures, and research data* (5th Ed.). Unpublished MS. Ottawa, Ontario: Saint Paul University.

Nucho, A.O. (1995). *Spontaneous creative imagery: Problem-solving and life-enhancing skills*. Springfield, IL: Charles C. Thomas Publishers.

Panagiotou, N., & Sheikh, A.A. (1977). The image and the unconscious. *International Journal of Social Psychiatry, 23*, 169–186.

Rainwater, J. (1979). *You're in charge: A guide to becoming your own therapist*. Los Angeles: Guild of Tutors Press.

Samuels, M., & Samuels, N. (1975). *Seeing with the mind's eye: The history, techniques, and uses of visualization*. New York: Random House.

Sheikh, A.A., & Jordan, C.S. (1983). Clinical uses of mental imagery. In A.A. Sheikh (Ed.), *Imagery: Current theory, research, and application* (pp. 391–435). Toronto: John Wiley & Sons.

Sheikh, A.A., Kunzendorf, R.G., & Sheikh, K.S. (2003). Healing images: Historical perspective. In A.A. Sheikh (Ed.), *Healing images: The role of imagination in health* (pp. 3–26). New York: Baywood.

Shorr, J.E. (1974). *Psychotherapy through imagery*. New York: Intercontinental Medical Book Corporation.

Shorr, J.E. (1995). *Psychotherapy through imagery*. New York: Fithian Press. (A revised and updated edition of Shorr, 1974.)

Singer, J.L. (2006). *Imagery in psychotherapy*. Washington, DC: American Psychological Association.

Watkins, J.G., & Watkins, H.H. (1997). *Ego states: Theory and therapy*. New York: Norton.

Young, J.E. (2005). Schema-focused cognitive therapy and the case of Mrs. S. *Journal of Psychotherapy Integration, 15*(1), 115–126.

Chapter Summary

Ego-state therapy is particularly suited to treat current emotional problems that are reenactments of earlier unresolved ego states. Current emotional problems are able to be resolved if the boundary between them and the hidden ego state is fluid and permeable. This chapter presents the major concepts associated with ego states, their development, and activation. The steps in doing ego-state therapy includes identifying hidden ego states, bridging ego states, and performing an ego-state shift. To bridge ego states and to shift to more adaptive states, ego-state therapy makes use of imagery that has the capacity to evoke feelings, memories, thoughts, yearnings, and sensations.

Introduction

Over the past two decades, ego-state therapy has become an increasingly recognized form of therapy, although it has been used in the past primarily by hypnotherapists to treat dissociative disorders (Emmerson, 2008). Ego-state therapy is derived from ego psychology, a branch of psychoanalysis. In his earlier writings, Freud (1901) viewed personality as comprising different layers of ego states such as the egoistic needs of children that are overlaid by altruistic impulses and morality. He believed that the former, a hidden ego state, could be activated and laid bare to modify a person's behaviours and perceptions. Later, Freud (1923) explained emotional disorders in terms of ego deficits and conflicts between the three agencies of the mind (Id, Ego, Superego). Fairbairn (1944) viewed emotional problems in terms of ego splitting and ego states. Splits in the ego were formed by the ego investing a part of itself in different situations relative to a significant other such as a parent. Berne (1961) provided important concepts such as ego boundaries, reactivating ego states, and ego cathexis, and a method to identify ego states. Klein (1961) introduced the concept of internal representations that she viewed as operating as ego states, and Young (2005) thought of schemas as being similar to ego states.

Ego-state therapy as it is practiced today is attributable to Watkins (1993). Watkins and Watkins (1997) and Lawrence (1999a, 1999b) have expanded the use of ego-state therapy to the treatment of the historical origins of a broader spectrum of psychologically based emotional problems and interpersonal dysfunctions. They assume that underlying these problems are covert problematic ego states. In treating these underlying ego states, it is assumed that the person's manifest behavioural and interpersonal problems will be indirectly treated as well. The first part of this chapter presents the major concepts, development, and activation of ego states. The second part presents the practice of ego-state therapy. The third part provides excerpts from a transcript that illustrate ego-state therapy.

Ego States: Major Concepts, Development, and Activation

This part of the chapter presents the major concepts related to ego states and the development and activation of ego states. Specifically included are: definition of ego states, ego-state sequences, and subpersonality; ego states and dissociation; ego states and psychic energy; development of ego states; activating ego states; ego states and psychopathology; characteristics of ego states.

Ego States, Ego State Sequences, and Subpersonalities

Watkins and Watkins (1997) define an ego state as "an organized system of behaviour and experience whose elements are bound together by some common principle and which is separated from other such states by a boundary that is more or less permeable" (p. 25). That is, ego states comprise behaviours and experiences (e.g., feelings, memories, desires) which form a whole and are held together by a common principle (e.g., the experience of childhood abuse), and are separated from each other by a boundary that is relatively easy to cross. Ego states are considered to be the product of state-dependent learning. Thus, when we experience or learn something, all the components (e.g., sensations, feelings, thoughts, images, memories, motor responses) of the self that were present at the time of the learning are linked and stored together forever. These linked components are called an ego state (Lawrence, 1999a).

Enduring ego states are to be distinguished from momentary ego states. The more enduring ego states are created by experiences that are traumatic, highly intense, chronic, or repetitive. Momentary ego states are those that occur sequentially and in close proximity to each other. For both types of ego states, associational linkages develop and these linkages are stronger when accompanied by intense affect or repetition. Lawrence (1999a) gives the following as an example of a momentary ego state:

> When the memory of an early childhood sexual trauma is uncovered, the patient will experience a series of different affective ego states in close sequence, paralleling the initial experience, going from intense apprehension, to outright terror, to feelings of dejection and helplessness. These momentary ego states unfold one by one, as if played on a video tape, forming ego state sequences, which can be highly predictable. (p. 5)

An ego-state sequence refers to the unfolding of a series of ego states that are associated to each other. The unfolding proceeds in such fashion that if one of the main ego states is activated, the other ego states will follow.

When a sequence of ego states "becomes sufficiently organized and dominant within a person to repeat itself frequently and regularly in certain situations, it is called a sub-personality" (Lawrence, 1999a, p. 5). A subpersonality is conceived of as having multiple ego states all of which are "linked together in a common pattern organized around some sort of central theme ... which may be a certain behavioural style, a predominant mood, an interpersonal objective, some basic premises about the nature of life" (Lawrence, 1999a, p. 5). The multiple ego states involved in the person's experience are united by the person's experience and world view.

Ego States and Dissociation

Broadly speaking, dissociation can include phenomena which range from daydreams and children's imaginary games to personality disorders (Shirar, 1996). In all forms of dissociation, one disconnects from oneself for a short period. From a narrower perspective, dissociation is "a separating process that extends throughout a continuum from normal and adaptive differentiation to the other extreme of pathological dissociation, like multiple personality disorder" (Watkins & Watkins, 1997, p. 39). Used in this sense, it is a defence mechanism. Dissociation can be an adaptive (normal) or a pathological process. As a normal process, dissociation protects persons from frightening situations, lowers their fears, and removes from within a person an area of conflict. In its pathological form, dissociation leads to dissociative identity disorders and amnesias. In between these two extremes, dissociation might lead to the development of covert or "hidden" ego states (Lawrence, 1999a; Watkins & Watkins, 1997).

Ego states differ from each other according to the degree to which the boundaries between them are permeable and fluid. Permeability refers to the ability of a primary ego state to access subordinate ego states. Fluidity refers to the shift from one predominant ego state to another ego state, often initially hidden. Ego states that are permeable and fluid communicate with each other, and ego states that are impermeable and rigid are not aware of the other ego state.

The concept of dissociation as used by ego-state therapy concerns the dissociated (covert, hidden) ego states that can be contacted or activated by the use of imagery. These are the intermediary and in-between ego states that are less rigid in their semipermeable boundaries, retain partial communication, interaction, and sharing of content. Although they remain covert, they can be activated "into the executive [observed, public ego state] position" (Watkins & Watkins, 1997, p. 33). The ego state of which the person is conscious and in which the energy and identity of self reside, is referred as the "executive ego state" (Watkins & Watkins, 1997, p. 26). The less dominant ego states are more or less dissociated. The relationship between the dominant ego state and the other temporarily less dominant ego states will depend upon permeability and fluidity at their boundaries (Lawrence, 1999a).

Ego States and Psychic Energy

To perform their tasks, ego states must be endowed with psychic energy. Ego states are not at one and the same moment equally energized. To explain the energy used by ego states and various psychological processes, Freud (1914, 1923) developed the *libido theory* that comprised both object-libido (e.g., psychic energy invested in a love object) and ego-libido (e.g., energy invested in oneself such as in narcissism). The libido invested in objects and in oneself was the same energy, only the direction of the energy is different (e.g., external vs. internal).

Federn (1952) revised Freud's theory by replacing the notion of libido with two energies, namely, ego cathexis and object cathexis. Ego cathexis is "the energy of selfness, and any item so invested was experienced as being within one's self, as a part of 'the me'" (Watkins & Watkins, 1997, p. 14). Object cathexis, on the other hand, "is an inorganic, 'it' energy" making the invested element or psychological process experienced as "not me" (Watkins & Watkins, 1997, p. 14). The distinction between object cathexis and ego cathexis has implications for the quality of ego states. Ego states invested with ego cathexis are experienced as part of "the me" and ego states invested with object cathexis are experienced as "not me."

Development of Ego States

Watkins and Watkins (1997) believe that ego states develop from one of three processes: normal differentiation, introjection of significant others, and reactions to trauma.

Normal Differentiation

Through normal differentiation, the child learns to make a host of discriminations. For example, at the level of interpersonal behaviours, a child learns how to relate to father, mother, teacher, peers, etc. The child learns entire patterns of behaviour which are appropriate when relating to mother, for example, or when at school. These patterns of behaviour and experiences are clustered and organized around some common principle. As such they can be thought of as ego states. The boundaries between these states and other personality patterns are permeable and flexible. The child is aware when he is with a parent or in school and can easily shift from one ego state to the other (Watkins & Watkins, 1997).

Introjection of Significant Other

Through the processes of the introjection of significant others and identification with them, a child internalizes a cluster of behaviours, feelings, sensations, motives, and thoughts which lead to the development of other-representations and self-representations which in turn lead to ego states. Ego states are the result of events experienced by the child. When a child experiences something, he experiences it as a whole and links and stores together forever all of its elements (e.g., sensation, memory) (Lawrence, 1999a).

Reaction to Trauma

The child may dissociate when confronted with rejection, abuse, or severe trauma. When reacting to such situations, the youngster "often removes the ego cathexis from part of himself, reenergizes it with object cathexis, and creates an imaginary playmate with whom he can interact" (Watkins & Watkins, 1997, p. 31). Such imaginary playmates are discarded or repressed by most children upon going to school. However, if such an ego state is merely repressed, later conflict or environmental stress may cause it to be reinvested with energy and reemerge, possibly in a self-punishing and malevolent form.

Activating Ego States

Ego states that begin to form early in life, referred to as residual infantile ego states, do not disappear but remain preserved in a latent state, waiting to be recathected and activated.

These hidden ego states can become energized and activated when a current situation (e.g., a critical boss) stimulates a past situation (e.g., a critical father) during which time the ego state (e.g., feelings of being demeaned) was developed. Hidden ego states may also be reactivated through the use of hypnosis, regressive techniques, and imagery (Federn, 1952).

Ego States and Psychopathology

Psychopathology, from an ego-state perspective, represents a failure to maintain an optimal permeability and fluidity between ego states (Lawrence, 1999a). In psychopathology, the boundaries between ego states are rigid. When the ego state does not have an opportunity to express itself, if it is suppressed, it will break through in order to have its needs met. The break through of the "problematic" ego state is viewed as symptomatology, or as psychopathology. The problematic ego state is called the "hidden" or covert ego state in the sense that it is disowned, unaccepted, or unacknowledged by the predominant ego states. Psychopathology may also occur because of a conflict between two or more major groups of ego states that believe that they are right and struggle relentlessly to dominate (Lawrence, 1999b). This overt struggle leads to a polarization of positions. Either the power shifts from one position to the other without a real resolution or the one might dominate for a period of time while the other fights covertly for domination.

Regardless of whether psychopathology is a manifestation of a "hidden" ego state breaking through or due to conflicts between groups of ego states, it is the person's maladaptive use of the dissociative process that allows the psychopathology and conflict to persist (Lawrence, 1998, 1999b). The dissociation can be a dominant ego repressing a hidden ego state, or it can be between two or more major groups of ego states.

Characteristics of Ego States

Ego states have several important characteristics (Lawrence, 1999a; Watkins & Watkins, 1997). First, ego states can be dissociated from each other, that is, one ego state can have no knowledge of the other, or when a person functions from one ego state, the other ego state is not implied. The components (e.g., feelings, thoughts) of the ego state might be dissociated from each other as well. For example, a survivor of childhood sexual abuse might be able to talk about the incident with no feelings attached to it.

Second, the relationship of dissociated ego states to each other depends on boundary variables such as permeability and fluidity. When the boundary between ego states is rigid, it will not allow information to pass from one ego state to the other.

Third, a dissociated ego state may erupt into consciousness without warning. It might be activated by experiencing a similar situation as to when it was formed. For example, a person talking to a boss who is critical of her work, might all of a sudden feel belittled, helpless, angry, and hurt.

Fourth, an ego state takes on the characteristics of the age in which it originated. For example, ego states that were created during the subject's adolescence will think like a teenager, be very defensive of their own independence, will not want to be told what to do, and will reject and be suspicious of grown-ups. These covert ego states will be hard for an adult to reach because the ego states seem to have been frozen in time. These ego states can be activated by imagery and hypnosis.

Fifth, an ego state was probably developed to enhance a person's ability to adapt and cope with a specific situation or problem. Thus one ego state might, for example, take the position of the dominant ego state to deal with parents, another ego state might assume the dominant position at the place of work. Thus different ego states become dominant depending on the situation.

Sixth, ego states are highly motivated to protect and continue their existence. They came into being to facilitate the adaptation of the primary person. Thus it is very difficult to eliminate a maladaptive ego state. It is far easier to modify the motivations of ego states and to change their behaviour constructively than to eliminate them.

Seventh, ego states act like "ground" and "figure" in Gestalt terms (Perls, Hefferline, & Goodman, 1951), with one ego state dominating while the others are hidden. Being hidden does not necessarily mean that it is a problematic ego state; it only means, that for a particular situation, a particular ego state, problematic or nonproblematic, is activated.

The Practice of Ego-State Therapy

This section presents the goals of ego-state therapy, its therapeutic conditions, steps, and techniques. The section ends with procedures for doing ego-state therapy and illustrates its use by providing excerpts from a transcript of a therapy session.

Goals of Ego-State Therapy

Ego-state therapy has three major goals. First, to undo the maladaptive dissociation between ego states in order to achieve optimal permeability and fluidity. Second, to promote cooperative, collaborative attitudes among the ego states rather than polarized postures. Third, to achieve greater integration of personality, the fundamental goal of ego-state therapy. Achieving these goals leads to optimal connection among the ego-state changes in behaviour in general, and changes in interpersonal patterns in particular. Ego-state therapy is possible when ego states are separated by a very permeable and fluid boundary (Lawrence, 1999a; Watkins & Watkins, 1997).

Therapeutic Conditions

In doing ego-state therapy, it is important for the therapist to establish safety and trust. Watkins and Watkins (1997) state that "trustworthiness is conveyed by the subtle impact of one's beingness, by nonverbal cues, and by honesty of expression" (p. 104). Second, the therapist must pace himself according to the readiness of the client. This requires that the therapist listen carefully to the client and follow his lead, understand when an intervention is appropriate and know when to be silent and let the client's inner forces resolve problems. A useful admonition is "follow before you lead" and use empathic responses to reflect what the ego state says (Watkins and Watkins, 1997, p. 103). Third, the therapist must make a commitment to the client, to tolerate a degree of dependency. In a good relationship, a certain degree of dependency is desirable. The patient who needs and trusts the therapist will be constructively and positively motivated. Fourth, the therapist has to resonate with each ego state and speak its language, that is, befriend the ego state and become its ally. It is important for the therapist to immerse himself into the experience of the ego state and to communicate from that position. The therapist has to become acquainted with the ego state, understand it, and build trust. When these are accomplished the therapist can challenge the client to move beyond a stuck ego state, to connect with another ego state, build bridges, and carry out shifts.

Therapeutic Steps

Ego-state therapy entails three interrelated and sequential steps, namely, identifying an ego state, bridging a current ego state to an earlier, similar ego state, and making a shift from a troubled ego state to a healthy or functional ego state.

Identifying an Ego State

An ego-state therapist begins by identifying a current ego state which may take the form of constantly feeling angry, depressed, anxious, guilty, victimized, needy, etc. A characteristic of a current ego state is that the affective, cognitive, motivational, and/or behavioural manifestations of an experience are disproportionate to the event itself. The sense is that the person is carrying over something from the past – unfinished business – which is influencing his response to a current situation. For every current ego state there is a hidden ego state that influences the person's responses. An example of a current ego state is a person becoming intensely angry when given feedback because the person feels he is being scolded and belittled. In this example, the person's response to the situation is greater than warranted by the event itself and presumably driven by a hidden ego state.

Ego-State Bridges

The second step is to link a current troubling experience (e.g., rage) or current ego state to an earlier ego state. The assumption is that the unresolved earlier ego state is impacting on the person's ability to deal in a more calm, objective, and adaptive way with current issues. This linkage of a current state to an unresolved ego state is referred to as "ego-state bridging" (Lawrence, 1999a, p. 9) or "affective bridging" (Watkins and Watkins, 1997, p. 101). An ego-state bridge involves amplifying a present ego state, tracing it back in time to when it was first experienced, and associating it with other components (e.g., feelings, memory). The bridge is a bridge in time, not to a different ego state. The therapist, for example, might ask the client when he felt like this for the first time. As much as possible it is important to identify an early childhood or adolescent experience. These earlier ego states are referred to as hidden ego states.

Ego-State Shift

The third step is to resolve the feelings, perceptions, sensations, etc., associated with the "hidden" ego state by developing a more capable ego state which will bring comfort and relief. This is accomplished by shifting from a problematic ego state – the hidden ego state – to some other ego state that can soothe or relieve the anxiety associated with the problematic ego state. In other words, the goal is to develop a new ego-state sequence so that whenever the problematic hidden ego state is activated, a more appropriate ego state is spontaneously activated in sequence. The assumption is that a more capable and appropriate ego state will predominate when a problematic ego state is activated. To develop a more capable and appropriate ego state the therapist might ask the client what the problematic ego state needs to be better, feel better, etc. The client is encouraged to bring in, through imagination, any person, thing, action, etc., that will make things better for the problematic ego state (Lawrence, 1999a).

Therapeutic Technique

Imagery is ego-state therapy's most powerful tool for conducting the processes of accessing the origins of psychologically based emotional, personal, and interpersonal problems and for treating them. Imagery is the medium by which ego states are bridged and by which one shifts from one ego state to another (Lawrence, 1999a). Practically, the client and therapist begin the therapeutic process by identifying a current ego state that is connected to a hidden ego state. The client is asked to describe the current experience in as great detail as possible. Following this, the client is asked, through imagination, to connect the current set of experiences to an earlier experience. Then, using imagery, the client is asked to imagine what would make the hidden ego state better. For the latter two steps, the client engages in an imaginary process. In shifting from the hidden ego state to a more capable ego state, the client is invited, through imagery, to let whatever needs to happen in the image to happen.

Procedures in Doing Ego-State Therapy

Watkins and Watkins (1997) provide many examples of ego-state therapy, and Lawrence (1999a) provides an exercise to experience a specific ego state, bridge an ego state with a hidden ego state, and shift from a problematic to a more capable and healthy ego state. From these cases and exercises and from our own experiences, we have deduced procedures for the use of ego-state therapy in working with individual clients and using the clinical material that they present. The following procedures serve as guidelines when using ego-state therapy for individual work.

Identify an Ego State

The first step is to identify an underlying troubling ego state. The therapy session begins with the client presenting and describing something with which he is struggling. The therapist invites the client to describe the current situation in as great detail as possible particularly with regard to feelings, motives, thoughts, sensations, memories, and behaviours. When the client has connected with his deeply felt experiences, described the current problem, experienced the feelings as strongly as they want to be, and the therapist has a good feel for the problem and assesses that the client's current problem is related to an earlier experience (a hidden ego state), the therapist may invite the client to engage in the ego-state technique by linking the current problem to an earlier experience. It is crucial that the client experience very intensely the feelings and sensations associated with the presented problem before moving into ego-state therapy in order to connect the current ego state with the problematic ego state.

Bridge an Ego State

In making a bridge between the current experience and a hidden ego state, the therapist asks the client to remain in touch with all of his feelings, sensations, thoughts, memories, and desires and to let them take him back in time to when he experienced this set of feelings and sensations for the first time. Although it is preferable for the client to go back to the earliest memory of such feelings, yet the client need not worry if it is not his earliest memory. As the client is in touch with these earliest experiences, he is to let an image form of this earliest memory. The client is then asked to place himself in the image or scene with as much detail as possible. He is asked to notice what is happening, what is being said, how he is feeling or what he is experiencing, what thoughts are going through his mind, how he sees himself relative to others, etc. The task is for the client to experience as fully as possible this earliest experience.

Ego-State Shift

After the client has described the image or scene and the associated experiences, he is asked to notice what is unsatisfactory about the scene or what is painful or disappointing about it. When the client is aware what the ego state needs to get relief, he is asked to *let go of the historical reality* and let the image unfold so that whatever relief needs to happen, happens. The client is instructed to play with it, to correct the problem in whatever way possible. The client is invited to bring into the image anyone from any time or any place to help the problematic (child) ego state have its needs met. The client is asked to let whatever needs to happen, happen so as to make it better or correct.

Application to Current Problem

When the early image seems resolved, the client is asked to bring his learning from that experience forward in time to the situation with which the client began the session. The client is asked to notice how he feels in the present situation. The client is invited to play with the image in the same way that he played with the previous early childhood image and to allow the same new, positive ego-state sequence to unfold as it occurred in the early childhood situation. The client is to play with it until it is resolved. The client can bring any persons from any time or any place to help him resolve the current situation.

Illustration: Sonja

Sonja (pseudonym), in her late twenties and recently graduated with an MSW as a case social worker, sought counselling because of an interpersonal problem with a male colleague. Below are a summary of the therapy session, a conceptualization of the problem, a description of the steps, and excerpts from a transcript illustrating its use.

Summary

Sonja reported that a colleague, Zdeno (pseudonym), was critical of her professional work and belittled her as a person. She began to question her competency as a therapist, felt hostile and angry towards Zdeno, and was distraught with herself for being hostile towards him. Sonja felt something similar in her early childhood when her father ridiculed her and called her stupid for being clumsy because of a neurological condition. In her late teens her father said that she would not amount to anything. His comments hurt her and she became very angry towards him. Her experience with Zdeno awakened early childhood and adolescent experiences of feeling demeaned, hurt, humiliated, and alone. To help Sonja access the hidden ego state and to equip her to deal with her current situation, ego-state therapy was used. To make the hidden ego state better, she imagined her father (in his later years) standing up for her, taking her side, acknowledging and accepting her, and she in turn accepting herself for her mistakes. Applying this to her relation with Zdeno, Sonja perceived herself taking distance from his critical comments and being open to what he had to contribute.

Conceptualization

Sonja's emotional reactions to Zdeno's belittling and demeaning statements are activations of her childhood experiences with a father who told her that she was inadequate, not good enough, and stupid. Associated with this ego state, are the ego states of wanting to attack, doubting her competency, and feeling angry at herself for feeling this way. These ego states form a sequence such that when Sonja feels put down by Zdeno, she begins to experience the other ego states mentioned above. The enduring ego state, feeling inadequate, was transformed by her father in affirming, acknowledging, and accepting her and by her acceptance of herself. With the development of a more resilient ego state, Sonja was able to distance herself from the negativity of Zdeno, be open to receiving from him what she found to be of value.

Steps in the Therapy Process

The therapy process comprised four steps, each of which was thoroughly explored before moving on to the subsequent step. The first step determined whether Sonja's interpersonal problems were related to the situation (e.g., a personality clash) or whether an underlying problematic ego state was activated (identifying an ego state). The depth of Sonja's hurt and hostile feelings, the need to protect herself, and her tendency to doubt herself and feel bad in having the negative feelings led to the inference of a problematic ego state.

The second step linked the current problem to a problematic ego state (ego bridging) that originated in early childhood in her relationship with her father, who ridiculed her, called her stupid, and said that she would amount to nothing. Sonja, on her part, felt humiliated, alone, and put down.

The third step entailed Sonja drawing on resources to make the situation better (ego shift) by developing a more capable ego state. It was to her father (of later years) to whom she turned to make things better. In the scene she imagined him standing up for her, accepting and acknowledging her, which in turn allowed her to accept herself.

The fourth step applied the healthy ego state to the situation with Zdeno (application). By taking distance from him, she was able to take what was of value from him and to be without defensiveness, feelings of humiliation, and the need to protect herself.

Transcript

In the following transcript excerpts, the therapist's responses, that were mostly empathic responses, summaries, or open questions, are in large part omitted for lack of space. In the transcript, C = Client, T = Therapist and the number following the letter represents the response number. The therapy begins with Sonja describing her interaction with Zdeno and her feelings towards him.

Step 1: Identifying an Ego State

C03:   Zdeno said that this couple came to you for therapy and your hypothesis might lead them to divorce. Are you ready to take on that kind of responsibility? The comment was so ridiculous and I responded by saying if this couple stays together because of therapy or if they divorce it is not my responsibility.

C04:   I felt hostile towards him and I wanted to tell him to shut up because I didn't need his unsolicited advice.

T04:   What else was happening within you?

C05:   I felt that my competency and professional integrity were being questioned.

C06:   Going in I felt very positive about my working hypothesis. With his comments I got really defensive and guarded and I questioned my own clinical competence. There was so much self-doubt, inner turmoil, and hostility, everything that I went in there with was upset.

T07:   Is there anything else about that experience?

C08:   My sense is when I try to illustrate my competence and demonstrate my learning, he has to squash them.

Step 2: Ego Bridging

T13:   If you take the whole of the experience, is there something in your earliest experiences that is similar to the way you experienced your colleague?

C13:   Well it is not really early. I do remember that my father never believed in me academically. I remember in high school talking about going off to college and my father made a comment that was very hurtful. He had kind of a goofy smirk and said, who the hell do you think you are going to college, a big shot (none of my siblings went to college). He said, you'll never make it in college. I was so rebellious that I had to prove to him that I could do it. And I did. From college I went to university and then to graduate studies. By that time he was old and frail, he was so proud of me and the past was swept under. All my life I can remember being called stupid, dummy.

T18:   Is there anything else that you remember?

C18:   You won't amount to anything. "That you won't amount to anything" I don't remember until teenage years. Stupid, dummy, or goof, these are names he used when I tripped over something because I was clumsy. I would spill something at the table or I couldn't judge the distance.

T20:   What did you feel like to hear all of this?

C20:   Extremely humiliating. I felt very alone, I couldn't measure up, very unloved, devalued, belittled, and then as I started to grow older and became more rebellious, I became very angry at him the way he treated me. I oscillated between being very hurt and being very angry.

T21:   Did you experience any other feelings?

C21:   I guess there is a small part of me that felt stupid, embarrassed, and ashamed.

C22:   I would have a lot of accidents. I was very clumsy. Every time I made a mistake or spilled something, I would say oops and that is what they used to call me, oops, and my father would mock me. I would get all nervous and clean it up. He would laugh and I would get embarrassed and put my head down and feel humiliated and unloved.

T23:   Do you feel some of that childhood experience now?

C23:   Yeah.

T24:   Stay with the whole of your feelings and if other feelings come, let me know about them.

C24:   (Pause.) I would laugh with the family because I wanted to be part of the joke, I wanted to feel that I belong, but I was just dying inside of sadness. And I never understood why he had to pick on me like that?

Step 3: Ego Shift

T26:   Take a minute to get in touch with the whole of this experience. When you are in touch with all of it, try to sense what you need to make it better?

C26:   I need him to acknowledge me and support me, to be on my side, be sensitive to my problems, to nurture me. I need him to affirm me for who I was and not to make fun of conditions that I was born with, I need him to build me up and not squash me.

T27:   Imagine something happening or someone to be with you so that you experience all of that is needed to make it better. Allow all of that to happen in whatever fashion it will.

C28:   (Pause, 75 secs.) I have this image of being around the table and my siblings are picking on me and my father standing up for me and when I spill something he saying that it is okay.

C29:   He stands up for me, supports me because of my limitations.

C30:   He tells my siblings that that's enough and when I spill milk reassuring me and not making a big deal about it.

C33:   I needed that. I already felt like some kind of freak and didn't understand why I was the only kid in the class with this condition and why I had to have all of these special appointments. I needed for him to stand up for me. The father that I knew in my older years and the relationship that I developed with him, did stand up for me and did believe in me and would never have allowed anybody to put me down or hurt me.

T35:   Stay with that and see how that feels for you.

C35:   It is such a good feeling; it is such a sense of relief from all of this worrying about what will be said or what will be the punishment.

T36:   What stands out most in the way he is for you?

C36:   (Pause, 15 secs.) He is gentle, patient, not angry?

C37:   I feel that I matter, that I can make mistakes and he will be there for me.

T46: How are the two experiences – your father accepting you and you accepting who you are – different for you?

C46: I need to embrace it and hold onto it when I feel threatened.

Step 4: Application

T47: Imagine holding onto what you know to be right and how you feel when critical comments are being made.

C47: (Pause, 30 secs.) It is a totally different experience when I am able to do that. I am able to respond versus defend. I am much more open and accepting. I am holding on to what I know to be right, true, and good.

T49: Stay with all of that and experience how good it feels being that way in that situation.

C49: It is so nice because I don't feel vulnerable, threatened, hostile, angry, and humiliated. It's kind of a spiritual experience, everything is in harmony. There is this transparent shield around me and everything coming in that is toxic and negative is being deflected away. I am able to contain myself and my composure and I am congruent.

C51: In that situation I am responding from what I know and feel to be good and true, to be me, to be my thought, to be my feelings, to be my judgment, to be my opinions, to be my assessments.

C53: My integrity is intact and I am standing strong, and firm, I am standing in belief of me and myself and yet there is still an openness to positive, but the negative is being deflected off this transparent shield.

C54: I can give back what I don't need and is not helpful and deflect what is counterproductive and hold onto what I know and what I feel and then complement it with positive input. There is room for an opportunity for change and growth but it is not undoing.

T55: Not letting the stuff get to you.

C55: That's right, there is a distance. There is the shield and all of the negative is bouncing off the shield and I am back here and I am maintaining my composure, my authentic me, what I came in with, what I know is not shakable.

C56: I feel connected to the colleague in a much more positive way because the negativity is not penetrating me. So I am able to take what is good and process what is good and there is an openness to that but I am able to take distance or deflect the negative. So there is whole sense of feeling connected, feeling part of. The experience can be positive now because there is some good in what he is saying.

Describing the Experience

In describing her experience of the technique, Sonja mentioned that she was able to connect the current experience to an earlier one. The most challenging part was to accept that she could not change her father or colleague, but she could change her reaction. She experienced a shift when she was able to take distance from the negative experience that in turn opened up a space for the positive. She realized that she did not have to play their game, defend herself, and be on guard. She found acknowledgment not from others but from within herself.

Something to Think About

1. What are ego states?
2. How are ego states and schemas similar?
3. How are ego states activated?
4. Compare an ego-state bridge and an ego-state shift.
5. When is ego-state therapy counterindicated?

References

Berne, E. (1961). *Transactional analysis in psychotherapy: A systematic individual and social psychiatry*. New York: Grove Press.

Emmerson, G. (2008). *Ego state therapy*. Williston, VT: Crown House Publishing.

Fairbairn, W.R.D. (1944). Endopsychic structure considered in terms of object relationships. In *An object-relations theory of the personality* (pp. 82–136). New York: Basic Books.

Federn, P. (1952). *Ego psychology and the psychosis*. New York: Basic Books.

Freud, S. (1901). *The interpretation of dreams*. Standard Edition (Vols 4 & 5). London: Hogarth Press.

Freud, S. (1914). On narcissism: An introduction. *Collected Papers* (Vol. 1, PP. 30–59). London: Hogarth Press.

Freud, S. (1923). *The ego and the id*. Standard Edition (Vol. 19, pp. 12–63). London: Hogarth Press.

Klein, M. (1961). *Narrative of a child analysis*. London: Hogarth Press.

Lawrence, M.A. (1998). EMDR as a special form of ego state psychotherapy: Part I. *EMDRIA Newsletter, 3*(4).

Lawrence, M.A. (1999a). The use of imagery and ego state therapy in holistic healing. Paper presented at the annual meeting of the American Association for the Study Mental Imagery, April.

Lawrence, M.A. (1999b). EMDR as a special form of ego state psychotherapy: Part II. *EMDRIA Newsletter, 4*(1).

Perls, F., Hefferline, R.F., & Goodman, P. (1951). *Gestalt therapy: Excitement and growth in the human personality*. New York: Delta Books.

Shirar, L. (1996). *Dissociative children: Bridging the inner and outer worlds*. New York: W.W. Norton & Company.

Watkins, H.H. (1993). Ego-state therapy: An overview. *American Journal of Clinical Hypnosis, 35*, 232–240.

Watkins, J.G., & Watkins, H.H. (1997). *Ego states: Theory and therapy*. New York: Norton.

Young, J.E. (2005). Schema-focused cognitive therapy and the case of Mrs. S. *Journal of Psychotherapy Integration, 15*(1), 115–126.

8   Solution-Focused Therapy

Chapter Summary

Solution-focused therapy is a practical approach to solving problems and attends to that which worked in the past. When the client is not able to ascertain what worked in the past, the therapist uses techniques such as the miracle question to draw the client's attention to potentials for a positive solution. The solution-focused therapist pays minimal attention to the theoretical origins of a problem and to using theory to design treatment. In the excerpts from an interview, Colleen demonstrates how solution-focused therapy helped her to deal with a practical problem with her sister. Although solution-focused therapy can be applied to a great range of problems, it is limited in working with problems that have an early onset such as in the experience of trauma.

Introduction

Solution-focused therapy (SFT) was pioneered by Steve de Shazer, Insoo Kim Berg, Eve Lipchik, and their colleagues at the Brief Family Therapy Center in Milwaukee, Wisconsin, in the 1980s (Lipchik, 2002). Prior to the development of SFT, de Shazer and his colleagues adopted the Mental Research Institute's (MRI) brief family therapy model, which had evolved out of communication theory, systems theory, and cybernetics and was developed at the Don Jackson's Mental Research Institute at Palo Alto in the late 1950s. The family therapies that emerged from this philosophy focused on problem-solving and designing strategies that outwitted resistance and brought about change with or without the cooperation of the family (Guterman, 2006).

In exploring problem behaviours of individuals, couples, and families, de Shazer (1988) observed that there are times when the problems are absent or appear less often. When he explored how the clients managed this, de Shazer became aware that they were able to identify some of their own resources and strengths that they used in solving the problem. These exceptions formed the basis for the client to see possible solutions towards moving forward. This chapter presents the essential components of solution-focused therapy. The first part presents theoretical aspects of SFT, the second part presents the practice of SFT, and the third part details the procedures for applying SFT. The last part illustrates the use of SFT for Colleen, who resolved a relational problem.

Theoretical Aspects

At the outset, SFT was heavily influenced by Milton Erickson's view of people as containing untapped and unconscious resources that require merely a slight shift to release them. The postmodern revolution changed theorizing from releasing resources (e.g., pent up anger) to changing the way people talk about their problems (Nichols & Schwartz, 2004). Structuralists, a form of postmodernism, believe that language shapes and creates reality. De Shazer and Berg (1993) took this idea further and stated that "language constitutes the human world and the human world constitutes the whole world" (p. 73). If indeed one accepts that language constitutes reality, then therapy becomes a simple procedure – change how people speak about reality. Indeed, the goal of SFT is to shift clients from "problem-talk" (e.g., "I'm trapped") to "solution-talk" ("I'm moving forward") (Nichols & Schwartz, 2004, p. 315). Lipchik (2002), however, disagrees with the idea that SFT can be reduced to nothing but language, adding that language is not intended to mean only words people speak, that is the form, but also refers to the substance of the communication.

Recently there has been a further shift from "words are magic" to look at the power of the therapist–client relationship. Butler and Powers (1996) assert that the real key to change is not the technique but the attitude of the therapist and the interchange between the therapist and the client. Others suggest that SFT works by highlighting the clients' strengths and successes and making them feel good about themselves – the cheerleader effect (Walter & Peller, 1996). This section organizes the conceptual material for SFT according to its definition, major tenets, and theory.

What is Solution-Focused Therapy?

Solution-focused therapy (SFT) is a "future-focused, goal-directed approach" that was developed inductively and is a highly disciplined, pragmatic approach rather than a theoretical one (de Shazer & Dolan, 2007, p. 1). Solution-focused therapy builds upon clients' resources and helps them to achieve their preferred outcomes by collaboratively designing solutions to their problems (O'Connell, 2001). SFT focuses on the present and future, not on the past; it focuses on what clients want to achieve through therapy, on their desired futures rather than on their problem-laden histories (Huber & Backlund, 1996). The therapists help clients to clarify what they want to happen in their lives, design strategies to bring them about, and co-construct solutions. The emphasis is on what the clients are doing that is right, on what the past has taught them, what works, and what they are able to do now (O'Connell & Palmer, 2003). Solutions refer to the changes that client make regarding their perceptions and patterns of interacting and the meanings they give to their experience within the context of their frame of reference (Berg & De Jong, 1986, p. 377).

Tenets and Rules of Thumb

Various authors have presented tenets, axioms, or rules of thumb that serve as guidelines for the practice of SFT (de Schazer and Dolan, 2007; Guterman, 2006; O'Connell & Palmer, 2003; Walter & Peller, 1996). The overarching tenet of SFT is that if it is not broken, do not fix it. This approach states that there are areas in a person's life that do not need change, they are best left alone. There are also times when the person's life is problem free. SFT does not look for underlying issues nor view the presenting problems as the tip of the iceberg. Rather, the therapist encourages the client to stop doing what does not work and to do more of what works. Changes are perceived as being incremental, that is, they take place in small steps. SFT assumes that there is more to the person than the problem. There are exceptions to the problem (e.g., an anxious person who has moments of calmness when walking the dog), and it is these exceptions that the therapist aims to help the client live from and organize her life according to.

The language of SFT is couched in solution terms, not in problem terms. The task is to help clients shift their thinking, words, and actions from being problem oriented to being solution oriented. For example, the clients endeavour to shift from "What I don't want" to "What I do want" and from "I'm trapped" to "I'm moving forward."

Theory and Solution-Focused Therapy

Attempts have recently been made to embed the practice of SFT within a theoretical framework. One of the theoretical orientations is *solution-focused counselling* by Guterman (2006), who is influenced by postmodern social-constructivist epistemology and by his training in rational-emotive therapy. Guterman incorporates techniques from cognitive-behavioural therapy and behaviour modification in his approach to solution-focused therapy.

Lipchik (2002) embeds SFT within the context of a constructivist theory that retains some "interactional/strategic concepts and integrates them with a biological perspective that includes emotions" (p. 14). Her theory, *solution-focused theory,* entails working with emotions and the therapeutic relationship. In describing her theory, she states:

> Human beings are unique in their genetic heritage and social development. Their capacity to change is determined by these factors and their interactions with others. Problems are present-life situations experienced as emotional discomfort with self, and in relation to others. Change occurs through language when recognition of exceptions and existing and potential strengths creates new actions. (p. 14)

From the above statement, Lipchik (2002) formulated 11 assumptions that shape the therapist's attitude towards the client and guide the therapist–client relationship. Many of the assumptions overlap with or flow into each other. Some of the assumptions are consistent with Walter and Peller's (1996) 12 assumptions. Lipchik's assumptions are presented in Table 8.1.

Regarding the first assumption, Lipchik cautions therapists from treating all clients alike and thinking that they know what the solution should be for the client. According to Lipchik, living systems (clients) are structure determined and therefore require unique treatment. The heart of SFT is the assumption that clients have the inherent strength and resources to help themselves (Assumption 2). The author debunks the idea of client resistance (Assumption 4), stating that it is less a statement about the client not collaborating and more a statement about the therapist's not understanding how to incite change in a way that allows the client to respond adaptively. From a constructivist and SFT viewpoint, there is no such thing as cause and effect (e.g., that negative thoughts about self cause depression) (Assumption 7). Problems and

Table 8.1   Solution-focused assumptions

1. Every client is unique.
2. Clients have the inherent strength and resources to help themselves.
3. Nothing is all negative.
4. There is no such thing as resistance.
5. You cannot change clients; they can only change themselves.
6. SFT goes slowly.
7. There is no cause and effect.
8. Solutions do not necessarily have anything to with the problem.
9. Emotions are part of every problem.
10. Change is constant and inevitable; a small change can lead to bigger changes.
11. One can't change the past so one should concentrate on the future.

Sources: Lipchik (2002), Walter & Peller (1996).

solutions are viewed as the unpredictable events of life and not caused. Assumption 9 argues for the inclusion of emotions as a subject of therapy very much as thoughts and behaviours are subjects of therapy. Lipchik states that "the failure to talk to clients about their feelings, and to connect with them on that level, could limit our understanding of them, their understanding of themselves, and the possibilities for solutions" (2002, p. 20).

The Practice of Solution-Focused Therapy

There are no explicit recommendations for applying SFT to clients with different presenting problems and within different settings because SFT therapists typically put their own spin on this approach. SFT therapists, however, have presented detailed descriptions of how they applied this approach to their clientele (Burns, 2005; de Shazer & Dolan, 2007; Guterman, 2006; Lipchik, 2002; O'Connell & Palmer, 2003; Thomas & Nelson, 2007; Walter & Peller, 1996). This section presents the characteristics of the SFT approach and summarizes both main and specific interventions.

Therapeutic Approach

Solution-focused therapy, like other forms of therapy, takes place within the context of a therapist–client relationship wherein the therapist empathically acknowledges the concerns and feelings of the client and develops rapport through a warm, positive, accepting relationship in which the client can feel understood, safe, and respected. This experience is considered to be in itself potentially transforming. Although techniques are inseparable from the therapist–client relationship, technical competence is secondary to the quality of the therapist's presence to the client presence (O'Connell & Palmer, 2003).

The SFT therapist and client collaborate in all aspects of therapy that include defining the problem and establishing the goals of therapy (Guterman, 2006). This is based on the postmodern view that reality is co-created in conversations between people. Second, SFT focuses on what is working rather than what is not working in the clients' lives. The assumption is that people have the natural resources, existing strengths, and problem-solving skills needed to solve the problems that bring them to counselling. Third, SFT focuses on the process and not on the content (e.g., depression) to be changed. The therapist's task is to identify and amplify exceptions to the problems rather than the problems themselves. Guterman (2006) states that it is not necessary to obtain extensive historical information or to know the cause of the problem. Lipchik (2002) disagrees with this position and indicates that obtaining historical information contextualizes the problem and facilitates its solution. It is assumed, as well, that the client is the expert on the content to be changed and the therapist is the expert of the change process; the therapist does not tell the client what to change, rather the therapist points to possible directions of change.

Solution-Focused Techniques

De Shazer and Dolan (2007) present a list of solution-focused interventions and techniques which they group according to main or specific interventions and techniques.

Main Interventions and Techniques

The main interventions and techniques are those used in all of the therapy sessions. These are presented with a brief description for each in Table 8.2. In utilizing the interventions and techniques, the therapist takes a positive, respectful, and hopeful attitude and a collegial stance towards the client. The therapist believes that the client possesses the resiliency, strength, wisdom, and experience to make changes.

Specific Interventions and Techniques

In addition to the main techniques, SFT employs four fundamental techniques, namely, the miracle question, scaling questions, constructing solutions and exceptions, and coping questions (O'Connell & Palmer, 2003).

The Miracle Question

The miracle question is a method of questioning that a therapist uses to aid the client to envision how the future will be different when the problem is no longer present. It also helps to establish goals. This is an adaptation of Erickson's (1954) crystal-ball technique. The idea underlying this technique was for the client, while in a trance, to create a future with the problem solved or without the problem. There are many versions of the miracle question and all usages are modifications of either the traditional or the standard versions.

Traditional version: (One might begin by asking "Is it okay if I ask you a strange question?") "Let's suppose that after we talk here today you leave and you go do whatever you usually do on a day like this. Then as the day goes by you continue doing whatever you usually do. Then you come home, you have dinner, perhaps watch TV, do whatever else you would normally do as the evening goes on. / Then it gets late, you get tired, you go to bed, and you fall asleep. / Then during the night ... while you're sleeping ... a miracle happens. / And not just any miracle. It's a miracle that makes the problems that brought you here today go

Table 8.2 Main interventions and techniques

Intervention	Description
Assessing presession change	Near the beginning of the first session, the therapist asks the client whether they observed any changes to the problem since they called to arrange the appointment. If changes have occurred the therapist explores these in detail with the client. If the client indicates that no change has taken place the therapist than asks a question, such as, "How can I be of help to you?"
Looking for previous solutions	Therapist helps the client to search for solutions to the problem that they used at another time, place, or situation.
Looking for exceptions	The therapist helps the client to look for something that happens instead of the problem, that is, for an exception to the problem, even if the client does not have a solution that can be repeated.
Questioning versus interpreting	Questions, not interpretations or confrontations, are a primary communication tool and as such are overarching interventions.
Using present- and future-focused questions	Questions asked are present and future oriented. This is based on the assumption that problems are best worked on in the here-and-now with an eye towards the future.
Setting solution-focused goals	The therapist helps the client to frame their goals as solutions and to establish clear, concrete, and specific goals that are manageable.
Providing compliments	The therapist acknowledges the difficulty of the client's problems, affirms and validates their progress and encourages them to continue to change.
Gently nudging to do more of what is working	The client is nudged to do more of what has previously worked, or to try something new of their own suggestion.

Source: de Shazer & Dolan, 2007, pp. 4–5.

away … just like that. / But since the miracle happens while you are sleeping you won't know if it happened / So … you wake up in the morning. During the night a miracle happened. The problems that brought you here are gone, just like that. How do you discover that things are different? What is the very first thing you notice after you wake up?" (de Shazer & Dolan, 2007, p. 42).

Standard version: "Imagine when you go to sleep one night, a miracle happens and the problems we've been talking about disappear. As you were asleep, you did not know that a miracle had happened. When you wake up what will be the first signs for you that a miracle has happened" (de Shazer, 1988). One might replace the word "miracle" by another word. For example, one might ask: "You come back from holiday and find that the situation has changed for the better, what will be the first signs for you that something amazing has happened?" (O'Connell, 2003, p. 8).

To help persons to productively use the miracle question, de Shazer and Dolan (2007) provide the following guidance: proceed slowly, pause after a main thought and wait for a response from the client. The suggested pauses for the traditional version of the miracle question are indicated by a slash (/).

According to de Shazer and Dolan (2007), asking the miracle question: (a) helps to create goals for therapy, (b) gives the person an opportunity to describe the emotions experienced after the miracle question, (c) prepares the client for a conversation regarding exceptions to the problem, and (d) helps the client to connect to those aspects of the miracle that are already happening in the person's life and/or improving. O'Connell and Palmer (2003) make the point that "the miracle question is not a fantasy question about a perfect day or a perfect life. It is a 'wonderful' ... question which bypasses problem talk and enables the person to describe the kind of life they want to lead" (p. 8).

Scaling Questions

These are tools that are used to identify useful differences for the client, assess the client's level of motivation and confidence, help to set small identifiable goals, establish priorities for action, and measure progress (O'Connell & Palmer, 2003). Traditionally the scale involved asking one question: "With ten (10) being the best things could possibly be and one (1) being the absolute worst they could be, where are things (the externalized problem) right now?" (Webb, 1999, p. 76). De Shazer and Dolan (2007) recommend that the phrase "absolute worst they could be" be changed to "when you decided to seek help." The use of "when you decided to seek help" in place of "absolute worst" as a reference point makes it easier to highlight and describe change (de Shazer & Dolan, 2007).

One introduces the scaling question when the client reports something that has happened since they called for an appointment or since the experience of the miracle. Part of this discussion entails the movement – including thoughts, feeling, interactions – from a lower score (e.g., 3) to a higher score (e.g., 6) on the scaling question. One can also discuss how the client made things improve and what is needed to advance one more step (de Shazer & Dolan, 2007).

De Shazer and Dolan (2007) suggested that the scaling question be renamed the "miracle scale" because it typically follows a description of the miracle question and therefore is part of the miracle. This change, however, would not be consistent with the idea that scaling questions may be used prior to asking the miracle question.

Constructing Solutions and Exceptions

The SFT therapist spends most of the session listening attentively for signs of previous solutions, exceptions, and goals. The therapist seeks to encourage the client to describe what different circumstances exist in that case, or what the client did differently. The goal for the clients is to repeat what has worked in the past, and for them to discover, acknowledge, and reclaim their own resources, strengths, and qualities and gain confidence in making improvements for the future. When this occurs, the therapist works to keep the solution-talk in the forefront. The therapist uses how and what questions such as "How did you manage to do that?" to help clients to think about what they did to accomplish something constructive (O'Connell & Palmer, 2003).

Coping Questions

Coping questions are designed to elicit information about client resources that will have gone unnoticed by them (Burns, 2005). To draw out such coping resources the therapist might say, "I can see that things have been really difficult for you, yet I am struck by the fact that, even so, you manage to get up each morning and do everything necessary to get the kids off to school. How do you do that?" The initial summary, "I can see that things have been really difficult for you," is for them true and validates their story. The second part, "you manage to get up each morning etc.," is also a truism, but one that counters the problem-focused narrative.

Advantage Questions

This type of question stimulates some "both–and" thinking by asking the client to consider what is positive about the negative (Lipchik, 2002). As an example, the therapist might ask the client what is the advantage of having a problem such as being overweight. The client might respond that the advantage is that they can eat as much as they want to without having to worry about it.

Procedures for Doing Solution-Focused Therapy

This section provides procedures for doing SFT in two different settings, namely, when one has the problem and when the other is the problem. When doing SFT it is important to focus on the process of arriving at a practical solution and less on the techniques. In understanding the process, the therapist will be able to creatively adapt SFT to the twists and turns that are often a part of every therapy session. The solutioning process comprises identifying the problem, establishing goals, looking for exceptions to the problematic state, discovering and formulating solutions, and encouraging continued work on the solution.

Procedures When One Has the Problem

The procedures in conducting single or multiple solution-focused therapy sessions when the person has the problem combine the five stages indicated by De Castro and Guterman (2008) and the steps outlined by O'Connell & Palmer (2003). These steps are now summarized.

Problem-Free Talk

The therapy session begins by problem-free talk, that is, by topics unrelated to the problem, to convey the message that there is more to the person than the problem. The problem-free talk may also reveal strategies, beliefs, values, and skills that are potentially transferable to other situations.

Presession Change

In the beginning of the first session, the therapist might listen for evidence of what the client has already done that works for her. This could be an emotion, attitude, or behaviour. The therapist affirms the client for her prior experience and learning. This sets the tone for the work to be done and conveys the message that the client is the agent of change.

Co-constructing a Problem and Goal

The therapist and client collaboratively work together to negotiate a solvable problem and an attainable goal that relates to a client problem, desire, need, or some other form of motivation (De Castro & Guterman, 2008). It is important that the problem and goal fit the client's world view. In constructing a problem and goal, the therapist uses questions that clearly focus on the client's preferred outcomes and indicate the direction and purpose of the work.

Identifying and Amplifying Exceptions

The solution-focused therapist listens for circumstances, instances, and times when the problem is not present or where the client is better able to manage it. That is, the therapist looks for exceptions to be found and seeks to understand what happens during those times and what the client is doing that is helpful, and assesses whether the client can do it again.

Scaling Questions

Scaling questions help the client to set identifiable goals, set priorities, and measure progress, and help the therapist to assess the client's level of motivation and confidence. The client is able to use this simple tool between sessions to assess the intensity of her problem.

The Miracle Question

If clients are not able to identify exceptions, therapists might ask them to consider small differences or changes or try to identify potential exceptions by asking questions such as, "What will it be like when you are coping better with the problem?" (De Castro & Guterman, 2008, p. 96). In this regard, the therapist might use the "miracle question" in order to identify potential exceptions and to identify "existing solutions and resources and to elicit realistic goals for themselves."

Assigning Tasks

Towards the end of the first and each subsequent session, the therapist provides feedback to the client in terms of a summation message and suggestion (Lipchik, 2002). Feedback might also be given regarding the client's participation in the session, what the client is doing that is helpful, and how the client's actions link with the stated goals. There might be a discussion as to what the client might consider doing before the next session, and the therapist might encourage the client to continue to do what is working, stop what is not working, or do something different.

Evaluating the Effectiveness of Tasks

During this stage the therapist helps clients to "identify and amplify exceptions derived from tasks that were given in the previous session" (De Castro & Guterman, 2008, p. 97). The therapist might ask the client what she did differently when she coped better with the problem.

Reevaluating the Problem and the Goal

At this stage, the therapist and the client evaluate the extent to which the identified exceptions serve as the attainment of goals and assess whether further sessions are required (De Castro & Guterman, 2008). If further treatment is needed, the client and therapist reconstruct the problem and the goal. In the case where the client says the goal has been reached but there is now a new goal, the therapist and client together modify the goal to make it more relevant to the client's problems, more specific, and more attainable.

Procedures When Someone Else is the Problem

Walter and Peller (1996) provide procedures for applying solution-focused therapy when someone else is the problem. The authors present four possible solutions for such cases: (a) accepting the fact that one cannot change the other, (b) exploring the future without a change in the other, (c) exploring a hypothetical solution and exceptions, and (d) exploring the goal beyond the attempted solution.

The steps for exploring a hypothetical solution would include the following: (a) exploring the problem, (b) establishing a preferred, hypothetical goal, (c) inquiring what the two might be doing differently if this is no longer a problem (hypothetical solution), (d) asking if there are times when the problem is not as intense as seen by the other and describe what this is like (exception frame), (e) inquiring how the person acts when the problem is less intense (exception frame), (f) affirming new actions or approaches to the problem (enhancing agency), and (g) inquiring about the chances that the other will think more favourably of the person and thereby both would have more of what they want in the relationship (bridging the exceptions as the goal of therapy).

Applications and Limitations

Solution-focused therapy has been applied to a wide spectrum of human problems including depression, substance abuse, eating disorders, drinking disorders, stammering, panic attacks, grief, suicide, sexual trauma, psychosis, and trichotillomania. It has been used with children, adolescents, adults, mandated clients, and palliative care in various settings such as private offices, schools, and hospitals. It has been used in social work, couple therapy, family therapy, and parent training (Burns, 2005; Guterman, 2006; Lipchik, 2002; Miller, Hubble, & Duncan, 1996; O'Connell and Palmer, 2003). Does this extensive application of SFT suggest that the technique is meant for everyone? Hardly so! Webb (1999) states that even at its best, SFT is not meant for every client, issue, or situation. For example, the healing process for sexual abuse survivors takes time as it involves past experiences. SFT, with its emphasis on the present and the future, can help clients live with the injury but it is not able to deal with painful issues of their past.

Illustration: Colleen

Colleen (pseudonym), in her mid-thirties, and a certified psychologist, sought counselling because of an interpersonal problem with her married sister. Below are a summary of the therapy session, a conceptualization of the case from an SFT perspective, a description of the steps of the counselling process, and an excerpt from the session.

Summary

Colleen began the session by reporting an interpersonal problem with her married sister, who tries to impose on Colleen her expectations and values regarding family loyalties. Colleen's solution is to take distance from her sister, stand firm with her decision to have different values, and be at peace with them. An added problem is that her sister keeps Colleen from having a relationship with her nieces and nephews. Colleen's solution is to take distance from her relationship with the children until they have a better understanding of their family dynamics.

Conceptualization

The problem was conceptualized in terms of Colleen not having a clear solution in mind, the need to establish goals, and the need to enhance personal agency regarding the problem.

Therapy Process

The therapy session incorporated main steps of SFT such as clarification of the problem (T02–C02), exploration of coping resources (T03–C03), goal setting (T04–C06), exploring exceptions (T07–C12), exploring a practical solution (T13–C30), and enhancing Colleen's agency (T31–C33) to deal with the situation.

Transcript

Colleen began the session by reporting an incident that occurred with her sister, who complained that Colleen has cut herself off from the family and does not respect family loyalties. In the transcript, C = Client, T = Therapist, and the number following the letter represents the response number. The words in italics (e.g., *clarification of problem*) indicate the step in the therapy process.

T02:   There are two issues for you. One is your relationship with your sister who tries to tell you what should be your values and how you should be and you resisting her impositions, and second, if it were not for your niece and nephew you would let go of the relationship. (*Clarification of problem*)

C02:   Yes, I would just have a casual relationship. She is upset because my values about my family and my loyalties to my family of origin are different from hers and she has a difficult time accepting that difference. I maintain a relationship now for the sake of the children. I am a big part of their life.

T03:   How are you managing to keep a relationship with your sister? (*Coping question*)

C03:   I am not really managing. I am still going to phone and invite the children to come for a couple of weeks in the summer. I am wondering if am I better to stay distant until things may calm down a little or do I just focus on the relationship with the children and hope for the best.

T05:   How would you like it to be with your sister? (*Goal setting*)

C05:   I would like her to respect my decisions, my life, the changes that I have made. I would like to be able to stand on my own two feet and be my own person in the relationship with her, and feel less need to defend myself for being different and for having moved away from my family and become my own person.

T06:   You would like her to let you be and respect you for your values and for the decisions that you have made in your life. (*Summarize goals, preferred choices*)

C06:   For her to focus on her own life and let me live mine.

T07:   Has this been a part of your relationship anytime in the past? (*Exploring exceptions*)

C07:   This has always been her vision of what family is – it is your siblings, your parents; they come first, before your partner, before your own children. I don't believe that.

T08:   Has this been her attitude for as far back as you can remember? (*Exploring exceptions*)

C08:   Yes as far back as I can remember. I don't see things the same way. Yes, they are my family, but my family, my husband and my children, are my priorities right now. I enjoy my family of origin but I don't feel that I owe them anything. My loyalties to them are different than hers.

T09:   Has it always been like that?

C09:   She has always felt that way as did I until about 10 years ago – family loyalties – whatever they needed, my role was to help or bail them out.

T10:   You and your sister were together on that, then. (*Exceptions*).

C10:   Yes, it's my family's belief system. You just never turned your back on your family.

T11:   At one point in time, you were able to share that value with her. (*Exploring exceptions*)

C11:   Yes, but that belief has shifted for me. When I left my family and started my own life and did my own therapeutic work, I realized that those loyalties were not healthy so I developed my own beliefs, my own values and become my own person outside of my family.

T12:   In a way you left them behind.

C12:   Yeah.

T13:   Given that your sister is not going to change and you can't change her, I am wondering, then, what are your options? (*Exploring a solution*)

C13:   The options are to stay distant and sacrifice the relationship with the kids and accept that this is my reality, that things are not going to change and I must find a way to manage within it. The second option would be to try to maintain the relationship for the sake of the children but with that goes exposure to her criticisms and judgments of me.

T14:   You are in a dilemma: on the one hand, you would like to maintain your relationship with her children and for you to do that means that you will be exposed to your sister's criticism and judgment of you?

C14:   I fear that she may manipulate them to feel that they are betraying her, not being loyal to her if they spend time with me. They would be torn between their loyalties to their mother and their love for me. I feel that I am better off to stay distant and hope that they will want a relationship when they are a little older.

T15:   You are looking at that as a practical solution – to let things be as they are and when they get older they may be able to see things for what they are and resume contact with you.

C15:   Yeah, but I think that they are probably thinking, why is she not calling us, is she upset with us?

T16:   You do not want her children to think that there is something between you and them because you have not contacted them.

C16:   Yeah, I don't want them to think or feel that I have distanced from them. I love them very much and I wish there was a way to have that contact with them yet not have to deal with their mother's issues.

T18:   Let us try something. If for some reason, this problem that you have with your sister were to go away or if someone passed a magic wand over it or if something miraculously happened, what is the first thing that you would observe?

C18:   That I would be at peace with my relationship, that I wouldn't need to defend myself, to be on guard.

T21:   How would she sense that you are at peace and not on guard?

C21:   I wouldn't be hostile towards her when she imposes judgment on me; I wouldn't be aggressive with her, I would be firm and consistent.

T23:   How might she respond to you being [that way] towards her? (*Linking exception to goal*)

C23:   I think that she would eventually be more accepting of me and our differences and perhaps be less judgmental and critical.

T25:   You would experience being more at peace, more firm but not angry or hostile. Her response to that then is that she is more accepting of you and letting you alone. (*Clarifying*)

C25:   Less oppositional, less combative – not so imposing.

T26:   Both of you, then, would gain if the problem was changed. You would gain by being more at peace, more firm, and she would gain in being able to accept you, let you be.

C26:   Yeah.

T27:   How capable are you to be at peace with yourself and firm with her?

C28:   I choose to react, I realize that her comment about me being distant is related to old familiar patterns and feelings. It goes back to my mother and feeling emotionally manipulated and guilty for becoming my own person.

T29:   Old feelings surface and you are aware that you respond to her based on the old feelings. You are able to manage this and respond to her differently – being more at peace, more firm, not having to defend yourself – she has to deal with you.

C29:   She has to accept that this is the way it is and it is not going to change. There doesn't have to be discord and hostility to have a relationship. There needs to be respect or at least tolerance for our differences. I need to accept our relationship for what it is. I need to give myself permission to be me and not get caught up in my family's attempts to manipulate me for individuating.

T30:   You said that you cannot change her but you can do things for yourself. You can be at peace, firm, and not withholding.

C30:   Exactly. And resist her attempts to draw me into old patterns.

T31:   Does this seem like a practical solution for you?

C31:   Yes, I think that it is something realistic that I can accomplish. I need to be aware of what gets invoked in me and respond more effectively. Yeah, I can do that.

T32:   Do you feel that in having come to the feeling that you can do this, that your purpose in coming here has been achieved?

C32:   Yeah, I think that I need to give myself permission to not have to defend myself, to be my own person and be at peace with who I have become despite my family's negative judgments of me. Intellectually I know that, emotionally I have some work to do.

T33:   You want to continue to work on that – to give yourself permission not to have to defend yourself?

C33:   Now that I understand why I am conflicted, why I am not at peace within, what the issue is, I know what I need to do differently and what I must continue to work on emotionally.

Describing her Experience

In the feedback, Colleen stated that she felt guided, not pushed, towards a practical solution to her problem. SFT helped her to come up with a solution that came from within her.

Something to Think About

1. What are the components of solution-focused therapy?

2. How has Lipchik integrated emotions into the practice of solution-focused therapy?

3. How do you respond to the criticism that solution-focused therapy is minimalistic?

4. When would you use the miracle question?

5. How was solution-focused therapy modified in working with Colleen's problem?

References

Berg, I.K., & De Jong, P. (1986). Solution building conversations: Co-constructing a sense of competence with clients. *Families in Society: The Journal of Contemporary Human Service*, 77, pp. 376–391.

Butler, W., & Powers, K. (1996). Solution-focused grief therapy. In S. Miller, M. Hubble, & B. Duncan (Eds.), *Handbook of solution-focused brief therapy* (pp. 228–247). San Francisco: Jossey-Bass.

Burns, K. (2005). *Focus on solutions: A health professional's guide*. London: Whurr Publisher.

De Castro, S., & Guterman, J.T. (2008). Solution-focused therapy for families coping with suicide. *Journal of Marital and Family Therapy*, 34(1), 93–106.

de Shazer, S. (1988). *Clues: Investigating solutions in brief therapy*. New York: Norton.

de Shazer, S. (1994). *Words were originally magic*. New York: Norton.

de Shazer, S., & Berg, I.K. (1993). Constructing solutions. *Family Therapy Newsletter*, 12, 42–43.

de Shazer, S., & Dolan, Y. (2007). *More than miracles: The state of the art of solution-focused brief therapy*. London: Haworth Press.

Erickson, M. (1954). Pseudo-orientation in time as a hypnotic procedure. *Journal of Clinical and Experimental Hypnosis, 2,* 261–283.

Guterman, J.T. (2006). *Mastering the art of solution-focused counseling*. Alexandria, VA: American Counseling.

Huber, C.H., & Backlund, B.A. (1996). *The twenty-minute counselor*. New York: Crossroad.

Lipchik, E. (2002). *Beyond technique in solution-focused therapy: Working with emotions and the therapeutic relationship*. London: Guilford Press.

Miller, S., Hubble, M., & Duncan, B. (Eds.) (1996). *Handbook of solution-focused brief therapy*. San Francisco: Jossey-Bass.

Nichols, M.P., & Schwartz, R.C. (2004). *Family therapy: Concepts and methods*. Toronto: Pearson.

O'Connell, B. (2001). *Solution-focused stress counselling*. London: Continuum.

O'Connell, B., & Palmer, S. (2003). *Handbook of solution-focused therapy*. London: Sage Publications.

Thomas, F., & Nelson, T. (Eds.) (2007). *Handbook of solution-focused brief therapy: Clinical applications*. London: Routledge.

Walter, J., & Peller, J. (1996). Rethinking our assumptions: Assuming anew in a postmodern world. In S. Miller, M. Hubble, & B. Duncan (Eds.), *Handbook of solution-focused brief therapy* (pp. 9–26). San Francisco: Jossey-Bass.

Webb, W. (1999). *Solutioning: Solution-focused interventions for therapists*. Philadelphia: Taylor and Francis.

Cognitive-Behavioural Therapy

Chapter Summary

The primary goal of cognitive-behavioural therapy is to help clients to change the manner in which they process information. The assumption is that a faulty information process leads to cognitive distortions and ultimately to emotional problems. Cognitive distortions manifest themselves in automatic thoughts and schemas that can be changed when they are identified, analyzed and checked against reality. This chapter summarizes procedures that may be used to help clients to identify and change their cognitive distortions. The thought record of one client tracking his automatic thoughts is presented. From this thought record, one of the client's schemas was ascertained, explored, and changed within the context of therapy.

Introduction

Cognitive-behavioural therapy has its roots in the writings of early Eastern and Western philosophers and in the writings, at the turn of the century, of psychiatrists and psychologists (Ellis, 1989). Epictetus (1756/1890) wrote that "people are disturbed not by things, but by the views which they take of them." Dubois (1904/1907) believed that incorrect ideas produced psychological stress, Janet (1898) held that hysterics had fixed ideas, and Breuer and Freud (1895/1965) believed that unconscious pathogenic ideas resulted in mental disturbances. Cognitive therapy was advanced by Kelley (1955), who demonstrated how "personal constructs" explained the role of beliefs in behaviour change, and by Salter (1949), who applied behavioural techniques to help unassertive persons cognitively retrain themselves. Arnold (1960) and Lazarus (1984) gave primacy to cognition in emotional and behavioural change. It is out of this backdrop that we see the emergence of cognitive therapies such as rational emotive therapy (Ellis, 1989), cognitive-behavioural therapy (Beck, 1976), innoculation therapy (Meichenbaum, 1977), and schema therapy (Young, 1999).

This chapter focuses primarily on Beck's cognitive-behavioural therapy because it is well known, has been applied to different emotional problems and populations, and its effectiveness has been extensively examined by research. Accordingly, this chapter is organized in the following way. Part 1 presents theoretical and conceptual aspects that include Beck's theories of personality and psychopathology. Part 2 presents the psychotherapy procedures and techniques. Working with automatic thoughts and schemas is presented and demonstrated in Parts 3 and 4, respectively. The chapter concludes with a summary.

Part 1: Theoretical Aspects

Theory of Personality

Beck formulated a theory of personality to explain the deeply engrained characteristics of personality disorders and their treatment using cognitive-behavioural therapy. The theory has been extended to include all of the emotional disorders (Beck, Freeman, & Davis, 2004). Beck's theory of personality is presented under the following topics: personality organization, automatic thoughts and schemas, perception-to-behaviour sequence, the internal control system, and changes in cognitive and personality organization.

Personality Organization

Two of the major influences on the development of personality and its processes, operations, and characteristics are social learning and information processing.

Social Learning

Social learning refers to learning that takes place within a social context where a person observes, imitates, and models the behaviours of others. Social learning and reinforcement play significant roles in the acquisition of behaviour and in the development of psychological distress. Social learning also influences the acquisition of schemas, the development of assumptions, and a person's interaction with the physical world and with people. In making assessments for treatment, cognitive therapists require a thorough examination of the person's developmental history and his own idiosyncratic meanings and interpretations of events (Beck & Weishaar, 1989b, p. 295).

Information Processing

Information processing refers to how the human mind as a system processes information through the application of logical rules and strategies. A person's beliefs and biases affect the manner in which information is processed. Persons with some kind of disorder, for example, systematically bias the information in a dysfunctional way that shapes the person's behaviour. The interpretation comes from a higher order of structuring – referred to as a schema – that attaches significance to events. The person will engage in a "feed-forward mechanism" to shape or mold events, data, or material in a way to fit a schema (Beck, Freeman, & Associates 1990, p. 31).

Automatic Thoughts and Schemas

In cognitive therapy, two interconnected levels of thoughts are addressed, namely automatic thoughts and schemas. Automatic thoughts are closer to consciousness whereas schemas are further removed from it. In therapy one typically begins by examining automatic thoughts which lead to the schemas from which the automatic thoughts emerge.

Automatic Thoughts

Automatic thoughts are the "moment-to-moment, unplanned thoughts (words, images, and memories) that flow through our minds throughout the day" (Padesky & Greenberger, 1995, p. 5). The thoughts emerge "automatically and extremely rapidly" and tend to be "specific and discrete" and "idiosyncratic" (Beck, 1976, p. 33). Everything a person thinks is an automatic thought. These thoughts are easily accessible. A problem arises when his automatic thoughts manifest as cognitive distortions. Cognitive distortions are automatic thoughts that are based on faulty reasoning and on deeply ingrained dysfunctional schemas. These distortions are irrational reactions that a person habitually has to situations, and he often is not aware that he sees the world in terms of these cognitive distortions. The common types of cognitive distortions will be presented later.

Schemas

Schemas are like rules or erroneous premises and assumptions that dominate how a person regards himself, others, and the world. Technically speaking, schemas are "relatively stable cognitive patterns [that] form the basis for the regularity of interpretations of a particular set of situations" (Beck & Emery, 1979, p. 12). Schemas develop early in life from personal experiences and identification with significant others. Further learning experiences reinforce early conceptualizations that, in turn, influence the formation of other beliefs, values, and attitudes.

Schemas constitute the matrix through which a person filters, differentiates, and organizes incoming information, and attaches meaning to the information. Schemas also select the information one attends to and govern what is remembered. Schemas are at the root of automatic thoughts and images. As a group, some schemas are active while others are latent during nonstressful periods. Depending upon the rules applied to an event, different schemas when activated will evoke different feelings and behaviours. Incorrect rules produce deviant interpretations of events and form the core of neurotic and personality disorders. Schemas may be positive and provide coping mechanisms or they may be negative and dysfunctional. Schemas are not in themselves conscious, but through introspection their content can be identified (Beck et al., 2004).

Perception-to-Behaviour Sequence

Underlying all emotional problems are sequences of different types of schemata that operate in a linear fashion (Beck et al., 1990). For example, exposure to a dangerous stimulus activates the relevant "danger schema" which begins to process the information that eventually leads to action. Perception of danger sets up the following sequence:

Cognitive → affective → motivational → action (motor)

A dangerous stimulus activates, in sequence, the affective, motivational, action, and control schemas. The person interprets the situation as dangerous (cognitive schema), feels anxiety (affective schema), wants to get away (motivational schema), and becomes mobilized to run away (action or instrumental schema). The task in assessing emotional disorders is to identify this sequence of schemas.

Internal Control System

Each person has an internal control system that modulates, modifies, or inhibits impulses. This system, too, is based on beliefs, many or most of which are realistic and adaptive. Whereas the impulses constitute the wants, the beliefs constitute the "dos" or the "do nots." An example of such a belief is "It is wrong to hit somebody weaker or bigger than you." This belief is automatically translated into commands, "don't hit" (Beck, 1976, pp. 41–46). The control functions are viewed as concerning self-regulation and involving external, primarily social, environment. One aspect of the self-directed regulatory processes is the way people communicate with themselves. These internal communications consist of self-monitoring, self-appraisal and self-evaluations, self-warning, and self-instruction. Self-appraisals and self-evaluations are important methods by which people determine whether they are on course. Self-appraisals may simply represent observations of the self, whereas self-evaluation implies making a value judgment about self: good–bad, worthwhile–worthless, lovable–unlovable. In doing cognitive therapy it is imperative to identify the appraisals, evaluations, instructions, etc., and link them to the deeper-lying cognitive schemas and structures.

Changes in Cognitive and Personality Organization

Beliefs that a client had prior to developing a pathology become more plausible and pervasive. For example, a belief such as "If you aren't successful, you are worthless" becomes more absolute and extreme. Moreover, "certain aspects of the negative self-image become accentuated and broadened, so that the patient begins to perseverate in the thought, 'I'm worthless'" (Beck et al., 1990, p. 37). In this process, some of the conditioned beliefs become broadened and include a broader array of situations. The ease with which this is done suggests that the client loses the capacity to look at the belief, weigh it with contradictory evidence, and reject a belief not supported by evidence. A person's personality influences how people use information about themselves and others, and when there is a disorder they use the information in a disordered way.

Theory of Psychopathology

Information Processing and Schemas in Mental Disorders

Social learning and information processing are involved in the development of both normal personality and mental disorders. The information-processing apparatus is thought to contain several related coding systems that select specific data, integrate them, interpret them, and store a selected sample. The coding systems draw on a specific memory residue that serves as a guide to interpreting current events (Beck & Weishaar, 1989a). In mental disorders, a specific, more primitive coding system is activated and takes precedence over the normal coding systems, thereby skewing the information process. This cognitive shift introduces a systematic bias into inferences and interpretation in various psychopathological conditions such as anxiety, and also accounts for the symptomatology associated with various psychological disturbances. For example, in anxiety, "the relevant coding system consists of the following parts: (a) hypervigilance for data relevant to danger; (b) selection of data relevant to danger; (c) overinterpretation of danger; and (d) increased access to danger themes in memory" (Beck & Weishaar, 1989a, pp. 22–23).

In the field of psychopathology, the term *schema* is applied to structures with a highly personalized idiosyncratic content that are activated during disorders such as depression and personality disorders. Schemas may be hypervalent or prepotent. Hypervalent schemas have a low threshold for activation, are readily triggered by a trivial stimulus, and inhibit and replace other schemas which might be more adaptive or more appropriate for a given situation (Beck et al., 1990). For example, when a person goes into a clinical depression, there is a pronounced "cognitive shift" which, in energy terms, means a shift "away from normal cognitive processing to a predominance of processing by the negative schemas that constitute the depressive mode" (Beck et al., 1990, p. 33). Prepotent schemas supersede more appropriate schemas or configurations in processing information. For example, in depression the negative schemas are dominant, resulting in a systematic negative bias in interpretation and recall of experience, whereas the positive schemas become less accessible.

Cognitive Distortions

Each individual has a set of idiosyncratic vulnerabilities that predispose him to psychological stress, to faulty information processing, and to the formation of cognitive distortions. These vulnerabilities appear related to personality structure and to a person's fundamental beliefs about the self and the world. During psychological stress, the information-processing system goes awry and there is a shift to a more primitive information-processing system, resulting in systematic errors in reasoning called cognitive distortions. Beck (1976) compiled a list of distorted rules or aberrant thoughts which lead to emotional disorders. Two examples of cognitive distortions are:

Overgeneralization: Making an unjustified generalization on the basis of a single incident. *Example*: A patient, based on a single failure, says "I never succeed in anything."

Magnification: The propensity to exaggerate the significance of a particular event. *Example*: A person with a fear of dying interprets every unpleasant bodily sensation as a sign of some fatal disease.

Psychiatric disorders are characterized by a systematic bias in information processing which distorts both external information, such as communication from other people, and internal information, such as bodily sensations during panic attacks. Beck and associates (1990) provide cognitive profiles with their systematic biases for some of the disorders. For example, in depression the systematic bias is "negative view of self, experience, and future," and in anxiety disorder it is "physical or psychological threat."

Part 2: Psychotherapy Procedures and Techniques

This section presents the goal of cognitive-behavioural therapy, its fundamental clinical processes, and the techniques used. In general, cognitive-behavioural therapy is a psycho-educational approach that aims to influence dysfunctional cognitions, emotions, and behaviours through a systematic and goal-oriented procedure, to teach new ways of thinking and behaving, and to develop new skills to manage symptoms. It focuses on the here-and-now and symptom removal, and emphasizes the importance of homework to keep track of thoughts and behaviours and to practice the new skills.

Goal of Therapy

The goal of therapy is for the therapist and client to work towards producing in the client a shift back to a functional level of information processing and thereby ameliorate the emotional problem. Theoretically, the process is initiated by disconfirming the client's faulty interpretations and conclusions regarding experiences that he considers personally relevant (Beck & Weishaar, 1989a). This is accomplished by drawing on two aspects of information processing. First, the therapist and patient draw on reality testing by refocusing the patient's attention to the evidence that is contradictory to his or her conclusions. Second, the patient's ability to admit different data into information processing is enhanced by challenging the patient to observe all of the relevant data in a situation, not simply the data that are consistent with the patient's dysfunctional beliefs. Similarly, setting up experiments to test beliefs broadens the patient's focus of attention and introduces alternative explanations. The patient returns to the normal coding system by allowing new information that is discrepant with previous beliefs to enter the information-processing system and by expanding his discriminating and evaluative functions.

Fundamental Clinical Processes

Four of the fundamental clinical processes are collaborative therapy relationship, Socratic dialogue, guided client discovery, and use of transference reactions. Case conceptualization (Kuyken, Padesky, & Dudley, 2009), although an important component of cognitive therapy, will not be presented, since the focus of the chapter is on techniques.

The Collaborative Therapy Relationship

The therapist and client together set the goals and the agenda for each of the sessions. They become co-investigators and examine the empirical evidence provided by the client to determine whether particular cognitions serve any useful purpose. They also subject prior conclusions to logical analysis. Biased thinking is exposed as the client becomes aware of other alternatives. This collaborative process is referred to as collaborative empiricism (Beck & Weishaar, 1989a).

The nature of the therapeutic relationship varies according to the severity of the emotional disorder. In disorders such as anxiety and depression, the therapist assumes the role of an authority and expert who knows the necessary procedures to help the client release the painful symptoms. In more severely disturbed clients (e.g., personality disorders), a warmer and a closer therapeutic relationship is required. The therapist spends a large part of therapy time getting to know the client and becoming familiar with his whole life (e.g., children, work). Rather then exploring the underlying beliefs of the client's problems, the therapist draws upon his own life experiences and wisdom and proposes possible solutions to the person's problems. The therapist becomes a psycho-educator and may educate the client regarding the nature of intimate relationships. The therapist, by showing consideration, tact, understanding, and sensitivity, in fact, becomes a role model that the client can emulate in his contacts with his friends and family (Beck et al., 1990).

Socratic Dialogue

Questioning is a major therapeutic device in cognitive-behavioural therapy, and Socratic dialogue is the preferred method. The therapist designs a series of questions to promote new learning. The general purpose of therapeutic questions is to clarify or define problems, assist in the identification of thoughts, images, and assumptions, examine the meanings of events for the client, and assess the consequences of maintaining maladaptive thoughts and behaviours. An implication in using the Socratic dialogue is that the client arrives at logical conclusions based on the questions that the therapist poses. The therapist poses the questions with sensitivity so that the client may look at their assumptions objectively and without being defended (Beck & Weishaar, 1989b).

Guided Client Discovery

Rather than directly pointing out information to the client, the therapist might guide the client to unravel the various facets of his present experiences and past history, to discover what themes may be running through his misperceptions and beliefs, and elucidate problem behaviours and discover errors in logic (Beck & Weishaar, 1989a). In the process of guided discovery, the therapist designs new experiences (behavioural experiments) that lead to the acquisition of new skills and perspectives.

Use of Transference Reactions

The therapist is vigilant for signs of anger, disappointment, frustration, etc., experienced by the client towards the therapist, and when they surface, the feelings are explored with the client. Negative feelings towards the therapist are allowed but not provoked. The client's transferences open windows to his private world. When the client's negative feelings are explored and brought out into the open, distorted interpretations that interfere with collaboration can be examined and rich material for understanding of the meanings and beliefs underlying the client's repetitious and idiosyncratic reactions can be provided (Beck et al., 1990).

Psychotherapeutic Techniques

Cognitive-behavioural therapists use a variety of well-developed and efficacious cognitive and behavioural techniques that are targeted for specific symptoms. The therapist provides a rationale for each technique used which enhances the client's participation in therapy by assuming responsibility for therapy. Cognitive strategies have been summarized in comprehensive books on cognitive therapy (Sudak, 2008).

Cognitive Techniques

Cognitive techniques are used to surface the client's automatic thoughts, analyze their underlying logic, identify maladaptive assumptions, and examine their validity. The automatic thoughts are tested by direct evidence or by logical analysis. However, maladaptive assumptions are less accessible to the client than automatic thoughts. Assumptions appear as themes in a client's automatic thoughts. Once an assumption has been identified, it is open to modification. The more commonly used cognitive techniques, decastrophizing, reattribution, redefining, decentring, and imagery (Beck & Weishaar, 1989b), are presented in

Table 9.1 Cognitive techniques

Technique	Description
Decastrophizing	Known as the "what if" technique, it helps clients to prepare for feared consequences by decreasing avoidance, enabling the person with coping plans, and identifying problem-solving strategies if an anticipated consequence happens.
Reattribution	Tests automatic thoughts and assumptions by considering alternative causes of events; encourages reality testing and appropriate assignment of responsibility; helpful for clients who perceive themselves as the cause of events.
Redefining	Means to state a problem in terms of the patient's own behaviour; in place of "nobody pays any attention to me" client says "I need to reach out"; helpful to mobilize a client who believes a problem to be beyond personal control.
Decentring	Means to change their belief that they are the centre of everyone's attention (e.g., being stared at) by focusing on the other rather than on self.
Imagery	Spontaneous images are used to provide data on the patient's perceptions and interpretations of events.

Source: extrapolated from Beck & Weishaar, 1989a, 1989b.

Table 9.1. The techniques are self-explanatory. A brief note, however, regarding imagery is in order. The cognitive domain comprises both thoughts and images. Some clients find it easier to access and report pictorial images rather than their thoughts. Different forms of imagery provide helpful information to understand the clients' conceptual system. For example, spontaneous images provide data on the patient's perceptions and interpretations of events.

Behavioural Techniques

Behavioural techniques are used to modify automatic thoughts and assumptions. These techniques are also used to expand clients' response repertoire (skills training), to relax them (progressive relaxation) or make them active (activity scheduling), to prepare them for avoided situations (behavioural rehearsal), or to expose them to feared stimuli (exposure therapy). Since cognitive techniques are used to foster cognitive change, it is important to know the client's perceptions, thoughts, and conclusions after each behavioural experiment (Beck & Weishaar, 1989b).

Questions are used to elicit a client's automatic thoughts, particularly those that occur during upsetting situations. For clients who find it difficult to recall thoughts, the therapist may use imagery or role-playing. Cognitive therapists do not interpret the thoughts, but rather explore them with the client. The more commonly used behavioural techniques are briefly summarized in Table 9.2. A brief note will be added regarding the use of homework assignments.

Homework assignments are particularly helpful to monitor and uncover one's automatic thoughts, to observe one's reactions in various situations, and to implement and practice skills such as challenging automatic thoughts. The assignments should be small, within the client's skill level, relevant and interesting, and their rationale clearly explained. For more elaborate situations, the client may use a worksheet, called a *thought record*, to record his daily activities and dysfunctional thoughts (Greenberger & Padesky, 1995).

Part 3: Working With Automatic Thoughts

Helping clients to address and work with their automatic thoughts is appropriate for emotional difficulties related to acute stresses in life such as anxiety and depression. This section provides procedures for using thought records to work with automatic thoughts and illustrates this procedure by summarizing the thought records of one client.

Procedures

Consistent with Beck & Emery (1979), Greenberger & Padesky (1995) provide a seven-task procedure for working with automatic thoughts. Their procedure, in essence,

Table 9.2   Behavioural techniques

Technique	Description
Homework assignments	Typically focus on self-observation, self-monitoring, structuring time effectively, implementing procedures for dealing with concrete situations, and practicing new skills.
Activity scheduling	This entails rating (on a scale of 0–10) the degree of mastery and pleasure experienced during each activity of the day; the goal is for the client to have an accurate assessment of mood changes, accomplishments, and degree of activity.
Graded task assignment	Client initiates an activity at a nonthreatening level while the therapist gradually increases the level of difficulty of assigned tasks.
Behavioural rehearsal, role plays, role reversal, modelling	These techniques are used (including *in vivo*) to practice and develop skills, particularly interpersonal skills; these can be videotaped for clients to use to assess their performance.
Diversion techniques	These techniques distance the clients from their emotional problems, reduce the strong emotions and decrease negative thinking; might include physical activity, work, play, social contact, and visual imagery.
Exposure therapy	Calls for the client to experience in reality or in imagination the feared stimuli for either a long or short period; this technique generates data regarding the client's thoughts, images, physiological symptoms, and self-reported level of tension experienced; this information is used to teach specific coping skills.
Social skills and assertiveness training	For clients who lack specific skills, the therapist helps them to gain the necessary skills. The skills to be acquired may involve anything from teaching clients how to properly shakes hands to practicing conversational skills.
Relaxation training	Use of progressive relaxation technique or imagery.

Source: extrapolated from Beck & Weishaar, 1989a, 1989b.

reflects Ellis's (1989) A-B-C-D-E method of changing irrational beliefs. In this model A = antecedent (situation); B = irrational belief (automatic thought); C = consequence (feeling); D = disputation (challenging evidence supporting hot thought); and E = effect (changed mood). In their practice, Greenberger and Padesky also use information from the client's thought records. The seven tasks are: (a) identifying and rating a current mood (e.g., anxiety) on a 100-point scale with 100 indicating intense feeling; (b) determining the situation or event that gave rise to the mood; (c) identifying a hot thought, with an emotional charge, connected to the mood; (d) assessing a hot thought for supporting evidence; (e) assessing a hot thought for disconfirming evidence; (f) formulating an alternative to the automatic hot thought; and (g) rerating the mood following the reformulation of the hot thought. These steps are illustrated in the summary of Sébastien's thought records.

Illustration: Sébastien

Sébastien (pseudonym), married, in his mid-thirties, and given a medical discharge from the military, sought psychotherapy to deal with both physical ailments and psychological symptoms related to depression, anxiety, low self-worth, and posttraumatic stress disorder. Over a three-week period, Sébastien completed thought records which were used to discern the schemas underlying the automatic thoughts. These records were discussed in weekly

Table 9.3   Summary of thought records

Situation	Automatic thought	Alternative thought	Mood Ratings	Before	After
1. Dreamed boss controlled neighbourhood	1. I have no control over my life 2. People will hurt me if I am not on guard	1. I have support within me and around me	1. Terror 2. Grief 3. Anxiety 4. Confusion 5. Disgust/ shame Mean	90 80 80 80 90 84	50 70 50 70 70 62
2. Person in authority not truthful	1. I sacrificed my life for them 2. Senior officials cannot be trusted 3. My life will be marginalized	1. Most people without checks are unethical 2. I have grown, matured, learned new skills 3. I have produced valuable work	1. Anxiety 2. Fear 3. Irritability 4. Intense sadness Mean	80 70 75 85 70	65 70 75 50 59
3. Booked vacation trip	1. The world is for others to enjoy 2. I can't take care of everyone on trip 3. I will never enjoy life around me	1. The world is for all to enjoy 2. We are all adults and have responsibility to care for ourselves 3. I am managing time better	1. Anxiety 2. Anger 3. Intense sadness 4. Worry 5. Fear 6. Frustration 7. Overwhelmed 8. Shame Mean	85 60 75 90 80 80 80 70 75	60 40 60 60 55 50 45 40 51
4. Preparing legal brief	1. I'm not in control of my life 2. I am of no value 3. Wasted 18 years of my life	1. I do have guaranteed income 2. Some people respect me 3. I want to live	1. Irritability 2. Shame 3. Terror 4. Grief 5. Helplessness Mean	75 70 80 80 80 76	50 50 50 90 80 64

therapy sessions to ascertain the situations that elicited the automatic thoughts, rate the moods associated with the thoughts, evaluate the evidence for the thoughts, formulate alternative thoughts, and rerate the mood. Representative entries from the thought records are summarized in Table 9.3. The last column presents the rating of his mood prior to and after the formulation of an alternative thought. The mean mood ratings per situation changed by 10 to 40 points when compared before and after the formulation of the alternative thought. Sébastien reported that preparing the thought records was revealing and helped him to moderate his perception of self and other.

An analysis of the automatic thoughts suggested that they were driven by two interrelated schemas. The first schema pertained to the self with feelings of being worthless, not valuable, and not deserving. The second schema pertained to others who were seen as not caring for Sébastien. The self schema served as the starting point for schema therapy that is presented in the following section.

Part 4: Working with Schemas

Padesky and Greenberger (1995) and Young (1999) provide practical strategies for working with client schemas. These are presented under the following topics: classification of schemas, schema processes, and procedures in working with schemas. A demonstration of working with schemas ends this section.

Classification of Schemas

Systems to classify schemas have been offered by Beck and Young. Beck and associates (2004) organize schemas according to their functions and content. These include: cognitive schemas, affective schemas, motivational schemas, instrumental schemas, and controlling schemas. Young (1999) identified 18 early maladaptive schemas and grouped them into five broad schema domains, namely, Disconnection and Rejection, Impaired Autonomy and Performance, Impaired Limits, Other-Directedness, Overindulgence, and Inhibition. These domains correspond to the five developmental needs of the child that are assumed not to have been met. People, in general, develop schemas, positive and negative, regarding self, other, and the world.

Schema Processes

Young (1999) has identified three processes that characterize schemas, namely schema maintenance, schema avoidance, and schema compensation.

Schema maintenance: This refers to the process by which the early maladaptive schemas are reinforced. This is accomplished by exaggerating, negating, and denying information that contradicts the schema, reinforcing self-defeating behaviours (e.g., selecting partners that are abusive), and by feeling hopeless in being able to change the schema.

Schema avoidance: Refers to volitional and automatic processes to avoid either the triggering of the schema or to the experiencing of the affect associated with the schema. Schemas are avoided by volitional or automatic attempts to block images or thoughts that might trigger the schema, blocking feelings triggered by the schema, and avoiding real-life situations or circumstances that might trigger painful schemas.

Schema compensation: This refers to processes that overcompensate for early maladaptive schemas. This is similar to the defence mechanism of reaction formation. The client reacts in a way that is opposite to what is expected given his early background. For example, children that were emotionally deprived might behave in a narcissistic manner as adults, thereby obscuring the underlying deprivation.

Procedures

Identifying and Triggering Schemas

One of the major tasks in working with schemas is to identify them and, if not in awareness, to trigger them. Various techniques have been designed to identify schemas. For example, one can review the thought records for recurring themes that are assumed to be schemas (Greenberger & Padesky, 1995). Second, one listens, in the initial interview, for presenting problems and symptoms and begins to form connections among specific emotions, life problems, symptoms, and schemas. One then develops hypotheses about possible themes and explores these for issues related to specific schemas such as disconnection and rejection. Third, one can look for schema-driven behaviours (e.g., avoiding intimacy) that are processes learned by clients to cope with and adapt to their environment based on the perceptions of self, other, and the world generated by the schemas. A schema is thought to be triggered when a high level of affect is aroused. These are referred to as primary schemas, as distinguished from secondary schemas with a low level of affect.

Schemas can be triggered by using experiential techniques such as imagery. With eyes closed, the client is asked to report whatever images come to mind. Or the client might be asked to imagine a situation that the therapist, from data previously obtained, believes will trigger a schema. Second, a client might be asked to discuss upsetting events currently experienced in his life. Third, the client is invited to discuss memories and distressing experiences of the past, particularly childhood experiences. Fourth, the therapist can use instances occurring in the therapeutic relationship to activate schemas, and when they occur, the therapist discusses these with the client (Young, 1999).

Changing Schemas

The second task in working with schemas is to design techniques to change them. This entails recognizing, evaluating, and testing clients' interpretations of experiences. The techniques have as their purpose to diminish the strength of dysfunctional schemas and permit the emergence of functional schemas (Beck et al., 1990, 2004). It is recognized that a certain level of affective experience is needed to bring about cognitive and schema change. Childhood material is particularly helpful in working with schemas as it opens up windows to understanding the origins of maladaptive patterns (Beck et al., 2004). The techniques used to change schemas can be grouped as cognitive, experiential, interpersonal, and behavioural techniques (Young, 1999).

Cognitive techniques: These techniques are used to systemize the process of schema change. Clients are taught techniques to enable them to battle schemas each time they arise outside of the session. Cognitive techniques, similar to those used to challenge automatic thoughts, include reviewing evidence that supports and does not support or contradicts the schema, considering alternative meanings of the evidence, and challenging schemas when they are activated in the therapy session.

Experiential techniques: These techniques are used to loosen up schemas and make them more accessible to change. Experiential techniques include a *creative imagery dialogue* with a significant person and *emotional catharsis* where a person is asked to access and express feelings generated by the use of role-playing, imagery, etc.

Interpersonal techniques: These are used throughout therapy with clients who display their schemas in the therapeutic relationship (e.g., transference). Interpersonal techniques include the therapeutic relationship, which can activate schemas itself, or one may provide a therapeutic relationship that counteracts early maladaptive schemas.

Behavioural techniques: These are used to change long-term, deeply engrained, self-defeating behavioural patterns. Among the behavioural techniques are *changing schema-driven behaviours* such as avoidance behaviours (e.g. going out with a partner who is more emotionally available) or *making environmental changes* such as temporarily leaving the house to create some breathing room.

Illustration: Sébastien

Summary

The purpose of this session was to challenge Sébastien's schema that he is worthless, useless, and without value. This was done by developing a worthless/worthwhile scale, positioning himself, his wife and three of his friends on the scale, and then comparing the scores. He became aware how his view of himself is very different from the views that others have of him.

Conceptualization

Sébastien's feelings of depression, anxiety, and anger towards others stem from an early childhood development of a schema that he is worthless. This schema was reinforced by the experience of those in authority who made it very difficult for him to secure the medical attention that he needed. The schemas were triggered by persons who represented critical, demeaning, and emotionally unsupportive parental figures. With a change in the schema, he changed his way of thinking from a black-and-white thinking to a more moderate way of thinking.

Therapy Process

The therapy began by identifying a schema, feeling worthless, and drawing a 100-point bipolar scale with a midpoint to represent the worthless/worthwhile continuum. To provide a point for comparison, Sébastien positioned himself on the scale and then his wife and friends. When viewing the scale, he was surprised to see how his view of himself differed significantly from the views that others had of him. He came to the realization that there is no black and white in thinking about issues such as worthlessness/worthwhile.

Transcript

In the following excerpts from one therapy transcript, the therapist's responses, that mostly consisted of giving directions, open-ended questions, and summaries, are in large part omitted for lack of space. In the transcript, C = Client, T = Therapist and the number following the letter represents the response number. The therapy begins with Sébastien expressing his wish to work on his feelings of not being worthwhile.

T02:   How do you experience not feeling worthwhile today?

C02:   When I reflect on how I struggled to get the needed medical and psychological services, and how those in authority portrayed me as being undeserving of getting the care that I needed, this reinforced the feeling of being worthless.

Form Baseline and Define Scale Points

T03:   We can work with that thought, if you wish. (Proceeds to draw a 100-point scale with 0 = being very worthless and 100 = being very worthwhile; hands the scale to client.) On this scale, where do you see yourself?

C03:   At 25% (Marks an X on line, writes 25% and adds his name.)

T05:   How do you want to describe the two ends of the continuum?

C05:   One end means worthless, helpless, fraudulent/fake, and undeserving.

T06:   And the other end?

C06:   Worthwhile, valuable, compassionate, genuine.

T07:   How would you describe the midpoint on this scale – at 50%?

C07:   (Draws an X on the line and numbers it 50%.) Acceptable, good, inoffensive.

Places Others on the Scale

(Sébastien and the therapist prepare a list of four people to determine how they see him on the worthless/worthwhile scale. These were identified as his wife, Suzanne, and three friends, Tom, Linda, and Richard. All of these persons say that he is a worthwhile, deserving, and useful person, which is based on their appreciation of what he has done for others and for himself. They proceed then to position their ratings of him on the scale.)

T10:   Where would Suzanne place you on the scale?

C10:   She would place me at the 100 point. (Places an X on the line and names it Suzanne.)

T11:   The next is Tom.

C11:   Let's say at 75. (Places an X on the line and writes his name.)

T14:   And Linda?

C14:   She would be around 85%. (Places X on line and names it Linda.)

T17:   And Richard?

C17:   Richard would be around 80%. (Places an X and writes his name.)

Making Observations

T20:   Let's look at the scale. What do you observe?

C20:   There is a big discrepancy between what other people think of me and what I think of myself.

C22:   It sets up the dissonance. I'd rather be in harmony as opposed to being in dissonance.

C23:   I would like to be up in the 75s, 80s.

Advantage to See Self as Others See Him

T24:   What would be the advantage for you to see yourself as others see you?

C24:   Less fatigue, less exhaustion, and I wouldn't be wrestling with major thoughts, I could pursue activities to make my life and others around me better. I would have more energy and be in harmony and enjoy life as opposed to fight against the negative attacks.

C28:   It would be like walking from a muddy stagnant swamp and having all of that washed away and feeling clean, free, less encumbered.

T30:   Is there anything else that you observe about the scale?

C30:   I am really alone. There is a lot of space between me and the others and it represents the darkness that surrounds me a lot that I have to fight against to go through each day.

Gains from Exercise

T46:   What has it been like for you to do this exercise?

C48:   The exercise definitely gave me insight into how hard I am on myself and how separate I see the world. The exercise also allowed me to see the world more on a sliding scale rather than completely black and white. The sliding scale before was just darkness for me and unattainable light for everything that is outside of me, and now I see a possibility that I can join some of those light areas because I don't have to be perfect, I don't have to be 100%.

T53:   Anything else?

C53:   To see people as separate and I can look at each person for who they are as opposed to lumping everyone together. People are individuals.

T55:   It is change from thinking in absolutes to thinking more in relative terms.

Describing the Experience

Sébastien found the task to be more difficult than he expected because it touched his emotions. He found it helpful to see how hard he is on himself when compared to others' views of him. He realized that one cannot talk in absolute but only in relative terms.

Something to Think About

1. How does social learning affect the ability to process information?
2. How are automatic thoughts related to schemas?
3. Emotional problems reflect cognitive distortions. Explain.
4. What is the purpose of assigning homework?
5. How did Sébastien proceed to change his schema of not being a worthwhile person?

References

Arnold, M. (1960). *Emotion and personality* (Vols. 1 & 2). New York: Columbia University.

Beck, A.T. (1976). *Cognitive therapy and the emotional disorders*. Toronto, Ontario: Penguin Books.

Beck, A.T., & Emery, G. (1979). *Cognitive therapy of anxiety and phobic disorders*. Philadelphia: Center for Cognitive Therapy.

Beck, A.T., Freeman, A., & Associates (1990). *Cognitive therapy of personality disorders*. New York: Guilford Press.

Beck, A.T., Freeman, A., & Davis, D.D. (2004). *Cognitive therapy of personality disorders* (2nd Ed.). New York: Guilford Press.

Beck, A.T., & Weishaar, M. (1989a). Cognitive therapy. In A. Freeman, K.M. Simon, L.E. Beutler, & H. Arkowitz (Eds.), *Comprehensive handbook of cognitive therapy*, pp. 21–36. New York: Plenum Press.

Beck, A.T., & Weishaar, M. (1989b). Cognitive therapy. In R.J. Corsini, & D. Wedding (Eds.), *Current psychotherapies*, pp. 285–320. Itasca, IL: Peacock Publishers.

Breuer, J., & Freud, S. (1895/1965). Studies in hysteria. *Standard Edition* (Vol. 2). New York: Basic Books.

Dubois, P. (1904/1907). *The psychic treatment of nervous disorders*. New York: Funk & Wagnell.

Ellis, A. (1989). The history of cognition in psychotherapy. In A. Freeman, K.M. Simon, L.E. Beutler, & H. Arkowitz (Eds.), *Comprehensive handbook of cognitive therapy* (pp. 5–19). New York: Plenum Press.

Epictetus (1756/1890). *Enchiridion. The collected works of Epictetus*. Boston: Little & Brown.

Greenberger, D., & Padesky, C.A. (1995). *Mind over mood: A cognitive therapy treatment manual for clients*. New York: Guilford Press.

Janet, P. (1898). *Névroses et idées fixes*. Paris: Alcan.

Kelley, G. (1955). *The psychology of personal constructs* (Vols. 1 & 2). New York: Norton.

Kuyken, W., Padesky, C.A., & Dudley, R. (2009). *Collaborative case conceptualization: Working effectively with clients in cognitive-behavioral therapy*. New York: Guilford Press.

Lazarus, R. (1984). On the primacy of cognition. *American Psychologist, 32*(2), 124–129.

Meichenbaum, D. (1977). *Cognitive-behavior modification: An integrative approach*. New York: Plenum Press.

Padesky, C.A. & Greenberger, D. (1995). *Clinician's guide to mind over mood*. New York: Guilford Press.

Salter, (1949). *Conditioned reflex therapy*. New York: Creative Age.

Sudak, D.M. (2008). *Cognitive-behavioral therapy for clinicians*. Philadelphia, PA: Lippincott Williams & Wilkins.

Young, J.E. (1999). *Cognitive therapy for personality disorders: A schema-focused approach* (Rev. Ed.). Sarasota, FL: Professional Resource Press.

10 Narrative Therapy

Chapter Summary

Narrative therapy is an action-oriented approach that helps people to resolve their problems by deconstructing old narratives and replacing them with new narratives that will be used to make decisions and take actions in the future. Although old narratives are similar to concepts such as self-image, critical parent, and superego, the term narrative is broader and more encompassing in that it is the product of familial, cultural, and societal influences. This chapter presents the meaning of narratives, how people organize their lives around dominant narratives that often are the source of their problems, and the methods therapists might use to help clients reconstruct preferred narratives. The case of Sonja illustrates how a client, with the help of a therapist, is able to move beyond living by old narratives and embrace a narrative in keeping with her sense of integrity.

Introduction

Psychotherapy could be described as helping clients to rewrite their life stories and to enhance their agency over their lives. Over a century ago, Breuer and Freud (1895/1955) invited patients, through the process of free association, to tell their stories. This process is similar to helping persons to rewrite their autobiographies by including omitted episodes and making the appropriate links so that they can live with the new story (Martin, 1986). Rogers (1942), sitting face-to-face with clients, advanced storytelling by becoming intimately engaged in the creation of their stories. The concept of storytelling was extended to couple and family therapy by White and Epston (1990), who viewed the therapy session as a story constructed by the therapist and the partners and/or family members. White and Epston have been highly instrumental in formulating and advancing a therapeutic approach that makes narrative its central concept. Narrative therapy draws upon postmodern themes for diagnostic purposes and upon existential themes such as self-agency, empowerment, and responsibility in its therapeutic work.

This chapter presents narrative therapy primarily as developed and advanced by White and Epston (1990) with contributions from Tomm (1988a) and Freedman and Combs (2000). The chapter begins with a brief summary of the theoretical influences that shaped White and Epston's approach to narrative therapy. It then presents the conceptual aspects pertinent to narrative therapy and its techniques and strategies. The chapter terminates with a transcript of a therapy session that illustrates the use of narrative therapy.

Theoretical Influences

As family therapists, White and Epston (1990) were particularly interested in the dynamics and the distribution of knowledge and power in the family, the authoring of the family story, and methods to understand and change the family system. To provide a framework for their approach, White and Epston adopted the concepts of *knowledge/power* from Foucault (1980, 1988), *storying* from Bruner (1986), *meaning making* and *interpretative turn* from Geertz (1983), and *news of difference* and *narrative structure* from Bateson (1979).

Knowledge and Power

Foucault (1980, 1988), in analyzing totalitarian societies, studied how knowledge and power affect and dominate people's lives. Foucault noted different classes of knowledge. One class is dominant knowledge, meaning those knowledges that "make unitary and global truth claims" (White & Epston, 1990, p. 20). These truths do not refer to those that are universally accepted but refer to the "objective reality" knowledges of modern scientific discipline. A second class of knowledge is the subjugated knowledges which comprise two distinct forms, namely erudite knowledges and local popular/regional knowledges. The erudite knowledges are those that existed prior to the ascendency of dominant knowledge that wrote erudite knowledge out of the record. Local popular/regional knowledges, the "naïve knowledges" (e.g., folk psychology), are located down low on the hierarchy and are currently in circulation but are denied or deprived of the space in which they could be adequately performed.

For Foucault, knowledge and power go together – where there is knowledge there is power, and where there is power there is knowledge. Moreover, power is not necessarily negative and repressive, it is also constitutive, that is, it influences and normalizes how people ought to think, behave, interact with each other, and live; it is prescriptive. Often for a client the dominant knowledge does not represent their lived experience, and in these situations a large part of their lived experience contradicts the dominant knowledge.

These classes of knowledge can be observed, for example, in what is occurring in psychotherapy today. The dominant knowledge is associated with empirically based therapies such as cognitive-behavioural approaches, while erudite knowledge is associated with psychoanalysis, which at one time was the dominant knowledge informing the treatment of emotional problems, but today is supplanted by empirical-based therapies and the psychology of common sense (folk psychology) that represents local knowledge.

To illustrate how these concepts analogously relate to client problems, one can take as an example a male client, Dominique, in his mid-thirties, who presented himself as being angry and depressed. He was brought up in a sociopolitical, cultural, and family context that strongly valued a career in the physical sciences over a career in the fine arts. In exploring – externalizing – his problem, the dominant knowledge became exposed and his preferred narrative became clear. He reluctantly pursued a physical sciences university path because of the cultural pressure, and yet his own preference was to pursue education in the fine arts. His preferred narrative was in conflict with the dominant narrative.

Storying of Experiences

By storying their experiences, people arrange their experiences of events in a linear sequence across time so as to arrive at a coherent sense of themselves and the world around them (Bruner, 1986). For example, a teenager, Francis, recently won an award in fine arts for his paintings. When talking about his current success, he states that he has always been interested in the fine arts, has won awards for his accomplishments in the past, and pictures himself becoming a great painter in the future. His past and present experiences and his hope for the future are coherently and lineally connected, and are put into the form of a continuous life story.

The ability to story one's experience provides the person with a sense of continuity of meaning in her life, as well as a means to order her daily life and to interpret further experiences. Since all stories have a past, present, and future, the "interpretation of current events is as much future-shaped as it is past-determined" (White & Epston, 1990, p. 10). Not all aspects of one's experience become part of the dominant narrative. A person excludes from her experience those experiences that are not congruent with the dominant story that she has of herself, and therefore these neglected aspects go unstoried and are never told or expressed (White & Epston, 1990). Stories are full of gaps. For the story to be performed, people draw upon their lived experience and their imagination to complete the story.

Meaning Making and the Interpretative Turn

Contrary to the explanatory models of psychologists that emphasized internal states (e.g., drives, traits) and their transformation into human expressions, Geertz (1983) aims his enquiry firmly at how communities construct meanings and on their categories. The belief is that people respond to and interpret each others' actions in terms of their own understanding of each others' actions and their own theory regarding these actions. This form of inquiry and understanding, referred to as the "interpretative turn," focused on "human agency" and the "intentional states" of a person rather than viewing her as being pushed by internal states (White, 2004, p. 24). Human agency means that people are active agents, mediators, and negotiators of their own lives. Intentional states mean that people live their lives according to certain intentions and purposes (e.g., values, commitments) in the pursuit of what matters to them.

News of Difference and Narrative Structure

"News of difference" (Bateson, 1979, p. 9) implies that change occurs when the person experiences something new and different, when something new is brought to the story. The new experience challenges the person to broaden her horizon (White & Epston, 1990).

Theoretical Aspects

Definition of a Narrative

In keeping with Brunner's (1986) definition, White and Epston (1990) define a narrative as a story by which people live their lives. The narrative forms a thread around a theme or a plot (e.g., Francis viewing himself as a painter) which intertwines the experiences of the past and present with anticipation of the future (White, 2007).

The narratives are like "structures" that provide a frame of intelligibility through which people make sense of their lives, link together events in an unfolding sequence according to a theme, and provide the basis for people to derive conclusions about what these events say about their and others' intentional states, including dreams, hopes, values, and beliefs (White, 2004). Thus, the interpretation that a person has of any event is determined by how it fits in with known patterns of events, that is, with her "interpretative method." A corollary to this is that those events that are not congruent and do not fit in with our life story, do not exist as facts (White & Epston, 1990).

The narrative contains the cultural values, meanings, expectations, and prohibitions that are passed on to the newborn to guide their life and to help them interpret experiences and events. The family or cultural narrative which has been passed on is largely unexamined. When it is examined, it may be the source of personal and interpersonal problems, because the narrative may not be consistent with the person's experience of self.

Classification of Stories

Although White and Epston (1990) have at times referred to dominant and alternative narratives, they focus more on the "constitutive or shaping effects" of all stories (White, 2004, p. 34). They view some stories as offering a broader range of options for action than other stories. In his practice, White (1991, 2007) gives primacy to the personal and authentic stories by which persons live their lives. These stories determine the meaning that the persons give to their experiences and largely determine which aspects of their experiences they select out for expression. The narratives, therefore, represent internal structures that shape actual lives and prefigure action. White believes that people are dependent upon social processes of acknowledgment for the "authentication" of their preferred identity claims. Authenticity, therefore, is not viewed as a personal achievement, as in the case of insight therapies, but as a social achievement whereby the person's new narrative is acknowledged, for instance, by friends, professionals, and family (White, 2004). For example, the teenage Dominique's dominant narrative when he was a child was that he be loyal to the values and practices of his parents and culture. Today his parents are pressuring him to pursue a career in the physical sciences. However, as a teenager, his preferred (alternative) narrative is that he is free to establish and pursue his own preference, and to pursue a career in the fine arts. Dominique's preferred narrative was socially supported (authenticated) by his school counsellor and by his friends.

Problems and Their Origin

Much like Foucault (1988), White and Epston (1990) view personal and interpersonal problems as resulting from a clash between a culture's dominant story and a person's preferred story. Problems may also arise from an opposition between significant aspects of a person's life experiences and the dominant story, or from the exclusion of essential aspects of one's life experience from the dominant story. The cut off or excluded aspects continue to maintain an influence on the person and have a potential for a unique and different outcome – a different story. A person's story needs to be rewritten by including the excluded experiences. For example, Dominique (cited above) was brought up believing that he did not have the freedom to make decisions regarding his life, and that now he must pursue a career in the physical sciences. The clash is between the parental expectation (dominant narrative) that he pursues a career in the physical sciences and his desire to pursue a career in the fine arts (preferred narrative). Under the dominant narrative, the freedom to make his decisions is denied him, and it now needs to be reclaimed and included in the writing of his new narrative.

The Practice of Narrative Therapy

The fundamental goal of narrative therapy is to help persons to shed false aspects of their way of life, access the neglected parts of their experience, and reconstruct their life around these neglected parts. The narrative therapist assumes that people have many skills, abilities, beliefs, and values that can help them to achieve the goal. The practice of narrative therapy entails externalizing the problem and exploring its history and effects, deconstructing and reconstructing narratives, and identifying emerging stories. The therapeutic procedures that facilitate this process include the use of questions and empathic responses, making distinctions, and being transparent.

Externalizing the Problem and Exploring its History and Effects

The single most dominant procedure in narrative therapy is to help persons to identify, articulate, and externalize the problem (e.g., depression). This entails helping clients to see that their personal and interpersonal problems are separate from both their person and their relationships, that their problems are not to be seen as something inherently wrong with them but are unwelcome and transient states driven by external factors (Dallos, 2006). Problems are to be considered as objects existing outside of oneself and experienced as being oppressive. The objectifying of the problem is referred to as "externalizing" the problem. The opposite is "internalizing" a problem, which means that the persons see their problems as related to internal states, dynamics, or processes (Payne, 2006, p. 12). To illustrate using the example cited above, Dominique has been referred to a narrative therapist because his parents find him to be rebellious, oppositional, and disrespectful of their wishes. The narrative therapist does not consider that there is something inherently wrong with Dominique; rather the problem is external to him and exists only because the teenager is expected to behave in a way that is alien to his preferred narrative as authenticated by his counsellor and his friends.

Externalizing the problem has also been referred to as taking distance from the problem, that is, standing back from the problem so as to see it more objectively and from other points of view. The ability to stand back from the problem is also referred to as "reflexive engagement with life" (White, 2004, p. 35).

Deconstructing and Reconstructing Narratives

Deconstructing Narratives

Deconstruction refers to the "procedures that subvert taken-for-granted realities and practices" (Tomm, 1993) and break down the influence of the problematic beliefs and practices (Madsen, 2007). The taking apart of the taken-for-granted reality reveals where a falsehood may be constructed and introjected as a truth to fill gaps, and explains the unknown in the natural inclination for narrative flow. (For Dominique, the falsehood is that his parents know what is best for him and that he does not have the ability to make his own decisions.) The narrative therapist assists persons to resolve problems by showing them the difference between the reality and the internalized stories of self, enabling them to deconstruct the meaning of the reality of their lives and relationships. By undermining "the dominant narrative that makes certain experiences problematic" the person is able to develop "a new story that enhances alternative knowledge" (Murray, 2000, p. 345).

Reconstructing Narratives

Reconstruction refers to rebuilding alternative perspectives, stories, behavioural practices, and relationship patterns that replace the old oppressive ones. Narrative therapists believe that constructing narratives is a means of making sense of the world and enabling persons to organize their experience into coherent accounts, to give meaning to the constant change in their lives, and to bring order to disorder (Murray, 2000). Narrative therapists believe, as well, that people are active agents in their own lives (White, 2004). (For example, Dominique reconstructs his narrative according to his preferences, believing that he has the capacity to do so.) In the reconstruction of stories, clients are encouraged to re-author their own lives according to preferred stories of self-identity and according to preferred ways of life. In retelling stories in therapy the clients find alternative ways of expressing them. The therapist seeks to engage the clients by richly describing and strengthening these new, preferred stories which are in line with how the person would like to be and live her life.

Identifying Emerging New Stories

As an alternative to externalizing the problem and deconstructing the disenabling stories, the therapist may pay attention to an emerging new story – the not-yet-spoken – and help the client or clients to live out of the preferred stories of themselves and their relationships. (For Dominique, a new story is said to emerge when he makes a statement to the effect that he is tired of relying on others and wants to rely on himself to make decisions about his life.) Freedman and Combs (2000) "listen for sparkling moments or hidden presences that would not have been predicted by the problematic story" (p. 350). They then ask questions about these moments and assess whether they might be openings for new stories. Freedman and Combs contend that stories are not equal, and they take a strong ethical stand against, for example, oppression, violence, and exploitation. In taking such a stand the authors seek the collaboration of the client or clients.

Therapeutic Re-authoring Procedures

The four commonly used procedures to deconstruct the oppressive stories and to reconstruct new, enlivening stories include the use of questions, empathic responses, making therapeutic distinctions, and being transparent (Meier, 2002).

Use of Questions

To construct new narratives, White (1991) uses two categories of questions: the "dual landscapes" of action and of consciousness in personal stories. The "landscape of action" comprises events, sequences, time, and plots. The "landscape of consciousness" entails the meanings or interpretations of the characters in the story. These include the desires of the characters, their characteristics and qualities, their intentions, and their beliefs. The elements of the landscape of consciousness coalesce into "lifestyles" and become enduring aspects of a personal story.

White (1991) uses landscape-of-action questions to differentiate past events from recent and distant events, and to obtain information regarding these time periods. These questions can be used to bring forth aspects of distant history, place them alongside and link them to aspects of recent history which are about current unique outcomes, immediate future possibilities, and distant future possibilities. White utilizes landscape-of-consciousness questions to encourage people to look at themselves through the events disclosed in the interconnected landscape of action. White selects questions about desires, qualities, intentions, beliefs, and commitments.

In his classification system, Tomm (1988b) divides questions into four major groups, using as parameters the therapist's intention when employing questions and the therapist's assumption about the nature of mental phenomena and the therapeutic process. Regarding the therapist's intention, questions can be thought of as *orienting questions* which provide the therapist with information, or as *influencing questions* which make changes in the client. Regarding the therapist's assumptions about the nature of mental phenomena and the therapeutic process, questions can be linear or circular. *Linear questions* are based on cause-and-effect assumptions and are associated, for example, with reductionism, causal determinism, and strategic approaches. *Circular questions* are based on cybernetic assumptions and tend to be associated with holism, interactional principles, systematic approaches, and so on. Descriptions of these questions with examples are presented in Table 10.1.

Empathic Responding

Empathic responding, seen from a social-constructionist perspective, engages both the client and therapist as active agents in the co-construction of meaning and in the re-authoring of life narratives. The advantage of empathic responding is that the therapist is constantly attuned to the clients' implicit messages and mirrors them back to the client. The main task of a therapist using empathic responses is to remain attuned to these messages rather than deciding which questions to ask. Empathic responding can help persons make distinctions and co-author a new story (McLeod, 1999).

Table 10.1 Tomm's categories of questions

Type of question	Description
1. Linear questions	Investigative in nature and orient the therapist to the client's situation. *Example*: "How long have you been depressed?"
2. Circular questions	Exploratory in intent and orient the therapist to the client's situation, seek to reveal the recurrent patterns that connect events to perceptions, feelings, etc. *Example*: "What do you do when he shows you that he is depressed?"
3. Strategic questions	Influence the person in a specific manner and by using them the therapist imposes his/her views of what "ought to be" upon the person/family. *Example*: "When will you take responsibility for your own life and get up without mom having to awake you?"
4. Reflexive questions	Facilitative in nature, the therapist acts as a guide; are intended to influence the client or family in an indirect way; are suited for an individual or family that is autonomous and cannot be influenced directly; are formulated to evoke the person or family to reflect upon the effects of their current actions and perceptions and consider new options.

Source: summarized from Tomm, 1988b.

Therapeutic Distinctions

A therapeutic distinction, derived from Bateson's (1979, p. 79) "news of difference," is an observation that shows something different, discloses the operating power-politics in the story, and "orients the observer in a healing direction" (Tomm, 1988a, p. 120). Questions have as their purpose to make distinctions, that is, to differentiate that which is pathologizing from that which is healing. Drawing a distinction is a two-fold process: First, it differentiates "an entity, an event, a pattern, or some other phenomenon from a background" (p. 118). Second, it entails "adopting a certain position, a behavioural stance, or a 'posture' in relation to the entity or phenomenon distinguished" (p. 119). Therapeutic distinctions – seeing a difference – serve as the basis for the construction of new stories.

Transparency

Transparency refers to therapists making known to the client or family their biases and ideas and trace them to particular experiences (Freedman & Combs, 2000). To achieve transparency, the clients are invited to ask the therapist any questions they wish. By thus being open with the client, it is hoped to minimize the power differential inherent in the therapist–client relationship.

Method In Working with Narratives

White and Epston (1990) developed a formal method by which to work with narratives in therapy. It is also possible to work with narratives in a more informal, spontaneous, and natural way that entails addressing narratives as they emerge within therapy. The method in working with narratives for the two approaches is similar and includes the following interrelated tasks: identifying the problem, externalizing (taking distance from) the problem, deconstructing the dominant story, reconstructing a preferred and new story, authenticating the new story, and acting in a new way.

Identifying and Exploring the Problem

The first task in working with narratives is to attentively listen to the presenting emotional or interpersonal problem, and to explore its history, prevalence, and intensity and to uncover its underlying hidden story so as to gain a clear understanding of the problem. The task is to bring the culturally imposed self-story to an awareness. The therapist pays attention to emotions, feelings, thoughts, preferences, and desires in order to identify the problem and to understand the factors that maintain it. It is important to view the problem within the context of the hidden story.

Externalizing and Taking Distance from the Problem

A second task is to help the client take distance from the problem or to externalize the problem with the goal of deconstructing the old story and reconstructing a new story. In externalizing the problem, clients are asked to view the problem as external to them and to recall the times when they successfully fought against the problem. In using the distancing technique and gaining a different perspective regarding the problem, the client might be asked, "If your best friend were listening to you, what might she say?"

Deconstructing the Old Story

A third task is to bring the dominant story to awareness so that it can be held up for examination and deconstruction. That which was taken for granted in the dominant story begins to appear simply as one view of oneself, not necessarily the correct view. The deconstructive move makes possible the replacement of a client's socially supplied life story with a story that incorporates the client's full life events and positions the client as the agent and responsible protagonist of her story. To gain agency over the dominant story, the client may be asked to recall the times when she successfully fought against the problem. Remembering these times allows clients to incorporate their strengths and past victories over problems into the stories they are now constructing about their lives. To assist in the deconstruction of the dominant narrative, the techniques of externalizing the problem and unique outcomes can be used. In using unique outcomes, clients are asked to recall events that have been dismissed and left out by the dominant plot. The recognition of events that cannot be integrated into the dominant plot serves to undo the dominant plot and open space for the development of a new and more complex plot that includes these now recalled but previously dismissed events and actions.

Reconstructing a New and Preferred Story

The fourth task is reconstructing a preferred, new story that begins when the client reports a new perspective regarding her problem or has identified an exception to the problem. The new perspective or identified exception to the problem forms the basis for the construction of the story and becomes woven into the new plot. Working together on the new plot enhances the client's agency, opens up for review past life events, and permits the client to alter assignments of self-responsibility for previous actions and alter the meaning of other's actions. These aspects are reconfigured in the new story.

Authenticating the New Narrative

A fifth task is to help clients to reclaim, strengthen, and authenticate their preferred and new story. The therapist helps the client to find people who experience the client in ways that manifest their preferred stories and who are supportive of them and can play a part in authenticating and strengthening the client's preferred stories emerging in therapy. Authenticating the new narrative implies the ability for clients to share their own stories with others and hear the stories of other people.

Acting in a New Way

The last task is for the therapist to help clients to reenvision a life plot that changes the meaning assigned to past events and happenings and serves to shape their future. The denouement of the new plot requires a different set of future actions. The altered meaning of the self generated by the new story calls into question future behaviours and plans that had been derived from the old dominant story (Parry & Doan, 1994).

Ethical Considerations

Several ethical issues present themselves when doing narrative therapy. First, therapists wield a heavy hand in making distinctions by the fact that they take a political position regarding the source of the problematic narrative. Outside of abusive and violent situations, how do therapists determine when they should take a political stand? How do therapists take a political stand and yet allow the unfolding story to be that of the client? Second, in deconstructing stories, the therapists need to exercise caution to assure that the person has the personal resources to carry out this task. Not all persons are equally capable of engaging in deconstructing the familiar. Third, in the rewriting or re-authoring of psychotherapy narratives, it is important the therapists be aware of cultural traditions. Fourth, it is important to give the person the space to create new stories and allow them to lead the way based on their preferred stories. Fifth, it is possible for a person to rework dominant stories more than once during their lifetime. For example, a story arrived at during adolescence might need to be reworked in a future developmental stage.

Illustration: Sonja

Sonja (pseudonym), in her late twenties and recently graduated with an MSW as a case social worker, sought counselling to resolve a conflict in competing for a position at work. Below are a summary of the therapy session, a conceptualization of the case, a description of the steps of the therapy process, and an excerpt from the session.

Summary

Sonja was brought up in a small-town family whose expectations were that girls complete high school, get a job, get married, and have children (the dominant narrative). Pursuing postsecondary education was considered to be for the privileged. Sonja's noncompliance with these expectations brought about feelings of disloyalty, selfishness, guilt, and sadness in moving on and leaving her family behind. In the session Sonja explored the holding power of the family (dominant) narrative and her own need to move on so as to fully use her talents and achieve her sense of personhood (the preferred narrative). Through self-reflection and support from her friends, Sonja realized that her desire to move on was a problem for her family and not her, a realization that freed and empowered her (self-agency).

Conceptualization

Sonja's angst about being promoted can be conceptualized as representing a clash between the dominant narrative and the preferred narrative and the conflict between letting go of her family and pursuing her life interests. To resolve the clash, it is imperative that Sonja understand the problem within the context of the dominant narrative, take distance from the problem, become aware of the new emerging narrative, and acquire self-agency to pursue the new narrative.

Therapy Process

The first step of therapy saw Sonja clearly identify the problem and situate it within current and past experiences. The second step explored how one aspect of the problem and the associated negative feelings were rooted in, and a consequence of, the dominant narrative that determined how people were to live their lives. The third overlapping step explored Sonja's preferred way to live her life, and this provided the basis for constructing a new narrative. These explorations brought about the awareness that in pursuing her preferred lifestyle, Sonja would be judged by her family as being disloyal, selfish, and thinking that she is better than others. Sonja did not identify with these thoughts but accepted that she was different. Realizing that her angst was rooted in letting go of her family, she felt free and empowered. Sonja was able to validate – authenticate – her own choices, and has friends who provide similar authentication of her choices.

Transcript

The session began with Sonja describing how her problem was related to the opportunity to be promoted at work. In the transcript, C = Client, T = Therapist, and the number following the letter is the response number. Some parts of the transcript have been omitted.

Identifying and Exploring the Problem and its History

T04: You sense that there is something holding you back from competing for the position.

C04: Yes, and it doesn't feel right, it doesn't feel normal. It is right there and I just need to walk to it and I am not doing that. I am not able.

T06: Although you have the encouragement of your manager and peers, yet you feel indifferent about it and feel an angst around it.

C06: I don't understand why it does not appeal to me the way that I thought it would.

Exploring the History of Problem

(The therapist explored whether the current problem was linked to earlier experiences.)

T08: I am wondering whether this is something that you have experienced in the past – that when new opportunities arose, you were thrilled at first but the thrill quickly faded?

C08: Yes, when I went off to university. I came from a small town and university wasn't the norm. It was for the privileged children, it was for kids whose parents were doctors and lawyers, who held expectations of their children to become educated. When I went off to university I was excited, I wanted it, but there was the same kind of tug, the same kind of pull. It is like – I wanted it but there was angst about it.

T10: You find the opportunity for promotion exciting and something that you want, yet you find yourself thinking that it is for the privileged.

C10: It was always a dream to become the executive director of this organization, but it wasn't for me. It was so far from what I ever imagined and now the opportunity is here. There is part of me that knows that I can do it but there is part of me that doesn't feel that I should go for it – (long pause) – that maybe it is not for me. It doesn't feel right to be there.

Deconstructing the Dominant Narrative and Co-constructing the Preferred Narrative

T13: What do you make of the thought that it is not for you?

C13: It doesn't make sense. On one hand I know that I can do it and I have people around believing in me, affirming me, and encouraging me to compete for it, yet there is a part of me that is being held back. There are two competing forces within me.

T14: These competing forces are holding you from moving forward.

C14: I need to break myself away in order to do this and to feel good about it. I don't understand this force that keeps tugging at me and pulling me.

Taking Distance from the Problem

T16: Is there anything that you can say or do to break away from this force that is holding you back?

C16: I have to stay with what I believe to be true. I know that I am capable to do that job.

T18: When you bundle all of this up – your dream, your conviction that you are able to do it, and wanting to be able to do it, your support from others – how are you with that?

C18: It seems right. I do want this and for the right reasons.

T19: Although in the back of your mind you hear something different, you are able to say to yourself that you can do it, that you want to accept it and move forward.

C19: Yes, there is part of me that wants this opportunity, wants the best for me, the best for my family, and all of the opportunities in life, yet there is this angst about actually having it.

T21: When you imagine having it, what do you feel?

C21: It feels like I'm moving away, moving on. It is like having to sacrifice other things in order to receive opportunities in life.

T22: I sense that in moving away you are breaking some family rule.

C22: Yes, it is very similar. When I mentioned going away to university, there was this sense that I was doing something outside of what was expected of me and in a way I was moving on with my life and leaving my family behind.

T24: Something within you is saying that you do not belong to the privileged and by accepting this promotion you are making the statement that you are one of the privileged. How is that for you?

C25: (Long pause.) There is a sense of selfishness for wanting so much, for wanting for more. There is a sense of guilt for going above and beyond, for feeling that I deserve to have more, that I am capable.

T26: This is touching on family expectations.

C26: Yes. In my family, my parents weren't educated, my siblings completed high school, and that was the expectation – complete high school, get a job, get married, have kids, and that was the expectation. To go above and beyond that, would be to put yourself in a position of being judged as better than, or privileged.

T27: You are being held back for fear of being judged as being better than them.

C27: Yes. I see it as moving on with my life whereas my family would see it as I am moving away from them and they can no longer relate to me and therefore they judge me to be better than them. I am not better, I am different. I have made different choices with my life. This allows me more opportunities in life. This opportunity is judged to be negative in my family. Like, I am not one of them because I have this opportunity and privilege.

T29: How do you see that?

C29: I just see it as being different. I am still who I am, I am still a sibling, a daughter, the same person. I chose to continue to grow and to develop myself and expand my opportunities in life and they haven't.

Self-authentication of Preferred Narrative

T31: How does that sit with you?

C31: I have to affirm myself for being different and for being my own person and remind myself that I am different in that I have grown, have become educated and successful in my life. I have made different and better choices with my life than perhaps my siblings have made. But I don't believe that I am better, I am different. I have to remind myself that I worked very hard for the privileges that I have in my life. I feel worthy of the privileges and opportunities. On the other hand, though, by me making these choices for my life and doing what I have done I have left them behind, I have let go of my family, their values, their judgment.

T33: How do you feel about that?

C33: I feel conflicted, I feel guilty for distancing, I feel disloyal, yet I also feel very proud in becoming who I am and accomplishing what I have accomplished given the level of resources that I had available. I feel very confident and very competent as a person and as a professional. I feel very good about who I am and what I have become and I feel very sad that the consequences of becoming are leaving my family behind and letting go of their shared values and expectations and judgment.

T34: In a way you wish that your family would pursue for themselves a similar journey and follow their ways as you have followed your way.

C34: I needed to move forward with my life, I needed to grow and change and pursue my talents and dreams and desires. Yes, I do wish that they could have followed – I wish that they could have exercised their potential as well.

T35: Feeling sad for them for not having taken the same opportunities that you did.

C35: Yes, feeling sad that they weren't able to pursue their talents and their dreams the way I did, that they did not believe enough in themselves, weren't capable of taking the risks and stayed stuck and resentful of my success.

Authenticating the New and Preferred Narrative

T37: When you look at what you have accomplished and how you made efforts to move away from the family and the feelings associated with this, how are you with it?

C37: I feel really good about myself and with what I have done with my life, what I have accomplished and what and who I have become, I feel very proud.

T38: Have you spoken about this struggle with any of your friends and has this helped you to move forward?

C38: Yes, I have good friends that I talk to about this and confide in. They are very supportive of me and of the person that I have become. They help me to keep grounded where I am at today and to continue to move forward, but also very empathic about the journey that I travelled to get to where I am.

T41: Is there anything that you would like to add to this conversation.

C41: The thing that I want to add is that the more I accomplish, the more I grow, the further that I develop myself personally and professionally, the more separated, the more distant I become from my family and I think that that is the root of my angst – is that to become me, I need to let go. I want my family to respect me for what and who I have become.

Describing the Experience

Sonja mentioned that the exercise was helpful for her to understand the root of her angst and to get unstuck. The experience was affirming for her. It empowered her (i.e. involved self-agency) to be authentic and keep moving forward with her life. Her motivation has shifted because she now realizes that she was held back by their negative judgment of herself, not for being better, but for being different. She feels freer to be true to herself without the guilt of being different and of living beyond her family's expectations. She has broken free from the dominant narrative so as to pursue her preferred narrative.

Something to Think About

1. Narratives are like threads that weave together human experiences. Explain.
2. How do power and knowledge relate in dominant narratives?
3. What are *therapeutic distinctions*?
4. What does it mean to externalize a problem?
5. How did Sonja emerge from the old narrative and engage in a new narrative?

References

Bateson, G. (1979). *Mind and nature: A necessary unity*. New York: Dutton.

Breuer, J., & Freud, S. (1895/1955). Studies on hysteria. *Standard Edition* (Vol. 2, pp. 1–305). London: Hogarth Press.

Bruner, E. (1986). Ethnography as narrative. In V. Turner & E. Bruner (Eds.), *The anthropology of experience*. Chicago: University of Illinois Press.

Bruner, J. (1986). *Actual minds, possible worlds*. Cambridge, MA: Harvard University Press.

Dallos, R. (2006). *Attachment narrative therapy: Integrating systemic, narrative and attachment approaches*. London: Open University Press (McGraw-Hill).

Foucault, M. (1980). *Power/knowledge: Selected interviews and other writings*. New York: Pantehon Books.

Foucault, M. (1988). Technologies of the self. In L.M. Martin, H. Guman, & P.H. Hutton (Eds.), *Technologies of the self* (pp. 16–49). Amherst: University of Massachusetts Press.

Freedman, J., & Combs, G. (2000). Narrative therapy with couples. In F.M. Dattilio & L.J. Bevilacqua (Eds.), *Comparative treatments for relationship dysfunction* (pp. 342–361). New York: Springer.

Geertz, C. (1983). *Local knowledge: Further essays in interpretative anthropology*. New York: Basic Books.

Madsen, W.B. (2007). *Collaborative therapy with multi-stressed families: From old problems to new futures*. New York: Guilford Press.

Martin, W. (1986*). Recent theories of narrative*. London: Cornell University Press.

McLeod, J. (1999). A narrative social constructionist approach to therapeutic empathy. *Counselling Psychological Quarterly, 12*(4), 377–394.

Meier, A. (2002). Narrative in psychotherapy theory, practice and research: A critical review. *Counselling and Psychotherapy Research, 2*(4), 239–251.

Murray, M. (2000). Levels of narrative analysis in health psychology. *Journal of Health Psychology, 5*(3), 337–347.

Parry, A., & Doane, R.E. (1994). *Story re-visions: Narrative therapy in the postmodern world.* New York: Guilford Press.

Payne, M. (2006). *Narrative therapy: An introduction for counselors.* London: Sage Publications.

Rogers, C.R. (1942). *Counselling and psychotherapy.* Cambridge, MA: Houghton Mifflin.

Tomm, K. (1988a). Interventive interviewing: Part III. Intending to ask lineal, circular, strategic, or reflexive questions? *Family Process, 27*(1), 1–15.

Tomm, K. (1988b). Therapeutic distinctions in an on-going therapy. *Dulwich Centre Newsletter,* Adelide, Australia (with Cynthia, Andrew and Vanessa), 116–135.

Tomm, K. (1993). The Courage to protest: A commentary on Michael White's work. In S. Gilligan & R. Price (Eds.), *Therapeutic conversations.* New York: W.W. Norton.

White, M. (1991). Deconstruction and therapy. *Dulwich Centre Newsletter,* Adelide, Australia, *3*, 1–22.

White, M. (2004). Folk psychotherapy and narrative practices. In L.E. Angus & J. McLeod (Eds.), *The handbook of narrative and psychotherapy: Practice, theory, and research* (pp. 15–51). London: Sage Publications.

White, M. (2007). *Maps of narrative practice.* New York: W.W. Norton.

White, M., & Epston, D. (1990). *Narrative means to therapeutic ends.* New York: W.W. Norton.

11 Self-in-Relationship Psychotherapy

Chapter Summary

This chapter presents a therapy model that gives primacy to relational and self needs. It assumes that underlying dysfunctional behaviours, emotional problems, and deep-seated negative and destructive feelings, are needs and yearnings that need to be given voice so that a person can deal with the problems and move forward. When these needs and yearnings are repressed or denied at an early age, other aspects of the client's personality are negatively affected, such as representation of self, other, and the world; the organization of the self and the psychic, relational patterns; and the development of intimacy, that is, balancing oneness and separateness. The case of Sofía illustrates that in addressing relational and self needs she is able to resolve her own inner conflicts and begin the process of reconnecting with a significant other.

Introduction

Within the domain of traditional psychoanalysis, there is a strong movement towards integrating relational theory into therapeutic approaches. This has been very clearly and artfully articulated by Wachtel (2008). This chapter presents a psychotherapeutic approach, known as *self-in-relationship psychotherapy* (SIRP) that has a relational focus. Unlike orientations such as transference-focused psychotherapy (Clarkin, Kernberg, & Yeomans, 1999) and relational psychoanalysis (Greenberg & Mitchell, 1983), that are based on psychoanalysis and object-relations therapy, and unlike relational therapy (DeYoung, 2003), that is based on self psychology and intersubjectivity theory, SIRP adopts concepts, processes, and techniques from object-relations therapy, self psychology, developmental psychology, and experiential psychotherapy, and integrates these within a self-discovery, person-centred, developmental, and relational approach.

The first part of this chapter presents the concepts and processes taken from object-relations therapy, developmental psychology, and self psychology that are pertinent to SIRP. The second part outlines SIRP's therapeutic procedures. The last part illustrates the therapeutic application of SIRP.

Major Concepts and Processes

Primary Motives

A person is born with two sets of primary innate needs, namely relational and self needs. Relational needs have as their purpose to establish and maintain relationships, whereas self needs have as their goal to expand, aggrandize, and enhance the self. The two sets of needs are played out together. With sexual awakening, the person also develops sexual needs.

Relational Needs

Relational needs comprise the need to bond with a significant caregiver and the need to separate from the caregiver and individuate (Mahler, Pine, & Bergman, 1975; Kaplan, 1978). The need for bonding (symbiosis) begins at birth, or earlier, and continues throughout all of life. The first expression of this need is seen in the fused (symbiotic) and dependent relationship of infant and caregiver (Mahler, Pine, & Bergman, 1975). Later this need shows itself as the need to interact with the caregiver, play with other children, be a cherished member of a family, have friends, have a lover, be part of a community, etc. In all of these relationships there is a need to feel that the other is present for and to oneself, to feel that there is a place for oneself in the heart of the other.

The infant, also, has the innate capacity and need to break out of and move away from the symbiotic relationship, to leave the "nest," venture forth, and become interdependent. This is achieved with the infant exercising its sense of omnipotence (being all powerful) (Winnicott, 1965a) and investing its energies (normal narcissism) (Kohut, 1977) in the service of these developmental tasks. The need to separate begins shortly after birth and is determined primarily by cognitive, social, and motor development. The need to separate is to be distinguished from the need to individuate. To individuate means to develop one's own interests, opinions, goals, meanings, values. It is to become an individual. The process of separation is first seen in the infant's crawling, standing, and walking behaviours. Later the tandem of separating and individuating are seen in the child's temper tantrums and assertions of his autonomy, his movement away from caregivers, choosing friends, forming his own opinions and values, choosing educational and career goals, and choosing a sexual partner.

Self Needs

Self needs, also referred to as narcissistic needs, comprise the innate desires to be (a) empowered and omnipotent and master of one's life and environment, and (b) feeling good, lovable, and worthwhile in one's own skin. The child needs the caregiver's admiration and affirmations to foster his sense of omnipotence, empowerment, and competency and to experience that he is a good, wholesome, and lovable person. Kohut (1977, 1983) refers to these as mirroring and idealizing transference.

Sexual Needs

Every person has an innate need to express themselves fully as a sexual being. Freud stated long ago that we are sexual beings from the very start of our existence, and that learning of sexuality begins at the mother's breast. Recent research has confirmed Freud's views (Haroian, 2000). Infants/children learn about sexuality in the way that they are touched, caressed, cuddled, and cared for from birth. Later, they learn about sexuality through exploring and learning how their bodies feel to themselves, exploring the bodies of children and adults, becoming attached to the parent of the opposite gender, observing how members of the family express affection and care for one another, hearing the words that family members use to refer to body parts, and from learning what constitutes sexually appropriate behaviour (Pike, 2000).

The sexual maturation of a child parallels the logical, orderly, and self-regulating pattern of development of other aspects of human behaviour such as dependency on family of origin, the development of a sense of an autonomous self, the confidence and desire to form an intimate relationship and begin a family of one's own. In infancy, the erotic response is global and undifferentiated; in childhood, it moves towards genital focus expressed in autoeroticism; in pubescence, the genital focus is intensified and sexual experience in itself is the paramount goal; and in adolescence, sexuality becomes a powerful force and manifests itself in sexual reciprocity and mutual sharing (Haroian, 2000; Webber & Delvin, 2005).

The acknowledgment and affirmation of an infant/child's relational, self, and sexual needs, and the extent to which they are realized, integrated, and moderated by interactions with caregivers, others, and reality (e.g., culture), affects all aspects of a child's personality including how they perceive the other, self, and the world, the organization and structuring of experiences, relational patterns and quality of intimacy, and coping strategies used to deal with the frustrations of unmet needs.

Internal Representations

In his efforts to emotionally bond with a significant caregiver and then to separate and individuate, the infant/child has both pleasant and unpleasant experiences. Pleasant experiences occur when the infant/child is emotionally responded to and tenderly held and when its primary needs are met (e.g., being fed), whereas unpleasant experiences occur when the infant/child is not emotionally responded to and its primary needs are not met. Due to the infant's immature ego and perceptual processes, it experiences the caregiver who responds positively to the child's needs as being a different person from the one who frustrates the infant. The pleasant and unpleasant experiences are organized to form two different internal representations of the caregiver. The caregiver who responds to the child's needs is perceived as being the good caregiver (object), whereas the person who frustrates the infant is considered as being the bad caregiver (Klein, 1936, 1959). This is summarized in Figure 11.1.

Parallel to forming internal representations of the caregiver, the infant also forms internal representations of self. When the caregiver responds positively to the infant's needs, he experiences pleasure and feels good about self, believing that the caregiver's positive responses are related to his good behaviours and actions. However, when the caregiver fails to respond to the infant/child's needs, he experiences displeasure and feels bad about self, believing that the caregiver's negative responses relate to his bad behaviours. The infant therefore forms two internal representations of self, the good-self and the bad-self (Klein, 1936, 1959) (see Figure 11.1). These representations of caregiver and self form the

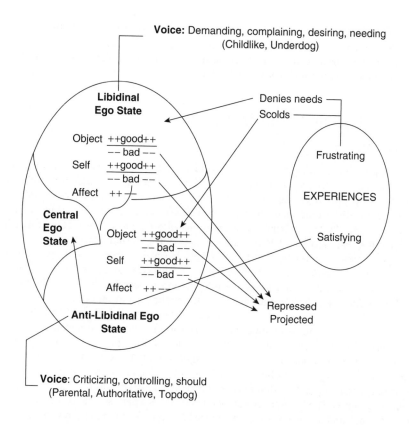

Figure 11.1   Psychic organization

Source: Meier & Boivin, 2006. © 2006, Novalis, Ottawa, Canada. Reprinted with permission.

substratum of the infant/child's psyche and personality and influence how the person views and responds to others.

Object Constancy and Affect Regulation

One of the infant/child's significant developmental tasks is to form constant positive internal representations of self and other. The representation of other is referred to as "emotional object constancy" (Mahler, Pine, & Bergman, 1975, p. 109). Such representations, formed from positive experiences with others such as caregivers, provide an "emotional psychological home" to return to for self-comforting and self-soothing when they feel emotionally distraught. When turning to this emotional psychological home, the person is better able to form a more realistic perspective on a situation, experience self more positively, and is better able to regulate his affects and their expression. Persons who have been maltreated, emotionally neglected, abused, and traumatized as children often lack an emotional psychological home to which they can turn to moderate their feelings and behaviours.

Internal Psychic Organizations and Functions

For each of his relationships, the infant/child forms internal representations of other (e.g., caregiver) and of self. The internal representations of other and self that are similar to each other collectively form "organized cognitive–affective–motivational systems" (OCAMS), that is, dynamic organizations that generate internal processes and interactions. These correspond to schemas (Young, 2003), internal representations (Klein, 1961), psychic structures (Freud, 1923), ego states (Fairbairn, 1944; Watkins & Watkins, 1997), and model scenes (DeYoung, 2003). Similar to ego states (Lawrence, 1999), the OCAMS comprise sensory, memory, affective, cognitive, behavioural, and motivational aspects that give direction to the person's actions, behaviours, attitudes, and values and influence information processing. The OCAMS, henceforth referred to as ego states, represent primitive and enduring, but mutable organizations that affect how well a person deals with the tasks and challenges of daily living. The OCAMS constitute the substratum for the development of the person's psyche and personality.

Although each of the infant/child's relationships leads to multiple ego states, ego states are typically considered in terms of a triad. For example, Freud (1923) refers to the triad as comprising the id, ego, and superego, Berne (1976) as child, adult and parent, and Fairbairn (1944) as libidinal, central, and antilibidinal ego states. For the purpose of this chapter, Fairbairn's triad will be adopted. The libidinal ego state encompasses a person's biological, physiological, sexual, relational, and self needs that are inherited at the beginning of physical life. This ego state, connected to the depriving and rejecting caregiver, also represents that part of self that is needy, perpetually frustrated, deprived, feels attacked, and insatiably craves for the fulfilment of its relational and self needs. The antilibidinal ego state is that part of self that encompasses parental, familial, and cultural demands, expectations, and prohibitions. When this ego state dominates, the person is hateful, vengeful, and bitter and critical of his own libidinal needs and cravings and controls by creating guilt feelings. The central ego state is the primary psychic and unitary self present at birth. It derives from the "ideal ego" and is still connected to those parts of the caregiver that were once gratifying. It comprises conscious and unconscious elements and relates to reality, and it is the voice of reason and compromise. It can become impoverished and enfeebled when the person has to deal with difficult life situations such as emotional rejection, physical abuse and trauma. In the process, part of the ego is dedicated to cope with the problem; consequently, part of it is not available to deal with the normal tasks of daily living and is left impoverished. The infant/child shapes its psychic organization according to that of the caregiver and significant others. The formation of the ego states, the processes that lead to their development, and their respective voices are illustrated in Figure 11.1.

Self Organization

Based on interactions with his caregiver, the infant/child develops notions about himself that are organized according to the two innate basic needs, that is, to be admired for being competent and to be loved for being a good person (Kohut, 1977). The infant/child's subjective experiences become organized to form a bipolar sense of self, namely, being admired and being loved. This bipolar organization of self influences how the person views and judges himself with respect to others and how he relates to them. The self, in reality, is the product of the central ego evaluating and judging itself with respect to how he complies to the expectations of others and their judgments about them. The person's sense of being admired and loved is related to these earlier experiences. Kohut (1977) refers to this bipolar organization as nuclear ambition (to be admired) and nuclear ideal (to be loved).

When the infant/child begins to relate to others, complies with their wishes and expectations, and puts aside his own strivings, the person begins to live inauthentically. When he lives according to his strivings the person lives authentically. A self that lives authentically is referred to as a true self, whereas a self that lives inauthentically is referred to as a false self (Winnicott, 1965a, 1965b).

Developmental Process, Failures, and Attachment Patterns

The working out of primary needs, the development of internal representations, and the acquisition of psychic and self organizations take place within the context of the changing infant/child and caregiver relationship. The infant begins his relationship with a significant caregiver in a state of total dependence, a state described as symbiosis (oneness, merger) (Mahler, Pine, & Bergman, 1975, p. 34) and a "nursing couple" (Winnicott, 1965b, p. 15). With the maturation of the perceptual processes and the caregiver's affirmations, the infant emerges from the fused state and embarks on the path toward separation and individuation. The developmental path extends over a two- to three-year period and comprises several subphases including symbiosis, differentiation, practicing, rapprochement, and consolidation/object constancy (Mahler, Pine, & Bergman, 1975). Each of these subphases carries with it significant developmental tasks, and if not negotiated, they will have significant negative effects on the infant/child in meeting its primary relational and self needs, developing internal representations of self, other, and the world, and forming internal structures. The negotiated as well as the failed developmental tasks (Table 11.1) act as prototypes or templates that influence how the infant/child, when an adolescent and adult, relates to others, the world, and self.

The manner in which an infant/child and caregiver negotiate the need for closeness and separateness determines how free the infant/child feels to turn to the caregiver when distraught. When this task is optimally negotiated, the infant/child trustingly returns to the caregiver for protection, security, and safety. When the caregiver is inconsistent in her/his emotional availability and responses, the infant/child will be preoccupied as to whether it is loved and does not trust that the caregiver will respond in a protective, caring, and safe manner. When the caregiver is cold and rejecting, the infant–child will avoid turning to the caregiver. These three responses represent behavioural stances that an infant/child forms regarding the degree to which they feel attached to the caregiver. These three stances have been described in attachment terms as secure, insecure preoccupied, and insecure avoidant attachments, respectively (Bowlby, 1988).

Relational Patterns and Intimacy

In the course of working out the fundamental relational and self needs, the infant/child forms and internalizes a pattern of relating to others that is formed in large part by the

Table 11.1 Developmental subphases: tasks and dysfunctions

Subphase	Developmental Tasks	Later Life Dysfunctions
Symbiosis (2–4 months)	a) Become emotionally anchored and bonded to caregiver b) Formation of inner core of self c) Form representations of other and self	a) Disconnection from other and self b) Yearning for connection
Differentiation (5–9 months)	a) Move towards active and separate functioning b) Differentiate self from caregiver c) Behaviour becomes outward oriented and goal directed d) Development of stranger anxiety	a) Fear to venture out b) Undifferentiated c) Fearful of others
Practicing (10–14 months)	a) Expanded locomotor capacity b) Interest in inanimate objects c) Increased exploration of the world d) Building fear resistance to separation from caregiver; seeks emotional closeness when needed	a) Feelings of inadequacy b) No goal, no direction c) Noncommittal; ambivalent; avoidant d) Fear of closeness e) Craving affirmations
Rapprochement (14–24 months)	a) Integrates good and bad objects b) Establish pattern of approach to caregiver; establishes boundaries c) Establishes of object constancy d) Begins to regulate affect e) Reverses splitting f) Differentiates self from others, beginning of gender identity	a) Failure to establish intimacy b) Prone to feelings of abandonment, rage c) Fails to regulate affect d) Enmeshes or cuts off e) Lacks relational boundaries
Consolidation (24–36 months)	a) Develops firm mental representations b) Develops notion of "self" separate from "love" object c) Achieves sense of individuality d) Acquires emotional-object constancy e) Emergence of superego precursors	a) Has limited sense of self; lives for others b) Maintains splitting c) Lacks affect regulation d) Lacks inner social controls

Source: extrapolated from Mahler & Furer, 1968, and Mahler, Pine, & Bergman, 1975.

modelling of the caregiver in helping the infant/child meet its relational and self needs. The relational patterns serve as a prototype for the infant/child's future relationships and shape his expectations about the way in which relational and self needs are to be met. The external manifestations of these internalized relational patterns have been labeled as cyclical maladaptive patterns (Levenson & Strupp, 2007) and projective identifications (Cashdan, 1988). A projective identification comprises a relational stance, metacommunication, and induction. For example, for the projective identification of *dependency*, the relational stance is that of "helplessness," the metacommunication is "I can't survive," and the induction is "caretaking" (Cashdan, 1988, p. 77). The internalized relational patterns manifest themselves particularly in couple relationships and in the therapist–client relationships as transferences.

Coping Strategies

The primary coping strategies of persons who have longstanding emotional problems include splitting, dissociation, projection, idealization, and villainization (depreciation) (Klein, 1936). These persons often blame others for their problems (projection), divide the world into good and bad people (splitting), and are out of touch with their emotional states (dissociation). When they meet another person who cares for and understands them, they will idealize the person, and when the person disappointments them or asserts their own needs in the relationship, splitting occurs, resulting in villainization.

Emotional States

In the pursuit of relational and self needs, if the infant/child experiences rejection, demeaning behaviour, and an emotionally unavailable caregiver, the infant/child may experience intense emotions that include feelings of betrayal, abandonment, anxiety, terror, and rage. When these feelings persist, they may turn into residual emotional states (e.g., chronic anxiety) that are carried into adolescence and adulthood and manifest themselves in behavioural problems and in disruptive relationships. These residual feelings may be triggered by situations similar to those experienced in infancy/childhood.

Emotional Problems

Emotional problems are construed in terms of a person's central ego state failing to mediate the libidinal relational, self, and sexual needs and the antilibidinal and reality demands, resulting in using coping strategies and adopting relational patterns that are ineffective and not satisfying. Emotional problems express themselves in terms of relational themes such as feeling abandoned and needing to be enmeshed and in self themes such as feeling inadequate and worthless. To deal with the deprivation of needs, the person might become disproportionately depressed, enraged, withdrawn, dissociated, and anxious, feelings that are either contained or acted out. Emotional problems are said to be chronic or residual when they have a long history and are continuously present, and they are said to be acute or intermittent when they are related to specific situations.

Summary

The self-in-relationship psychotherapy model is presented in Figure 11.2. The core of this model comprises the relational, self, and sexual needs that are achieved within the context of a changing infant/child–caregiver relationship. In the pursuit of these needs, the infant/child is challenged to negotiate the developmental tasks of bonding and separating/individuating, form representations of the other and of self, and develop the psychic organization. To deal with the obstacles in the pursuit of primary needs and the emotional

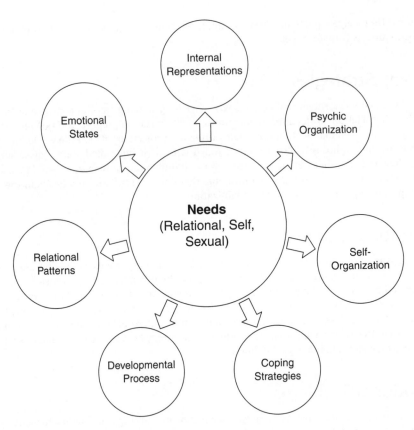

Figure 11.2   The self-in-relationship psychotherapy model

reactions, the infant/child acquires coping strategies and patterns of relating. When the infant/child is not able to effectively surmount the obstacles, he might develop emotional problems construed in terms of relational and self problems. In therapy, all problems presented by the client entail each of these dimensions, in varying order, and need to be addressed.

Therapeutic Process

Goals of Psychotherapy

The goal of psychotherapy is to help clients rediscover and reclaim primary relational and self needs that have been compromised and to help them reorganize their relationships according to the emerging life-giving needs. A second goal is to transform the psychic organization so that the central ego state acquires the capacity to harmonize the needs of the libidinal ego state with the demands of the antilibidinal ego state and of reality. This transformation takes place within the context of the therapeutic relationship where the therapist both nurtures and nudges the client to move towards greater personal growth and meaningful relationships.

Primary Candidates

The primary candidates for SIRP are clients with long-standing relational, self, and emotional problems that were brought about by emotional neglect, abuse, significant losses, tragedy, and/or trauma experienced in early childhood, adolescence, or adulthood. Appropriate candidates must be able to manage the physical aspects (e.g., finances) of their lives and their symptoms (e.g., rage, drug abuse). SIRP is the therapy of choice for these candidates because it addresses the fundamental needs for emotional connection, safety, security, and predictability that were interrupted by experiences that resulted in the development of dysfunctional psychic organization and ineffective coping strategies.

Qualities of the Therapist

It is important that psychotherapists working from a SIRP model of therapy possess the capacity to create a safe, protective, and secure place for clients to explore their experiences, and that the psychotherapy provide a holding environment (Winnicott, 1965a) to help clients contain their emotions, particularly when they become enraged, feel abandoned, and regress into childlike behaviour. Psychotherapists must have the fortitude, emotional maturity, and resiliency to feel and endure different kinds of emotions not only in the clients but also in themselves. They must possess the interpersonal skill to nurture clients and permit them to become dependent when appropriate, and the skill to act as a catalyst to nudge clients forward according to their readiness and ability. It is taken for granted that psychotherapists possess the Rogerian (1961) qualities of empathic understanding, congruence, and unconditional positive regard, and that the therapist offers the client a real person willing to be in relationship with them.

The Psychotherapy Process

Psychotherapeutic change is a process by which the client makes incremental gains and moves forward across time. Meier and Boivin (1998) named these significant gains in terms of phases that include problem definition, exploration, awareness/insight, commitment/decision, experimentation/action, integration/consolidation, and termination (see Chapter 1). SIRP postulates that successful psychotherapy includes recognizing, accepting, and exploring the problem, gaining insight into its underlying dynamics and processes, and taking action to make changes based on these insights. The action taken may be a change in regulating one's feelings, adopting a new attitude, changing behaviours and relational patterns. SIRP addresses the components (themes) of a disorder (not the disorder directly), such as a sense of powerlessness, need to connect, or sense of obligation, to mention a few (Meier, Boivin, & Meier, 2006).

Techniques

SIRP focuses on the here-and-now and works moment-to-moment within an empathic, self-discovery, person-centred, and developmental approach in the context of relationships, be they client–therapist, couple, caregiver–child, etc. Empathic understanding, introspection, and clarification are fundamental techniques used by the therapist; interpretation and confrontation are used when addressing client inconsistencies. When required, experiential-based techniques are incorporated. For example, one might use task-direct imagery to help a client move out of a "dark hole," the Gestalt Two-Chair technique to resolve a conflict between two ego states, and so on (see earlier chapters). One introduces these techniques when one assesses a high probability that the client will engage in the technique and benefit from them.

Procedure

Self-in-relationship psychotherapy begins by defining the presenting problem and completing a psychosocial history that focuses on relational and self issues experienced in the family of origin, school, workplace, social relationships, and intimate relationships. One pays particular attention to the problem, often expressed as an emotional state, such as anxiety, and ascertains its history, chronicity, and extensiveness. The presenting problem and associated affects are understood as reflecting dysfunctional relational patterns, failure to negotiate separation and individuation, conflicted psychic organization, and ineffective coping strategies. One listens carefully to all of this to determine the developmental arrest (e.g., failure to separate) that serves as the beginning and target of the therapeutic work. After having defined the problem and identified the developmental arrest, one begins to surface, understand, and transform the processes and dynamics underlying the arrest. In every situation, however, one begins with the problem presented that is viewed as a failure to secure primary relational and/or self needs. The problem typically reflects one or more of the dimensions presented in Figure 11.2. The process of therapy after defining the problem and identifying the arrest might be as follows for two of the dimensions.

Dysfunctional relational patterns: In exploring dysfunctional relational patterns, one pays attention to their communication style (e.g., attacking, defending), residual emotional state (e.g., anger, fear), coping strategies (e.g., splitting), perception of the other (e.g., mother, child), attempts to draw the other into their dysfunctional pattern (e.g., projective identification), and underlying relational and self needs.

Conflicted psychic organization: Dysfunctional relational patterns might reflect parallels in a conflicted psychic organization where one part is libidinally needy and the other part cannot tolerate and accept such neediness. This internal conflict might replicate itself in relationships where a person is not able to accept the neediness of others and pulls away from such demands, only to have the other person pursue for connectedness with greater vigor.

Illustration: Sofía

Sofía (pseudonym), in her mid-thirties, professional and married, sought help to explore the possibility of reestablishing a relationship with her mother with whom she had a falling out.

Below are a summary of three consecutive therapy sessions, a conceptualization of the relational problem, a description of the therapy process, and excerpts from therapy sessions demonstrating the use of SIRP.

Summary

Therapy focused on Sofía's relationship with her mother. Sofía viewed her mother as a selfish person incapable of giving needed love and affirmation. To maintain a relationship with her mother, Sofía, as a child and adolescent, compromised her own needs and was not able to get what she needed from the relationship. Sofía left home in her late teens to pursue her own life and gradually disconnected herself emotionally from her mother and the family. The relationship deteriorated when the mother absented herself from a significant event in Sofía's life. Sofía sought help to explore possibilities to establish a real relationship based on the realistic needs of both her mother and herself.

Conceptualization

The main elements in conceptualizing Sofía's relational problem with her mother include primary relational and self needs, representation of mother and self, the separation–individuation process, self organization and psychic organization. From infancy to late adolescence, Sofía compromised her relational need to separate to maintain a relationship with her mother. As a child and adolescent, Sofía was not affirmed or validated in her growing needs for independence, autonomy, and being her own person (relational needs), particularly when they conflicted with those of her mother. In the process, Sofía was not able to balance her relational need for connection with her mother and her relational need for separateness and individuation (the developmental process). Sofía felt responsible for her mother and felt guilty when she asserted her autonomy and independence and disconnected from the family (antilibidinal ego state). Based on these early experiences, Sofía began to entertain negative feelings that she is not lovable, important, or good enough (self representation) because the mother did not honour and affirm Sofía's self needs. Later Sofía began to see her mother as a selfish person and not able to put the needs of others ahead of her own (mother representation). Sofía was left yearning for a meaningful, accepting, and affirming relationship with her mother (relational need) and struggling to affirm herself as being a good, lovable, and caring person valued in her own right (self need). The therapeutic task was to help Sofía complete the separation–individuation process, resolve psychic conflicts, enhance feelings of self-esteem, and develop capacities to meet relational and self needs.

Therapy Process

The therapist, using a self-discovery, person-centred, and developmental approach, empathic responses and summaries, and focusing on the here-and-now, helped Sofía define and clarify the relational problem and explore the associated thoughts, feelings, and needs. This exploratory work led to a new awareness that her relationship with her mother was not real and that Sofía felt guilty in distancing herself and disconnecting from her family. Sofía envisioned becoming reconnected by being empathic toward her mother for her limitations, seeing the situation through the eyes of her mother and siblings, wanting to let go of the guilt and focus on what she accomplished and who she has become, shifting from expecting affirmations from others to affirming herself and establishing a comfort zone between relating with her mother and being her own person.

Transcript

In the excerpts from the transcripts that follow, the therapist's responses, that were mostly empathic responses, summaries, or open questions, are in large part omitted for lack of space. In the transcript, C = Client, T = Therapist, and the number following the letter represents the response number. The therapy begins with Sofía expressing a desire to try to rekindle a relationship with her mother.

Session 1

Relational Need: for Connection

C05:   There is a part of me that thinks that I should try again to have a relationship with my mom. She's older and her health is not great and I am not sure whether or not I will have regrets if she should die without [my] trying to establish some kind of a relationship with her.

C07:   She is the woman that gave birth to me, raised me, and was in some ways a good mom. I think that in her own mind she believes that she did everything she could.

T10:   What is missing for you in this relationship?

Representation of Mother

C11:   Me. My mother is all about herself. She doesn't know how to be a real mother, she isn't capable of putting other people's needs before herself. Her needs usually came first so it left me wanting, yearning, and angry.

T12:   You yearn for that which you did not receive from her?

Relational Need: for Connection

C12:   Yearning for a mother who was aware of, attuned to, and available to meet my needs, who would put my needs before her own. When we had a falling out 10 years ago it was that same scene all over again, it was all about her. It was the most important day of my life and she couldn't give me that day because of her own selfish needs.

T14:   What is the yearning like for you today?

C14:   It is very sad, it makes me ache, it makes me feel like I have missed out and that there is something missing.

C20:   I don't believe that she is capable of experiencing others as important, worthy, and meaningful and of connecting to a person in a healthy way; so she couldn't relate to my experience.

Self Representation and Self Need

T21:   You would like to have experienced that you are important.

C21:   I thought that I was until this incident happened. It forced me to look back over our relationship and realize that my importance to her was never valued in its own right. There had to be something in it for her in order for it to be considered important.

T22:   How do you cope knowing she is not able to give you the love and acceptance you want?

C22:   I embrace my relationships with my friends, my own family, my husband, my children. I feel that I am genuinely important and valued in these relationships. When I go over my mother's relationships with my siblings, my father, and her own parents, and when I am able to see that there is nobody who comes first, then it doesn't become so personal. I am aware that this is not about me, it is about her.

T23:   How does knowing that help you get through it?

Psychic Conflict

C24:   I just remind myself of who I am and the good person that I am, all that I have to give and the meaningful life that I have. It is a tentative way to alleviate the ache but I never feel completely settled. If I stay with my logical mind that tells me that she is not capable of giving me what I need, then I am okay. But when I connect with my heart, it is hard for me to soothe that ache.

Session 2

Representation of Mother: Transformed

C01:   I realize that I want a real relationship with my mom and that the relationship that I had and that may be available to me is not a real relationship. I do not believe that my mother is capable of this. That understanding shifts things a little bit for me. I feel a little more at ease knowing that.

Relational Need: for Connection: Transformed

T05:   How is it for you knowing that you might not be able to have a real relationship with your mother?

C05:   I feel sad that I am missing out on that, that I won't ever experience that with my own family of origin. I have developed real relationships with friends, with my husband, with my own children.

C07:   I did not realize until moving away from my family of origin what real relationships are, how meaningful they are, how my needs can be met in these relationships.

Self Need: be Valued

T22:   If you were to speak to your mom, what would you say to her?

C23:   I wish that I could feel important to her, to feel valued in her life and accepted by her for who I am and the person that I have become.

Balancing Need for Connection and Individuation, Being True to Herself

T24:   What is standing in the way for this to become a reality?

C25:   (Pause, 25 secs.) We don't speak the same language anymore, we don't share similar interests and we don't have a lot in common. I can't relate to their life.

T26:   You have grown apart.

C28:   (Pause 10 secs.) I needed to disconnect to come out and discover me and be myself and I cannot reconnect now that I am out.

T29:   What would be the price to reconnect?

C29:   Having to go back to old patterns, trying to fit into their world, to make sacrifices, having to undo.

C35:   It would be like becoming unravelled, undone, and knowing that it is not where I want to go and that is not a healthy place for me to be. I feel that when we talk and I feel a lot of resistance to being pulled back into old patterns.

T36:   To reconnect means to become undone.

C36:   Yes, and a real sense of discomfort with the pull. So, when I resist, that's the disconnection.

C37:   It would mean me being untrue to myself and trying to be something that someone else needs me to be in order to be in a relationship.

T39:   Any other thoughts or feelings?

C39:   (Pause, 15 secs.) I wonder if I can hang on to me and yet maintain a relationship where I am accepting of who they are without feeling that my own sense of self is being threatened or compromised.

Session 3

C01:   I was thinking a lot about what I would need to be in these relationships with my mother, with my siblings, and where I need to move toward in order to be able to do that.

T02:   What has come up for you as you are thinking about this?

Separation—Individuation Process: Transforming

C02:   I need to see the situation differently, I need to look at this not so much as me being denied but rather me being more accepting of both whom I have become and who my family are. If I can accept who they are and also accept who I am and have become, then I won't need to defend myself for moving away. I think that I will be better able to have a realistic relationship based on what is versus what I would like and feel more comfortable in my own skin and find a way to relate from a distance.

Psychic Organization: Transforming

C03:   I realize that I harbour guilt for moving away and distancing myself from my family, becoming my own person, and although I have always sort of seen it as though they harboured resentment toward me, I feel guilt as well in leaving them behind. I need to let go of the guilt, I need to embrace what I have done and to affirm myself for the good things that I have done for myself and not expect any affirmations from them.

Self Needs: Move from Other to Self Affirmation

T04:   Letting go of the need for affirmation from them and affirming yourself for what you have accomplished and have become.

C04:   I have not been able to do that in large part because in some ways I feel guilty for moving on with my life and that I created that distance.

Psychic Organization: Transforming by Becoming Empathic

T05:   How do you reconcile the fact that you evolved, they did not?

C06:   I need not feel guilty for that. In fact I need to be proud of what I have done and of what I have become and the choices that I have made and feel sad and empathic toward them for the choices that they made with their life and not to compare my accomplishments with theirs and see it as different.

T07:   Do you have any other ways to deal with your guilt feelings?

C08:   (Pause 15 secs.) Probably by being more empathic towards them, by understanding that the resentments that they harbour toward me or their disinterest in my life are not a reflection of me but rather a realization of what they have not accomplished.

T09:   You do not need to defend yourself for the things that you have achieved.

C09:   No, when I understand that, I am able to empathize with their sense of helplessness and sadness for the things that they have not done.

C10:   It also helps me to understand what it must be like for them to see where I am at in my life and to see me through their eyes and then I am able to connect with their sadness and not feel guilty but feel more empathic toward them and the things they have not done with their life.

T12:   How does all of this fit in with you having a more realistic relationship with your mom?

C12:   I think that I could have a relationship with her if my expectations of her were realistic, by being empathic and understanding of who she is and what she is capable of giving, and by being more accepting and affirming of myself and not having to defend who I am or what I have become, so that I can be in a relationship at a comfortable distance and feel comfortable within my own skin but also being accepting of what she is able to give.

Something to think About

1. How does self-in-relationship psychotherapy pay attention to subjective realities?
2. Object constancy contributes to affect regulation. Explain.
3. How does working with the psychic organization lead to the resolution of emotional problems?
4. Failure to separate and individuate leads to intimacy problems. Explain.
5. How did Sofía reconcile her relationship with her family?

References

Berne, E. (1976). *Beyond games and scripts*. New York: Grove Press.

Bowlby, J. (1988). *A secure base*. New York: Basic Books.

Cashdan, S. (1988). *Object relations therapy: Using the relationship*. London: W.W. Norton & Company.

Clarkin, J.F., Kernberg, O.F., & Yeomans, F. (1999). *Transference-focused psychotherapy for borderline personality disorder patients*. New York: Guildford Press.

DeYoung, P. (2003). *Relational psychotherapy: A primer*. New York: Brunner-Routledge.

Fairbairn, W.R.D. (1944). Endopsychic structure considered in terms of object relationships. In *An object-relations theory of the personality* (pp. 82–136). New York: Basic Books.

Freud, S. (1923). The ego and the id, *Standard Edition* (Vol. 19, pp. 12–63). London: Hogarth Press.

Greenberg, J.R., & Mitchell, S.A. (1983). *Object relations in psychoanalytic theory*. Cambridge, MA: Harvard University Press.

Haroian, L. (2000). Child sexual development. *Electronic Journal of Human Sexuality*, 3, 1–45 (ww.ejhs.org).

Kaplan, L. (1978). *Oneness and separateness: From infant to individual*. New York: Simon and Schuster.

Klein, M. (1936). Weaning. In *Love, guilt and reparation and other works, 1921–1945* (pp. 122–140). New York: Delta.

Klein, M. (1959). Our adult world and its roots infancy. In *Envy and gratitude and other works, 1946–1963* (pp. 247–263). New York: Delta.

Klein, M. (1961). *Narrative of a child analysis*. London: Hogarth Press.

Kohut, H. (1977). *The restoration of the self*. New York: International Universities Press.

Kohut, H. (1983). *The analysis of the self*. New York: International Universities Press.

Lawrence, M.A. (1999). The use of imagery and ego state therapy in holistic healing. Paper presented at the annual meeting of the American Association for the Study of Mental Imagery, April.

Levenson, H., & Strupp, H.H. (2007). Cyclical maladaptive patterns: Case formulation in time-limited dynamic psychotherapy. In T.D. Eells (Ed.), *Handbook of psychotherapy case formulation* (pp. 164–197). New York: Guilford Press.

Mahler, M., & Furer, M. (1968). *On human symbiosis and the vicissitudes of individuation.* New York: International Universities Press.

Mahler, M., Pine, F., & Bergman, A. (1975). *The psychological birth of the human infant.* New York: Basic Books.

Meier, A., & Boivin, M. (1998). *The seven-phase model of the change process: Theoretical foundation, definitions, coding guidelines, training procedures, and research data* (5th Ed.). Unpublished MS. Ottawa, Ontario: Saint Paul University.

Meier, A., & Boivin, M. (2006). Intrapsychic conflicts, their formation, underlying dynamics and resolution: An object relations perspective. In A. Meier & M. Rovers (Eds.), *Through conflict to reconciliation.* Ottawa, Ontario: Novalis.

Meier, A., Boivin, M., & Meier, M. (2006). The treatment of depression: A case study using theme-analysis. *Counselling and Psychotherapy Research, 6*(2), 115–125.

Pike, L.B. (2000). *Sexuality and your child: For children ages 0 to 3.* University of Missouri–Columbia: Department of Human Development and Family Studies.

Rogers, C.R. (1961). *On becoming a person.* Boston: Houghton Mifflin.

Wachtel, P.L. (2008). *Relational theory and the practice of psychotherapy.* New York: Guilford Press.

Watkins, J.G., & Watkins, H.H. (1997). *Ego states: Theory and therapy.* New York: Norton.

Webber, C., & Delvin, D. (2005). Sexuality throughout life. http://www.netdoctor.co.uk/sex.

Winnicott, D. (1965a). *The maturational processes and the facilitating environment.* New York: International Universities Press.

Winnicott, D. (1965b). *The family and individual development.* London: Tavistock Publishers.

Young, J. (2003). *Schema therapy: A practitioner's guide.* New York: Guilford Press.

Epilogue

This book presents eleven commonly used therapeutic techniques together with the theory from which they emerged, the procedures for their administration, and an illustration of each technique. How can one account for such a divergent group of techniques, assuming that each is therapeutically effective? We will attempt to answer this question with reference to four of the dimensions for comparing techniques presented in the first chapter, namely, therapy as process, therapeutic content, psychic organization and target for change, and the therapeutic relationship.

Therapy as Process

One can make sense of the divergent techniques used in therapy if one considers therapy to be a process that sees a client move from being in a troubled situation to having resolved the situation. This process is characterized by the achievement of significant tasks, called phases. Four of these phases are exploration, awareness, action, and integration. Clients typically arrive in therapy at different places in working through their problem, that is, they arrive at differing phases regarding their troubled situation. For example, one client might be psychologically derailed by flashbacks and require help to explore and gain awareness as to the source of the flashbacks, while another client has given a lot of thought to their problem and requires help to put their awareness into action. Techniques such as experiential focusing, ego-state therapy, and self-in-relationship psychotherapy are very useful to help a client explore the underlying dynamics of the problem (e.g., flashbacks) and gain insight into the problem, whereas solution-focused therapy, cognitive-behavioural therapy, and task-directed imagery are helpful to learn new ways of acting and behaving (e.g., being assertive). Thus, one can make sense of the multitude of available techniques when therapy is viewed as a process that requires specific technical aid to help a client to move from one phase to the next.

Therapeutic Content

When the therapeutic approaches and their techniques are viewed as a whole, we observe that they address a wide spectrum of therapeutic (psychological) content. This ranges from a focus on emotions, bodily felt feelings, cognitions, and desires/aspirations to metaphors, narratives, and behaviours. All of these are part of every person's experiences. Specific techniques have been developed to address these differing therapeutic contents. Metaphor therapy has detailed guidelines in how to work with metaphors, and experiential focusing has guidelines how to work with bodily felt feelings. To provide a rationale for these differing contents, it is necessary to develop a theory that demonstrates how these therapeutic contents relate to each other and the order in which they need to be addressed in therapy. It is not helpful to reduce the contents to a few concepts such as hot cognitions and emotional needs. It appears that it would be helpful from both therapeutic and research perspectives to consider emotions, needs/aspirations, and cognitions as three interdependent systems that interact in the formation of behaviours, attitudes, values, and so on. It is assumed that in addressing these contents therapy will unfold according to the process referred to above. In providing a rationale for the therapeutic contents, one is at the same time providing a rationale for the divergent techniques and the role they play in the therapy process.

Psychic Organization and Processes, and Targets for Change

All therapeutic approaches accept, at least implicitly, that experiences form internal organizations such as schemas and ego states that influence both adaptive and maladaptive behaviours. Therapeutic approaches, however, differ in the extent to which these organizations are addressed in therapy and become the target of change. Some of the therapeutic approaches such as experiential focusing, metaphor therapy, and Gestalt Two-Chair, design techniques to bring into awareness experiences that have been encoded sensorially, perceptually, and symbolically. The target of change for these approaches is the psychic organization. Other approaches such as solution-focused therapy and narrative therapy designed techniques to address problems that the client is aware of. These are addressed at a conscious and rational level. The target of change for these approaches is the development of new and adaptive behaviour. Thus therapeutic approaches and their techniques differ according to whether they address psychic organizations and/or overt behaviours.

The Therapeutic Relationship

All forms of therapeutic approaches acknowledge that the therapeutic relationship is important for the technique to be effective. However, they differ on the type of relationship that needs to be offered. When viewed broadly one can identify three types of client–therapist relationship. One type is where the therapist and client work collaboratively as detectives and researchers to identify the problem and systematically determine what strategies are needed to solve the problem. This is seen in solution-focused, narrative, and cognitive-behavioural therapies. A second type of client–therapist relationship is where the therapist offers a set of interpersonal qualities that facilitate the therapeutic process. Person-centred therapies, such as empathic responding, advocate that the therapist be empathic, genuine, and congruent, and actively listen and be present to the client. The belief is that the provision of these qualities by themselves is therapeutic. A third type of relationship is where both the therapist and the client are actively engaged in a dynamic, lively, and at times emotional encounter. There is a working out of an issue at the emotional and motivational (e.g., relational needs) levels rather than at the intellectual, logical, and practical levels. This type of therapist–client relationship is seen in self-in-relationship psychotherapy and Gestalt-oriented therapies where self and relational issues (e.g., transferences and countertransferences) are worked through. Gestalt therapists maintain that all relationships, including therapy, take place at the contact boundary.

Conclusion

From the above descriptions, it can be seen that all techniques potentially contribute towards therapy. However, the techniques and the theory from which they emerge, tend to have a narrow focus and are keyed to specific psychotherapeutic content at a particular point in the therapy process, and work with psychic organization and/or overt behaviours. It appears necessary to define the therapist–client relationship differently. Rather than seeing the relationship, technique, and theory as separate constructs, it might be useful to view, as integral to the relationship, a therapist's grasp of a theory and the ability to use it to guide assessment and treatment, and techniques as an extension of the therapist's ability to deal with day-to-day problems. The therapist–client relationship, therefore, comprises his/her personal and interpersonal qualities, grasp of theory, and ability to create and/or apply techniques. This view is akin to parenting, which comprises personal and interpersonal qualities, understanding of children, and ability to guide their growth and development. All three qualities constitute parenting, and when one or more of these qualities is absent, parenting suffers. Therapy is analogous to parenting in that the therapist also needs to possess personal and interpersonal qualities, an understanding of emotional problems (a grasp of theory), and an ability to guide the process. Therapy suffers when one or more of these attributes are absent or where one dominates the others. For example, a therapist may know theory but not be able to relate emotionally to the client and not have the skills to apply the theory to the client's problem.

To explain the array of therapy techniques and their usefulness in the therapy process, it is important to develop a theory that integrates the psychotherapeutic contents, links psychic organization and actual behaviour, and bridges subjective experiences and objective realities. Such a theory would contribute enormously in viewing therapy as an integrated and a unified process. Theory needs to be embodied and alive. Techniques are not the therapy, they are aids to therapy. Techniques are meaningful when they bridge the conceptualization of a client's problem with the therapeutic goal to be achieved.

Glossary

Acknowledgment: Affirmation or validation of the child's self-directed actions, behaviours, and thoughts.

Active imagination: Ability to loosen one's conscious focus, enter into a state of reverie, and allow images and sensations to emerge and become elaborated regardless of whether they are socially acceptable or unacceptable.

Advanced-level accurate empathy: Empathy that gets at what clients say not only explicitly but also implicitly and which is only half expressed.

Antilibidinal ego state: Part of self that encompasses parental, familial, and cultural demands, expectations, and prohibitions. When it dominates it is hateful, vengeful, bitter, and critical of its own libidinal needs and cravings, and controls by creating guilt feelings.

Automatic thoughts: Minute-to-minute, unplanned thoughts, words, images, and memories that pass through our minds throughout the day.

Being: Essential existence of the organism that is present from birth.

Boundary disturbances: Disturbances in relationships where a person may merge with another, incorporate the other, or exclude the other.

Central ego state: Primary psychic and unitary self present at birth.

Circular questions: Orient the therapist to the client's situation, seek to reveal the recurrent patterns that connect events to perceptions, feelings and so on.

Clearing a space: Create an internal environment that is receptive and open to fully experience the problem or feeling.

Client-generated metaphors: Come from within the client's experience and are coded with symbolic attributes which contain meaning and significance for the client.

Cognitive distortions: Systematic errors in reasoning brought about by the breakdown of the information-processing system with a consequent shift to a more primitive information-processing system.

Cognitive schemas: Deeply engrained and stable cognitive patterns that comprise rules or erroneous premises and assumptions that dominate how persons regard themselves, others, and the world.

Cognitive shift: A move away from normal cognitive processing to a predominance of processing by negative schemas.

Confluence: Process by which persons merge with the environment and are not able to tell what belongs to them and what belongs to the environment.

Contact: The meeting between two separate and independent persons at which I experience "me" in relation to whatever is "not me" and where I experience "me" as distinct from "you."

Contact boundary: The point in the contact between two independent persons at which something transpires and happens.

Coping questions: Illicit information about client resources that will have gone unnoticed by them.

Deconstructing narratives: Procedures that subvert taken-for-granted realities and practices.

Developmental process: Entails becoming attached to the caregiver and then separating from them and embarking on the path to becoming individuated, an individual. This process comprises subphases that carry with them unique developmental tasks to be achieved.

Direct referent: Inward bodily feeling that a person can turn to at any time to resolve problems.

Dissociation: Process of disconnecting from oneself for a short period of time. Can include phenomena which range from daydreams and children's imaginary games to personality disorders.

Dominant narrative: Cultural, societal, and family expectations, values, demands, and behaviours that a person is expected to live by.

Early recollection metaphors: Association, on a bodily feeling, of a current problem situation (being noisy; snoring), with an early memory image (noisy, because of childhood pneumonia; coughing).

Ego states: Primitive, enduring, internalized, but mutative, organizations formed from the child's relational experiences that affect how well a person deals with the tasks and challenges of daily living.

Ego-state bridging: Involves amplifying a present ego state and tracing it back in time to when it was first experienced.

Ego-state shift: Movement from a problematic ego state (the hidden ego state) to some other ego state that can soothe or relieve the anxiety associated with the problematic ego state.

Empathic cycle: Process of listening to the client, observing his/her behaviours, resonating with what is said, and communicating your understanding and checking for its accuracy.

Empathic understanding: Moment-to-moment sensitivity in the here-and-now of the inner world of the client's private personal meanings "as if" it were the therapist's own, but without losing the "as if" quality.

Exceptions: Ability of the client to identify some of their own resources and strengths that they used in solving a problem and which forms the basis for them to see possible solutions towards moving forward.

Executive ego state: Ego state of which the person is conscious and in which the energy and identity of self reside.

Externalizing the problem: Problems considered as objects existing outside of oneself and experienced as being oppressive.

Fantasy: Mental creation which has little or no connection with reality.

Fluidity: Shift from one predominant ego state to another ego state, often initially hidden.

Focusing: Attending to a body felt sense that at first is unclear so that something new emerges.

Guided imageries: Pre-recorded specific imagery scripts wherein clients are asked to journey through the script and then at the end of the script to share their experience.

Hidden ego state: Problematic ego that is hidden in the sense that it is disowned, unaccepted, or unacknowledged by the predominant ego states.

Human agency: People are active agents, mediators, and negotiators of their own lives.

Imagery: Mental recreation of an experience that resembles in some respects the experience of actually perceiving an absent object or an event.

Individuation: Developing one's own interests, opinions, goals, meanings, values and becoming a separated and differentiated individual.

Information processing: Processing information through the application of logical rules and strategies.

Intentional states: Intentions and purposes according to which people live their lives in the pursuit of what matters to them.

Internal conflict: Self's failure to mediate the needs of being and self-image that results in a conflict between the two.

Landscape of action questions: Explore the events, sequences, time, and plots of a narrative.

Landscape of consciousness questions: Explore the desires, intentions, beliefs, meanings, characteristics, and qualities of the characters of a story.

Libidinal ego state: Person's biological, physiological, sexual, relational, and self needs that are inherited at the beginning of physical life and represent that part of the self that is needy, perpetually frustrated, deprived, feels attacked, and insatiably craves for the fulfillment of its relational and self needs.

Lineal questions: Investigative questions that orient the therapist to the client's situation.

Linear correspondence: Relationship of items characterized by linear, logical, cause-and-effect relationships.

Linguistic metaphor: Image that is used to convey meaning of the situation to which it refers.

Metaphor: Figure of speech in which a word or phrase literally denoting one kind of object or idea is used in place of another to suggest a likeness or analogy between them (as in *drowning in money*) (*Merriam-Webster Dictionary*).

Miracle question: Method of questioning that helps the client to envision how the future will be different when the problem is no longer present and to establish goals.

Modernism: Trend of thought that rejects previous traditions and affirms that human beings with the help of scientific knowledge, empirical methods, and technology are able to improve and reshape their environment.

Narrative: Forms a thread around a theme which intertwines the experiences of the past and the present with anticipation of the future.

Nonlinear correspondence: Pattern and organization characterized by nonlinear causal chains (e.g., A is to B as C is to D).

Object constancy: Positive internal representation of a significant other such as a caregiver that is formed from positive experiences with that person and provides an "emotional psychological home" to which the person can turn to comfort and soothe themselves when distraught.

Organismic self-regulation: Striving for tension reduction and a balance between the conflicting forces represented by an external demand and an internal need.

Organismic valuing process: Inherent ability to positively value experiences that a person perceives as enhancing his organism.

Permeability: Ability of primary ego state to access subordinate ego states.

Postmodernism: Rejects the assumed certainty of scientific endeavors to understand and explain reality and asserts that reality is co-created in conversations between people.

Preferred narrative: Personal values, expectations, and behaviours that a person wishes to live by but that are often counter to the dominant narrative.

Primary-level accurate empathy: Entails communicating a basic understanding of what the client is feeling together with the experiences and behaviours that underlie these feelings.

Reconstructing narratives: Rebuilding alternative perspectives, stories, behavioural practices, and relationship patterns that replace the old oppressive narratives.

Relational needs: Need to bond with a significant caregiver and the need to separate from the caregiver and to individuate.

Relational patterns: Patterns of relating to others that have been internalized and serve as prototypes for the infant/child's future relationships and shape the expectations about the way in which relational and self needs are to be met.

Retroflection: Individual turns the energy to be used for adaptation inward upon himself and treats self as he wanted to be treated by others (e.g., caresses self).

Scaling questions: Tools used to identify useful differences for the client, assess the client's level of motivation and confidence, help to set small identifiable goals, establish priorities for action, and measure progress.

Self (Gestalt):   Creative process which leads the individual to actualizing behaviours. It represents that part of personality concerned with wants.

Self-actualization: Innate tendency that subsumes all other needs and aims to develop all capacities in ways that maintain or enhance the organism and move it towards autonomy.

Self-image: Part of personality that says what an individual should do and which hinders creative growth.

Self needs: Innate desires to be empowered, omnipotent, and master of one's life and environment and to feel good, lovable, and worthwhile.

Self organization: Internalized notion of self derived from child–caregiver interactions that are organized according to the two innate basic needs, to be admired for being competent and to be loved for being a good person.

Sensory encoding: Storing experiences at the level of the senses; this is also referred to as bodily memory.

Social learning: Learning that takes place within a social context where a person observes, imitates, and models the behaviours of others.

Solution-focused therapy: Future-focused and goal-directed approach that builds upon clients' resources and helps them to achieve their preferred outcomes by collaboratively designing solutions to their problems.

Solutions: Changes that clients make regarding their perceptions and patterns of interacting and the meanings they give to their experience within the context of their frame of reference.

Spontaneous imagery: Image that is freely evoked while the client is relaxing, listening to music, or looking at an object or a painting.

Structuralism: Form of postmodernism that argues that language shapes and creates reality.

Symbolic encoding: Storing experiences at the level of symbols, images, metaphors, scripts, and narratives that embody a wealth of affective, cognitive, motivational, and value-related information.

Task-Directed Imagery: Form of imagery designed to help a client to achieve a personal or relational goal by first empowering the client and then asking the client to proceed from this empowered position to confront and resolve a current personal or relational problem.

Therapist-suggested imagery: Imageries that have been selected, in advance, for their therapeutic value, with the client being asked to focus on the image and report what is experienced.

Unfinished business: Nagging, unresolved, unexpressed, or withheld feelings, memories, and events of hurt, anger, and resentment towards another person.

Index